The Descent

THE DESCENT

Witnessing Russia's Spiral into
Madness under Putin

MARC BENNETTS

BLOOMSBURY CONTINUUM
LONDON · OXFORD · NEW YORK · NEW DELHI · SYDNEY

BLOOMSBURY CONTINUUM
Bloomsbury Publishing Plc
50 Bedford Square, London, WC1B 3DP, UK
Bloomsbury Publishing Ireland Limited,
29 Earlsfort Terrace, Dublin 2, D02 AY28, Ireland

BLOOMSBURY, BLOOMSBURY CONTINUUM and the
Diana logo are trademarks of Bloomsbury Publishing Plc

First published in Great Britain 2026

Copyright © Marc Bennetts, 2026

Marc Bennetts has asserted his right under the Copyright, Designs and Patents Act, 1988, to be identified as Author of this work

All rights reserved. No part of this publication may be: i) reproduced or transmitted in any form, electronic or mechanical, including photocopying, recording or by means of any information storage or retrieval system without prior permission in writing from the publishers; or ii) used or reproduced in any way for the training, development or operation of artificial intelligence (AI) technologies, including generative AI technologies. The rights holders expressly reserve this publication from the text and data mining exception as per Article 4(3) of the Digital Single Market Directive (EU) 2019/790

Bloomsbury Publishing Plc does not have any control over, or responsibility for, any third-party websites referred to or in this book. All internet addresses given in this book were correct at the time of going to press. The author and publisher regret any inconvenience caused if addresses have changed or sites have ceased to exist, but can accept no responsibility for any such changes

A catalogue record for this book is available from the British Library

Library of Congress Cataloging-in-Publication data has been applied for

ISBN: HB: 978-1-3994-2169-0
eBook: 978-1-3994-2164-5
ePDF: 978-1-3994-2167-6

2 4 6 8 10 9 7 5 3 1

Typeset by Lumina Datamatics Ltd
Printed and bound in Great Britain by Clays Ltd, Elcograf S.p.A.

To find out more about our authors and books visit
www.bloomsbury.com and sign up for our newsletters

For product safety related questions contact productsafety@bloomsbury.com

For T, who was with me for almost all of it
For M, who arrived later and gave it new meaning
And for my parents, who started it all

CONTENTS

	Preface	ix
1	Dislodged Memories	1
2	'Look Around This Place'	12
3	A Pact with The Devil	27
4	'He Is Reacting to Pictures in His Own Head'	40
5	False Hopes	57
6	He Who Sobs with Joy	71
7	'Putin *Khuilo*!'	83
8	'No More Time for Truth-Seeking'	93
9	Making The Gate Wider for Fascism	102
10	Madman for Hire	117
11	'He Was Killed by The Hatred Poured Into The Air'	124
12	'When They Beat You, Say Thank You for The Lesson'	141
13	Holy Water and HIV	153
14	Exorcizing Putin	170
15	A City Soaked in Terror	179
16	Deliver Us from Evil	191
17	'What Does It Matter If I Am In Pain, If I Am Nothing?'	210

| 18 | 'Just Switch Your Brains On' | 219 |
| 19 | 'Always Cold: Nothing is Allowed' | 227 |

Acknowledgements — 234
Endnotes — 235
Index — 252

PREFACE

I originally intended to write this book in strict chronological order, tracing Russia's descent into violence, hatred and war under Vladimir Putin. But the Kremlin's invasion of neighbouring Ukraine in February 2022 was an event of such monstrous proportions that, like a black hole, it melded together events, time and even memory itself. Accordingly, I decided that while I would try and adhere to my original plan, it would often be necessary to move forwards and backwards along the timeline to add context and understanding. That is, of course, if such things can ever be truly understood: I am not entirely sure that they can.

I had spent 25 years in Russia, almost half of my life and the vast majority of my adult years, before leaving in May 2022, perhaps for ever. After a quarter of a century in Moscow, people often ask me, quite understandably, if I feel Russian. The answer to that is a definitive no. Yet, despite witnessing up-close the devastating consequences of Russia's war in Ukraine, I still feel a link to the country that I called home for so many years. It is, however, one that is perhaps best compared to the conflicted emotions experienced by the friends or relatives of criminals who have committed senseless acts of extreme brutality. Why did they do it? What possessed them? And how do I deal with these stubborn feelings of attachment?

On an individual level, though, I have nothing but the deepest disgust and contempt for Putin, for those who support his regime and for Russia's invading troops. When I began this book, one of my biggest challenges was to control my hatred: without doing so, I would have likely produced 80,000 words of unreadable bile. I hope I have avoided that trap but I make no apologies for any anger that has spilled over onto these pages.

Conversely, I have only respect for those Russians who have stood up to the Kremlin, often at the cost of their own lives or freedom. It is up for debate whether Russia's opposition movement could have done more to stop Putin. It is my view that the opportunities were limited and by the time it became clear how high the stakes were, it was already far too late. In any case, I am opposed to collective guilt; attempts to portray the entire population of Russia as responsible for their army's war crimes are inaccurate, as well as self-defeating.

This is not a book about how Putin came to power or a profile of his best-known domestic critics, such as Alexei Navalny. These topics have been covered extensively elsewhere, including in my own work. Instead, it is an attempt to portray what it was like to live through the Kremlin's suppression of all forms of independent thought as Putin led his country towards all-out war in Ukraine.

Despite the use of the word madness in my title, I can offer no precise definition of the term. Yet madness, like evil, is so very easy to recognize when witnessed. And I am certain that I encountered both in Russia, in multitudes. Under Putin, a significant slice of Russian society has been gripped by a collective delirium of the type that brought about the witch hunts in medieval Europe, or the fainting spells and mass hallucinations that have been documented in the modern era among teenagers and other highly susceptible groups.

Of course, a diagnosis of madness doesn't let Russia off the hook for its crimes, including against those inside the country who have called for a cure. It does, however, make political analysis and policymaking all that much harder: how do you rationalize the irrational or guard against the pathologically unpredictable?

The Descent was written after my departure from Russia, but it draws on my reporting and my experiences in the country between 1997 and 2022, as well as my many subsequent visits to Ukraine's war-ravaged towns and cities.

1

Dislodged Memories

The Russian artillery shell hurtled through the evening gloom before crashing into an advertising hoarding close to our car. Shrapnel cracked the vehicle's windscreen and slammed into its hood as the blast reverberated through the desolate streets of Kherson, a front-line city in southern Ukraine. Flames lit up the dark: we were so close to the explosion that I briefly experienced the impact as a physical force. My driver, Oleksandr, and I were unhurt, but shaken. He put his foot down and we sped away into the night, hoping that another missile wasn't already flying towards us. I had never planned to become a war correspondent, but here I was, in one of the hottest spots of the conflict, dodging shells and documenting destruction.

It was November 2023, almost a year to the day since I had witnessed the liberation of Kherson by Ukrainian troops after eight long months of Russian occupation. Grateful residents, some crying tears of relief, had crowded the main square to greet their triumphant soldiers as they drove into the city. 'Putin Kaput!' read one hastily written sign. The joy didn't last long. After being forced to retreat from Kherson, Russian troops dug in on the left side of the Dnipro, the mighty river that cleaves the wider region. From there, they bombarded Kherson's residents with relentless artillery attacks, pounding its streets apparently at random.

A once bustling city famed across Ukraine for its succulent watermelons, Kherson had become a place of terror, where death could arrive at any time. At night, the unlit streets were a cacophonous landscape of wailing air sirens, incoming missiles and baying packs of stray dogs whose owners had either been killed or fled to safer regions. Drones flew almost unhindered over the city's streets, seeking out fresh targets and barely a day went by without a civilian dying or being injured in a Russian strike: I later found out that a passer-by had been badly hurt by the shell that almost hit our car.

This wasn't my first close call since I had begun reporting on the war. Yet, like many journalists who were covering the conflict, I had become dangerously desensitized to danger. A few months earlier, as I sat in a hotel courtyard in eastern Ukraine, a Russian S-300 missile had roared overhead with a sound like the heavens cracking open before exploding in the near distance, a cloud of black smoke rising into the sky. Elsewhere, in the same region, Russian troops had lobbed, almost casually, an artillery shell towards our car as we drove quickly down a rough-hewn track that was within range of their lines. The shell detonated with a flash somewhere to our right. In Bakhmut, a town that has since been razed to the ground by the Kremlin's forces, a rocket exploded half a block away as I interviewed people queuing for humanitarian aid, filling the air with the sudden stench of munitions propellant. The locals were so used to the daily soundtrack of war that they didn't even flinch.

As we made our way through Kherson's war-shattered streets, I considered the motivations of the Russian soldiers who loaded and fired these missiles. Many, I knew, had bought into Vladimir Putin's great lie about Ukraine being a Nazi state and falsely imagined themselves in the role of their grandfathers, defending Europe from fascism. Others believed Putin when he said that the war was necessary to prevent an attack on Mother Russia by Nato. Some were there simply for the money, seizing the opportunity to earn far more than they could ever expect to make at home. In addition, there were the former convicts – including serial killers, rapists and child abusers – who had been released from Russian prisons to slaughter Ukrainians, 'liberating' entire towns and villages by wiping them from the face of the earth.

Perhaps most depressingly, however, I was certain that a significant number of the troops had not given any real thought as to why their country was waging war in neighbouring Ukraine. These soldiers were not so much brainwashed zombies as unfeeling grunts whose lives had been shaped and twisted by the nihilism and cynicism that is perhaps the defining nature of Putin's regime. '*Da pokhui*' – 'I don't give a fuck' – they would most likely reply if confronted with the senselessness of Russia's invasion. It would, I reflected later, have been an insult to have been killed by these men.

My suspicions weren't based on guesswork. I could picture all too well these soldiers who had brought destruction to Kherson and other towns and cities across Ukraine. During my years in Moscow, I had spoken to dozens, perhaps hundreds of Russians like them. I had argued with them and tried to understand them. On occasion, I had drunk with them. '*Da pokhui*' was an all-too-common response to everything from human rights abuses to electoral fraud: a pathological indifference to almost everything, including their own lives.

I had married and brought up a child in Russia, adapting to the daily rhythms of life in Moscow until they became more familiar to me than those in Britain. I had watched the same television programmes as the Kremlin's invading troops, the hate-filled broadcasts that were beamed into homes across Russia's vast territory, stirring old and new animosities and convincing millions that there was no alternative to Putin's rule. As the years went by, I watched with mounting disbelief as Putin resurrected the demons of the Soviet regime, plunging Russia once more into dictatorship. After the Kremlin annexed the Black Sea peninsula of Crimea from Ukraine in 2014, the mood in Russia grew steadily darker. Joseph Stalin, the Soviet tyrant whose name had been almost taboo for years, became fashionable again. His face was suddenly everywhere, from newly erected monuments to t-shirts and the souvenirs on sale at Moscow's international airports. I watched as crowds of people, their children alongside them, flocked to central Moscow to cheer as nuclear missiles rumbled through the city streets on Victory Day, the national holiday commemorating the defeat of Nazi Germany. 'We can do it again,' read car stickers and internet memes. Sometimes, they were accompanied by an image of a Russian tricolour raping a US flag.

State media, taking its cue from the Kremlin, ramped up its attacks on opposition figures or 'national traitors' as Putin had taken to calling them. Acquaintances that I had considered too intelligent to fall for the Kremlin's crude and violent propaganda, began to parrot its talking points on the West and on Ukraine. 'Only Putin can guarantee Russia's sovereignty,' a man I had known for years told me, after the Kremlin had rewritten the constitution to allow Putin to remain in power until at least 2036. I had once considered him a friend, but as I looked into his eyes, I realized that I no longer knew him.

I grew used to Russians asking me if I was a spy: usually as a good-natured, if irritating, joke, but on occasion more aggressively. My workdays were often spent talking to dissidents who had been tortured by the Kremlin's security services. One opposition activist told me how he had been broken, physically and emotionally, by prison guards who had forced him to shout: 'Putin is our President!'. My articles annoyed the Russian authorities so much that one year, I was singled out by a state media study that said I had the most negative attitude towards Russia of any British journalist.[1] Of course, when the study said my reporting was negative, what it really meant was that it was critical of Putin, the Kremlin and the corrupt officials who were busy purchasing luxury properties in Europe and the United States while preaching to their people about the evils of the West. My Russian friends told me that such high-level condemnation meant I was doing a good job. 'Congratulations! That's real success,' one wrote to me. I received half a dozen similar messages. Less than a decade on, almost all of those Russians are now living in exile, forced out by Putin's bid to reshape their homeland in his own malevolent image.

In February 2022, just days after Russian troops and tanks had poured into Ukraine, I was arrested while reporting on an anti-war protest near Red Square. Perhaps unwisely, I had tried to distract police who had seized a couple of protesters by flashing my press accreditation at the officers and asking questions. I'd done this in the past at opposition rallies and sometimes my brief interventions had allowed demonstrators to wriggle free. But not on this occasion: the mood was turning ugly and a hefty officer in a black mask grabbed me and pushed me into a nearby police truck. 'Charge him with resisting police,' he shouted. As I sat down on a hard wooden seat inside the truck alongside a dozen or so other detainees, the grim thought occurred to me that this was probably the worst time to be arrested as a British journalist in Russia since the height of the Cold War.

We were held in the truck for about four hours and then driven to a police station in northern Moscow. I was separated from the others and led into a small room where two men in plain clothes were waiting for me. They did not identify themselves, but everything about them suggested they were from the Federal Security Service (FSB), a successor agency to the KGB, the Soviet secret police.

'What do you know about Russia?' was their first question. I asked them how long they had and one of them made a show of looking at his wristwatch. 'For ever,' he replied. I gave them a quick potted history of Russian political history from 2000, when Putin first came to power, finishing off with a brief summary of the structure of United Russia, his ruling party. 'How do you know all that?' one of them asked. 'I had a quick read of Wikipedia before I left the house,' I replied. But they weren't in the mood for sarcasm. 'What do you think about Putin?' the other demanded to know. I shrugged. 'What difference does it make to you?' But they were adamant. 'We want to know. The sooner you tell us, the sooner you can get out of here.'

A police station in Moscow didn't seem like the best place to reveal my true feelings. I wasn't going to lie, though. I considered my reply. 'It must be very hard to manage such a large country effectively,' I said, eventually. My interrogator gave me the thumbs up, as if I was a contestant in some bizarre quiz show who had just provided the correct answer. I was later released without charge, but it was an unsettling experience. Everything we thought we knew about reporting from Russia, about the unspoken rules that Western journalists would not be arrested, or harmed, was suddenly up in the air.

We weren't the only ones who were confused. A few days after the invasion, I called a Kremlin adviser in the hope of gaining some insight. He appeared to be as shocked as everyone else. 'Can you speak?' I asked him, unsure if his phone was being tapped. 'I can speak, but the problem is that I have nothing to say. I have no idea what is happening,' he replied. When I pushed him for an opinion, he said he believed that Putin had decided to create a new political system, one that would have nothing in common with the West. He refused to go on the record, however.

In the early weeks of the war, Moscow made it a crime to publish 'fake news' about the actions of the Russian army in Ukraine, a move that essentially made it illegal to report the truth.[2] A few days later, I attended a nervy breakfast at the British embassy for journalists. As rumours swirled that Putin was about to announce martial law, a move that could close borders and have citizens of 'hostile' countries locked up in internment camps, we were told that it was time to make decisions about our own safety and that of our families. It was made very clear that if anything happened to us, the British special forces would not be parachuting into Russia on a rescue mission. After that meeting, as I walked back into central Moscow with two other Western journalists who had also started families in Russia, it became clear that our lives in the country were over, perhaps for ever. So, this is what it feels like to live through history, I thought.

There was a sense that events were rapidly spinning out of control. The afternoon before my arrest, I was coming home from our local shops when a vast motorcade sped past on its way from the nearby Kremlin. 'Something's up,' a passer-by said, as we both stared at the fast-moving stream of black vehicles with tinted windows. Putin was almost certainly a passenger in one of the cars. I tried to put myself inside the Kremlin dictator's head, as I have done so many times over the years while Russia lurched from crisis to crisis, but it was harder than ever that day. I was still wondering what the motorcade might signify when an editor called me from London. Putin had just put Russia's nuclear forces on high alert.[3] I hurried home, absurdly trying to hold my shopping in one hand while using the other to check on my phone what Russian state media was saying. Was it time, I wondered, to get to the nearest bunker? Come to that, where was it? Should I call my family and friends in Britain to warn them?

After the fake news law came into force, my employer, *The Times* newspaper, decided that it was too dangerous for me to remain in Russia and asked me and my family to leave. By this stage, all direct flights between Russia and the West had been cancelled and the scramble for seats meant that there were very few options left. The paper eventually booked us onto a flight to London via Dubai for the following day. Not that long ago, it had been possible to buy a return ticket from Moscow to London on a discount airline for around £70. Now, Russia was more isolated than it had ever been. Even at the height of the Cold War there had been regular flights between Western Europe and Moscow.

Yet leaving Russia after 25 years was not so easy. My wife and daughter are both Russian citizens and I was reluctant to uproot them overnight. There were also practical issues to consider. Where would we live in England? How would we pack decades of our lives into three suitcases? What would we do with Misha, our tabby cat with a broken tail that we had rescued from the streets of a small town near Moscow? These were, of course, minor issues compared to the multitude of horrors in Ukraine, but that didn't make it any less stressful. Eventually, our suitcases overflowing and our heads pounding with the implications of leaving so suddenly, we gave up. 'Fuck it – let's stay,' I blurted out, just hours before our flight was due to depart. My suggestion met little resistance.

Once we had taken the decision to remain, a great calm descended upon me. Over the next few days, however, as friends and fellow journalists fled Russia to destinations that ranged from Argentina to Uzbekistan, I began to wonder if I had made a mistake. It suddenly felt very lonely in Moscow. For the next week or so, every time I heard footsteps on the stairwell or the clanking of the lift in the early hours, I wondered if the sounds signalled an unwelcome visit from the FSB, and arrest. I held on for three more months, using a pseudonym for some of my articles. It was unclear whether officials would charge foreign reporters who violated the new censorship laws, but there didn't seem to be much sense in taking the risk. It was unsustainable though. Two months into the war, I received a message from one of my editors: 'Our security team thinks you could be arrested,' it read. 'Call me.'

I left Russia a few weeks later and my wife and daughter followed shortly after. Yet, even as I was leaving, despite the risks, I wondered if such a drastic exit from Russia was really necessary. After all, while the Kremlin had imprisoned its own journalists, it had so far refrained from locking up Western correspondents. Any doubts about the wisdom of the move were, however, dispelled in March 2023 when Evan Gershkovich, an American journalist at the *Wall Street Journal*, was detained on trumped-up espionage charges while on a reporting trip in Yekaterinburg, a city 1,000 miles east of Moscow. In an ominous sign of the times, he was the first Western reporter to be arrested by Russia since the Cold War. He spent 16 months in Russian prisons before finally being released in August 2024 as part of the biggest prisoner exchange between Moscow and the West for almost 40 years.[4]

I preferred to think of my departure as a retreat from Moscow, rather than an escape. Yet I have not been back since and I am not sure that I ever will. In December 2022, the Russian embassy in Britain wrote on social media that I have been 'banned from entering Russia for several years'.[5] No further confirmation was forthcoming, however.

As Oleksandr and I drove back to our hotel in Kherson, the only one still operating in the city, I considered again how close I had come to being killed or maimed by soldiers from a country where I had spent so long. It was an unpleasant thought, but also one that triggered a process of remembering. Since my unplanned departure from Moscow, I had tried to suppress my memories of Russia. They were too raw and too painful: my recollections of even the good times – and there were many – tainted by the suffering that Russia had caused in Ukraine, as well as my reluctance to accept that the Moscow I once knew was likely gone for ever.

We arrived back at the hotel and I went to my room to try and relax. Like other reporters in Ukraine, I had grown used to sleeping through air raids and the dull thud of shelling. But, as I lay in my bed that night, it wasn't the missiles that kept me awake. A sudden cascade of memories from my life in Moscow came pouring back, as if the artillery shell that had almost killed me had dislodged the mental barrier I had imposed to keep them at bay.

Everyone had known that Putin was leading Russia towards catastrophe, but no one could have guessed the path to escalation would be so very short. If Russian bombs have twisted Ukraine's landscapes into grotesque, barely recognizable shapes, then Putin's war on dissent at home has also transformed Moscow, purging it of the artists, civil society activists and non-conformists who once made it such a vibrant place. 'I used to live in Moscow, you know?' I jokingly reminded a friend who had remained in the city when she absent-mindedly began to explain to me the location of a place I knew well. 'So did I,' she replied, despairingly. 'So did I.'

As I finally began to drift off to sleep that night in Kherson, a downbeat song by the Soviet rock band Kino, whose lyrics had helped me learn Russian back when Putin was still an obscure official, began to play on repeat in my head, like a mantra. '*I knew it would be bad/but I didn't know it would be so soon,*' Viktor Tsoi, the group's vocalist, had sung.[6] And what, it occurred to me, as I recalled my decades spent in Moscow, the torrent of memories punctuated by the boom of artillery duels, could be more appropriate?

My final interaction in Moscow with a Russian citizen after 25 years in the country was a fittingly grotesque encounter with a veterinarian official whose office was behind a metal door in a corner of the city's Vnukovo airport. The documents to take our cat to Britain were all in order, but I still needed final permission to remove him from Russia, something that was only possible on the day of my departure. I banged on the metal door. A few moments later, it was yanked open and the vet ushered me into his office. His eyes were red and he had the sweaty, dishevelled appearance of someone who has clearly been drinking most of the night. On his desk, there was a small metal bust of Stalin. 'Did Stalin also like animals?' I asked, jokingly. 'Only fried ones,' the vet replied. And, like that, my life in Russia was over. The vet stamped my papers, and I was ready to leave. A couple of hours later, I was on board a Turkish Airlines flight heading out of the country. I had flown out of Moscow dozens of times since my arrival in Russia half a lifetime ago, but I had always known I would return. This time, I could not be sure that I would ever see the city again. We ascended swiftly, Moscow's familiar landscape growing smaller and smaller. I had not planned to grow old in Russia, but I was sad to be leaving like this. I had wanted our departure to be planned carefully, at a time of our own choosing and on our terms. But at least, unlike millions of Ukrainians, I wasn't fleeing into the unknown. My home had not been destroyed by Russian missiles and my friends and family had not been murdered by Putin's sadistic troops. The plane entered the clouds and Moscow was no longer visible. I was gripped by a sudden weariness and I slept for most of the flight, only awakening when the plane touched down.

There are many things that intrigue me about Russia. Even after so long in Moscow, I remain curious about its culture and its people. But since the start of the invasion of Ukraine, the only questions that really concern me are these: why is it that a country of 144 million people, the homeland of some of our planet's greatest minds, has allowed itself to be ruled by the same former KGB officer, a man of unremarkable intellectual ability, for a quarter of a century and counting? How and why did Russia slide so quickly into violent nationalism? Was this always Putin's plan? Or did he, as a disillusioned ex-Kremlin adviser suggested to me, submit to madness and paranoia during his decades in power?

Other countries have undertaken unjustified invasions, but rarely have they gone to war with such obvious contempt for the lives of their own soldiers. How did Putin suck millions of Russians into his own distorted view of reality? One where priests bless nuclear weapons, where convicted murderers lecture children on patriotism and parents reject their sons and daughters because they oppose the slaughter of civilians in Ukraine. And, most importantly, how much longer will Putin's regime last? How and when will it fall? And when it does, what kind of Russia will emerge from its ruins?

2

'Look Around This Place'

The pulsating rhythms boomed across central Moscow as The Prodigy took to the stage in front of around 200,000 delirious fans just off Red Square. 'I'm a firestarter, twisted firestarter!' shouted Keith Flint, the British group's frantic vocalist, his eyes lined with heavy black mascara and his hair spiked up. Police struggled to hold back a sea of pogoing teenagers. Some eventually gave up and joined in with the dancing.[1]

Flint leapt into the air, revealing the Union Jack patch on the back of his denim jacket, as the walls of the nearby Kremlin reverberated to the heaviest basslines ever to have been heard at the ancient seat of Russian state power. Just behind the stage was the tomb of Vladimir Lenin, the leader of the 1917 Bolshevik revolution that ushered in seven decades of communist rule. This area of Moscow had once witnessed Soviet Army parades: vast displays of tanks, missiles and troops that were intended to send an unsubtle message to Western countries about the Kremlin's military might. It was from Red Square that Soviet soldiers had also headed directly to the front to defend Moscow from invading Nazi forces after a parade that was overseen by Stalin in 1941.

It was September 1997 and I had been in Russia for eight months and in Moscow for just three weeks. Occasionally, music, location and time come together in glorious synchronicity and that evening in the very heart of the Russian capital was a potent symbol of the changes that had swept the country since the disintegration of the Soviet Union fewer than six years earlier.

'Fuck them, and their law,' yelled Maxim, The Prodigy's rapper, as guests at the nearby National Hotel, where Lenin had stayed for a while after the revolution, danced energetically on their balconies. This was so far from the Russia that I had grown up hearing about that it felt for a moment, as strobe lights illuminated the Kremlin's famous towers, that we had all slipped into an alternative dimension.

The Prodigy's violent, frenzied and anarchic music was the perfect soundtrack to the chaos that gripped Russia in the 1990s under President Yeltsin, as crime rates rocketed, living standards slumped and millions put their faith in new ideologies to try and fill the gaps left by the now discredited Soviet system. But it also encapsulated the exuberance of the era. After having spent so long being forced to at least pay lip service to the ideas of Marx and Lenin, Russians were high on their newfound freedoms. The entire country often felt like one massive economic and social experiment. National television, now rid of the suffocating censorship that had turned Soviet media into a soporific parody of itself, had become a genuine force. One of the most popular programmes was a political satire that was based on Britain's *Spitting Image* and mercilessly mocked Yeltsin and his inner circle. Only a few decades before, even the mildest criticism of Soviet leaders had been enough to result in imprisonment in a gulag labour camp, or worse.

In another indication of change, the nightclubs around Red Square were infamous for their anything-goes atmosphere, as young people shook off the stifling atmosphere of the Soviet period in a heady cocktail of sex, music and alcohol. In the summer, scantily clad patrons spilled out of the clubs onto the streets around Lubyanka Square, home to the headquarters of the FSB state security service. One evening, I saw a group of young men break-dancing close to the spot where a statue of Felix Dzerzhinsky, the Soviet Union's first secret police chief, had stood before it was torn down by pro-democracy protesters in 1991. One of them was wearing a USA baseball cap decorated with the Stars and Stripes. Such startling symbolism was everywhere you looked.

Yet there was also a far darker side to Yeltsin's presidency. The conflict in Chechnya, where Russian troops killed and tortured civilians with almost total impunity, was a bloody stain on his time in office. Likewise, Yeltsin's use of the army to remove rebel lawmakers from the country's legislature in 1993 was evidence that while the Soviet Union may have been no more, the Kremlin still preferred brute force to diplomacy. His government's economic 'shock therapy', a policy that was supported by US advisers, had also plunged millions into poverty after Soviet price controls were lifted, sparking hyperinflation, while corruption was rampant, including among top officials.

It became common to see pensioners touting their possessions to survive, once-cherished items piled on the ground near metro stations or in filthy underpasses, for sale to the highest bidder. On the outskirts of Moscow, near the kiosks that sold alcohol and cigarettes around the clock, gangs of children or crippled soldiers begged for money. Contract killings rocketed, as criminal gangs settled their differences with extreme violence. Police officers had more interest in securing bribes to supplement their meagre salaries than combatting crime. 'They gave us guns and said: "do what you gotta do,"' an indignant police officer told me once in Moscow, after he had tried, unsuccessfully, to shake me down for a bribe. 'Do you know what we earn?' his fellow officer said, angry at my refusal to cough up some cash. Then they asked me if I could teach their children English.

As the economy collapsed, people went without their wages for months on end. Some struggling factories paid their employees with the goods they had produced in lieu of salaries. The workers were then expected to try and sell these items, which could be anything from shoes to sausages to windowpanes, as best they could. For several months, one factory near Moscow paid its employees with flare guns. Local gangs bought them up and converted them into lethal weapons. 'Once, my mum received mackerel from the fish-canning factory where she worked in place of her salary,' a friend told me. 'We ate mackerel soup until we burst, but we couldn't afford much bread to go with it.'

Others moonlighted as unofficial taxi drivers, simply driving around the streets of their hometowns until someone flagged them down. In Moscow, you rarely had to wait for more than a minute before a car skidded to a halt. You then negotiated the price and off you went. Every week I met an incredible and varied cast of characters who were trying to make ends meet, from nuclear physicists and doctors to army officers. Once, an off-duty ambulance stopped for me. There was still blood on the stretcher when I jumped into the back. A few weeks after that, some new Russian friends I was with paid a bus driver $20 to alter his route and drop them off at their house during a snowstorm.

Later, Putin claimed that he too had briefly been forced to work as an unofficial taxi driver in his free time to provide for his family.[2] His comment was widely mocked in the West, but it is unsurprising that his words were taken at face value by millions of his fellow citizens: Russia in the 1990s was a society in total freefall. Yet not everyone was living badly: a new class of businessmen, as well as those Westerners with the nerve for the cut-throat world of Russian commerce, grew massively wealthy, very quickly. 'Russia is on sale now, and those who arrive late will have to pay more,' wrote the *Harvard Business Review*.[3]

In return for vital support for his floundering re-election campaign in 1996, Yeltsin also handed over Russia's assets to the oligarchs, the new breed of tycoons who had taken advantage of the economic mayhem of the Soviet collapse to seize control of state enterprises, from oil companies to television stations. With their vast fortunes and control of media outlets, the oligarchs were Russia's shadow rulers, orchestrating events with a barely disguised contempt for the country's fledgling democracy. Or *dermokratia* – shitocracy – as many Russians had begun to refer to their new political system. That night in central Moscow as The Prodigy ramped up the beats near Red Square, I knew I was witnessing something deeply symbolic. What I didn't, and couldn't, realize was that the era of unprecedented social freedoms in Russia was grinding to a halt. As if the path of history had taken a wrong turn with the collapse of the Soviet Union and was now correcting itself, something far darker than even Yeltsin's warped version of democracy was on its way. A quarter of a century on, my very recollections of that concert now seem unreal, like a false memory or a fever dream.

I'd arrived in Russia in January 1997 when I was 26. Since dropping out of university halfway through my first year, I had travelled around South America and spent time living in a huge, squatted house in New Cross, a district of London that is south of the River Thames. I played guitar in a noisy rock group, stayed up for days at squat parties, and wrote an unpublished novel. Unsurprisingly, I was unemployed for most of the time, but I had always had my eye on Russia. Pre-internet, despite being almost penniless, I purchased the broadsheets three or four times a week; more if there was major news from Moscow. I spent countless lazy afternoons in south London poring over articles about Russia. Back then, the notion that I would one day become *The Times*'s correspondent in Moscow was not something that would have occurred to me, even in my wildest fantasises.

Growing up during the Cold War, the Soviet Union had been a constant presence throughout my childhood, its very existence synonymous with the nightmarish prospect of global nuclear conflict. 'What would you do if you heard the four-minute warning?' my classmates and I sometimes asked each other, as we considered what actions we would take in the short time that would be left before the Soviet warheads rained down. During the Christmas holidays of 1979, I watched televised footage of Soviet tanks rolling into Afghanistan. It is my first real memory of international affairs.

I didn't know much back then about the realities of the communist system, but the brief glimpses of Red Square I caught on the news were an intriguing window into another world. There was so little information available about everyday life in the Soviet

Union that my imagination filled the gaps. When school lessons grew too tiresome, I tried to waste time by lying to my teachers that I was a devout communist, something that was guaranteed to draw most of them into lengthy tirades against the evils of the Soviet system.

But Russia, I soon discovered, wasn't just about geopolitics. I was in my early teens when my parents gave me *The Master and Margarita* by Mikhail Bulgakov, a surreal Stalin-era novel about a visit by the devil and his diabolic cohorts to Moscow. My parents had no connection to Russia; like many young people in the 1960s, they had first heard of the book when it provided the inspiration for the lyrics to 'Sympathy for the Devil', the epic, bongo-driven song by the Rolling Stones. Although much of the novel went over my head at the time, I was captivated by the depictions of Satanic mischief in Soviet Russia. My parents could not have known that I would later end up spending 25 years in Moscow, often wandering the very same streets as Bulgakov's fictional demons. And, on occasion, encountering some very real ones. In an ironic twist, our final apartment in Moscow overlooked a huge mural of Bulgakov that had been painted onto the facade of the neighbouring house.

In August 1991, as communist hardliners staged an unsuccessful coup to reverse Soviet leader Mikhail Gorbachev's democratic reforms, I was trekking in Venezuela. One afternoon, when I emerged from the jungle into a tiny village, I picked up a newspaper and saw images of Yeltsin on top of a tank in Moscow. My Spanish wasn't great, but I understood enough to realize that momentous changes were underway in Russia. The coup leaders had put Gorbachev under house arrest in Crimea, claiming falsely that he was too ill to perform his duties. But the coup was badly planned and its leaders had apparently not considered that they would face resistance. Huge crowds flooded the streets of Moscow and other cities to defend Gorbachev's reforms, while some Soviet troops openly sided with the protesters. Within days, the last-ditch attempt by Stalin's heirs to plunge the country back into its totalitarian past was over. Yeltsin banned the Communist

Party three months later and by the end of the year, the Soviet Union had ceased to exist. History comes at you fast in Russia, and often when you least expect it. That was something I would later experience for myself, time and time again.

I first began to think about moving to Russia in the mid-1990s after splitting up with a girlfriend. We remained good friends, however, and when she moved to Prague to teach English, I visited her on numerous occasions. Her students were from Georgia, a mountainous country on the coast of the Black Sea that had achieved independence from Moscow after seven decades under Soviet rule. It had also recently witnessed an armed conflict in Abkhazia, a Russian-backed breakaway region. The received wisdom was that the break-up of the Soviet Union had been a largely bloodless affair, yet its collapse had clearly resulted in deep fissures throughout the region.

Some of my ex-girlfriend's Georgian students had been driven from their homes during the fighting, while others had taken up arms. They were a colourful group, and we often drank with them in the evenings after lessons and compared our lives in Britain and Georgia. Naturally, the men were still on edge and beneath the laughing and the jokes there was an undercurrent of simmering violence. One of them, Aleksi, had lost an eye in the conflict and had a deep red scar down one side of his face. One night, as we were walking home from a bar through the Czech countryside, Aleksi suddenly lost control and began punching and kicking another student over a perceived insult. It seemed for a moment, until we could restrain him, that the night might end with a serious injury or worse. But having been pulled away, Aleksi appeared to almost instantly forget the insult that had caused him to lash out and he and his fellow student walked the rest of the way home with their arms slung around one another's shoulders.

In the bars and cafes around Prague, I also met Armenians, Belarusians, Russians and Ukrainians, all of them eager to talk about their experiences amid the turbulence of the Soviet collapse. Their stories were often violent, and frequently sad, but I was enthralled. After I returned to Britain, I began to wonder what it would be like to live in a country where all the old certainties had been abandoned and history was being made every week. There wasn't much happening for me in London at the time and swapping the bland stability of Tony Blair's Britain for the unpredictability of Russia began to seem increasingly attractive. Why not head eastwards for a while? I could teach English in Russia for a year or so and then move on, perhaps to south-east Asia. It seemed like an achievable ambition and one that would allow me to see more of the world. Things didn't turn out quite like that.

It was less than six months since a fragile peace had been established in Chechnya, when I flew into St Petersburg, the cradle of the Bolshevik revolution, to take up a job teaching English. I knew only a handful of words in Russian and had only the vaguest idea of what to expect. I was met at the airport by a taciturn driver who took me to a cluster of tower blocks on the frozen outskirts of the city. There, I was introduced to Lyudmila, the woman who was to oversee my lessons. She spoke barely any English, and she had a scarf wrapped around the lower half of her face, making it even harder to understand what she was saying. I later found out that she had been embarrassed about a foreigner seeing her blackened, crumbling teeth.

Lyudmila showed me to the one-room flat where I was to stay, gave me the key and left. It was a typical, threadbare Soviet-era flat, but it was a step-up for me. Since leaving home at the age of 17, I had lived in squatted houses and bedsits – this was the first time I had ever had an entire flat to myself. Around 6 a.m. the next morning I was woken up by the clanking of a tram outside my window. I got up and looked down at the lines of early morning workers, the scene illuminated by the sodium street lamps amid a swirling snowstorm. I realized I didn't even know the name of the street I was now living on. Telephone calls to Britain were so expensive that I would only be able to afford one long call home a week. I had wanted a complete break from London, to immerse myself in the rapidly shifting realities of post-Soviet Russia, but having arrived, the experience was briefly crushing. I couldn't guess back then, of course, that I would spend the next 25 years gazing at snowstorms through the windows of a succession of Russian flats. If I had known, would I have packed my things and booked a ticket on the next flight home? I suspect so. But I stayed and my life is now inextricably intertwined with Russia, for better and for worse.

My fellow teachers were remarkably uncurious about Russia. Before long, bored of endless conversations about lesson plans, I began spending my evenings wandering alone around Nevsky Prospekt, the tsarist-era street that cuts through the centre of St Petersburg. Once, while seeking shelter from an icy wind, I ended up at the city's main train station. A gigantic Soviet-built edifice, its cavernous central hall was fitted with multiple wooden benches, providing somewhere for weary travellers to rest while waiting for their connections. It also acted as an unofficial shelter from sub-zero temperatures for the city's homeless population. That evening I somehow got talking to a few of them. My Russian was still extremely basic, but I was able to make myself understood and grasp at least some of what they were saying. A huge, grizzled man, who looked to be in his forties, told me he had served in Afghanistan. Before I left, he rolled up a sleeve to show me a tattoo of Joseph Stalin on his arm. I couldn't help but notice the needle marks scarring his skin. As a teenager, I had let my imagination run wild about Russia, but I had never considered the existence of junkie Stalinists.

I returned to the station a few times over the next few months, picking up useful Russian swearwords with every visit. I much preferred learning Russian in informal situations like this; I'd had just a handful of lessons in St Petersburg before I decided to teach myself the language, using a dictionary to make sense of newspapers and the lyrics to Russian rock music and then testing out the new additions to my vocabulary in everyday situations. Before long, I was speaking well enough to hold my own in conversations, even if I had to occasionally fake understanding to keep discussions flowing.

During my wanderings, I had also discovered a squatted building that doubled as an arts centre just a short walk from the train station. It hosted a club that was popular with the city's punks, hippies and dropouts. A smoky venue with a cheap bar, it wasn't that different from the clubs that I had once visited in London. The only difference was that these clubgoers were the children of Soviet army officers, dissidents and, in some cases, New Russians – the nouveau riche who had amassed huge fortunes, often through dubious means. The first time I visited, the club's speakers were pumping out 'Fuck tha Police,' the anthemic hit by N.W.A., the American hip-hop group. I hadn't expected to find such places in Russia, but things were changing fast.

I quickly made a few friends. One of them, Sergei, spoke almost perfect English, complete with an arsenal of American slang. He had perfected the language while serving time in New York for a crime that he was reluctant to go into detail about. A moody man in his mid-thirties with tattoos on both arms, he was cynical about Russia's leaders, but intensely passionate about its people. 'Look around this place,' he told me once, as we sat drinking tea in a canteen in the centre of St Petersburg, the street outside barely visible behind a snowstorm that masked the city's streets like static. 'Every single person here has an intense life story to tell. It's probably fucking tragic, and barely believable, but this is a city where everyone has experienced so much that we are all walking novels.'

A year in Russia, I ascertained, would be woefully insufficient to gain a proper understanding of the country. Russian society had been turned on its head. People who, just a decade or so before, had been members of Soviet youth movements were now bankers, while once-respected academics who lectured on Marxism–Leninism were now scrabbling to make ends meet within a capitalist system they had spent their entire lives condemning. If I'd had a journalist's notebook, it would have been full before my first year in the country was out. I decided to stay on.

My employer had other ideas, though. When my contract was up, the head of the school where I taught called me to tell me that it was not being renewed. The reason for my dismissal? An important client had complained after seeing me drinking beer at the train station with '*bomzhi*'. The word is the Soviet acronym for tramps and stands for *Bez Opredelyonnogo Mesta Zhitelstva* – Of No Fixed Abode.

'We have our reputation to consider,' the school director told me. And that was that. With no work and my visa running out, I flew back to London for the summer. That could have been the end of my time in Russia, but I was desperate to return. Life in Britain was dull and uneventful after the months I had spent in St Petersburg. After a few weeks, I applied for another teaching position with a different school in Moscow. I did not mention my fondness for chatting to *bomzhi* and the day after the interview they called me to say I had the job. I flew to Moscow in the autumn of 1997, just in time to catch The Prodigy's historic concert beneath the Kremlin's walls.

I had moved to Russia to work as a teacher, but what I really wanted to do was write. Yet I had no meaningful knowledge of how one went about becoming a journalist. I had grown up in Knowle West, a notoriously rough council estate on the outskirts of Bristol, where I attended a comprehensive school that was eventually closed down after it was rated among the worst ten in the country for academic results.[4] The estate was also home to Adrian Thaws, better known as Tricky, a future member of Massive Attack, the internationally acclaimed trip-hop group, and a solo star in his own right. Years later, Tricky would also fall for Moscow, spending long periods of time in the city and even recording tracks with Russian rappers. There must have been something in the water in Knowle West in the 1970s and 1980s.

When I was 18, I moved to London to study English Literature and International Relations at university, but quit after my first term, unable and unwilling to adapt to the discipline of serious study. Unsurprisingly, when I arrived in Russia, I lacked contacts in the media or any real idea of how one went about making them. Instead, I spent the first few years of my time in the country testing my limits for alcohol abuse, waking up too many times in strange flats in the suburbs of Moscow or St Petersburg, with only hazy memories of how I had got there.

One evening, in the summer of 1998, I was invited to a party at a nuclear power station not far from Voronezh, a city that was closer to the border with Ukraine than it was to Moscow. I had been keen to see more of Russia beyond its two biggest cities and I had moved there for a few months that spring when a teaching vacancy became available. Located in central Russia's Black Earth Region, named after its famously fertile soil, Voronezh was where Peter the Great had established Russia's first shipyard in the late seventeenth century. By the time I arrived, however, like most provincial cities in Russia, it was run-down and economically depressed. Russian dialects are relatively uniform, but it was in Voronezh that I first encountered the soft 'g' pronunciation that has more in common with the Ukrainian language than the Russian spoken in Moscow.

Pavel, a middle-aged teacher who was one of my students, was going out with a female security guard at the Novovoronezh atomic power plant and he took me along to the party. We set off in the late afternoon and drove through the Black Earth countryside. When we arrived, we were waved through a security checkpoint and pulled up outside a small building in sight of the Soviet-built nuclear facility. We were greeted by three security guards, including Pavel's girlfriend, an older woman with blonde hair. There was pop music on the radio, snacks and a fire bucket full of samogon, a potent, homebrewed alcoholic drink.

As the evening wore on, two truck drivers arrived. As far as I could make out, they were there to pick up some nuclear waste, but not before they had sunk a few rounds of samogon. Inevitably, they wanted to know exactly what I was doing at the party, in

Voronezh and, indeed, in Russia. I must have said the right thing because very soon, I was sitting in the front seat of their truck, just metres away from the barbed wire fence around the nuclear power plant. I had let on that I was unable to drive and the truckers had decided to teach me there and then. I put my foot down on the pedal and the massive vehicle lurched forwards a few feet. This was just 12 years since the Chernobyl nuclear disaster and I had visions of crashing into the power station, sending a plume of radioactive smoke into the air. I had no idea how plausible that danger was, but an alert sounded in my alcohol-frazzled brain. I clambered out of the driver's seat. Undeterred, one of the truckers took over and we did a few drunken laps of the perimeter of the nuclear plant, occasionally veering dangerously close to the security fence. Was anyone at all in charge of Russia these days? I wondered, as the next day we drove back to the city along potholed roads that looked like they hadn't been repaired since World War Two. As Yeltsin sank into alcoholism, I wasn't the only one having such thoughts.

At the time, being from a Western country was generally an advantage in Moscow: being able to utter 'I'm from Britain' was a ticket to many things, from salaries that most locals could only dream of, to entry into nightclubs with the strictest bouncers. But it would be wrong to say that the distrust of the West that had been encouraged by the communist regime had vanished entirely. In Voronezh, the janitor at the House of Culture where I taught English took every opportunity to lecture me on the evils of the West. It was easy to see why he was bitter: he was an educated man in his fifties who had lost his job at a state-run company after the break-up of the Soviet system and had been reduced to sweeping up after me and my few, relatively well-off, students. On my last day at the school, he gifted me a communist-era book called *Britain without Fog*[5] (it is a common myth across the former Soviet Union that the British Isles are perpetually shrouded in fog). 'You should know the truth about your country,' he said. The book, which was published in 1985, contained chapters about the Troubles in Northern Ireland, the crackdown on the

Greenham Common anti-nuclear protests, mass unemployment and the far-right National Front movement's attempts to infiltrate the British Army. One photograph showed a demonstrator holding up a sign that read 'I am ashamed to be British.' It didn't tell me anything new, and the rhetoric was so hyperbolic as to be laughable, but it was another useful reminder that not everyone in Russia was in thrall to the West.

Around a year later, in March 1999, Nato began bombing Yugoslavia, a Russian ally and a fellow Orthodox Slav nation, in a bid to prevent ethnic cleansing in Kosovo. Yevgeny Primakov, the Russian prime minister, was on a plane to Washington in the hope of securing billions of dollars of aid from the International Monetary Fund when he was informed that American air strikes were about to begin. He ordered his plane to turn around halfway over the Atlantic in protest.[6] In Moscow, anti-American sentiments soared and an angry mob smashed windows at the US embassy. 'Yankee go home!' a group of Russian men shouted at me one day in the street while I was speaking English to a friend. They laughed as they said it and there didn't appear to be any real malice behind their words. I told them that I was British and that I had never even been to America, something that was true at the time. Apparently chastened, they apologized and insisted on buying my friend and I beers. I decided not to remind them that Britain was also a member of Nato.

If that incident passed off peacefully, that wasn't the case a few weeks later in Voronezh when I got into an altercation with locals who held me personally responsible for the bombardment of Yugoslavia. I'm not sure if they thought I was American, or whether they were just better informed about Nato's member states than their ideological allies in Moscow. Either way, I didn't see the punch coming and I landed heavily, fracturing my left arm. It was when we arrived at the hospital that things got really bad though. There were stray dogs in the unlit corridors and a drunk doctor grilled me about Nato. 'Why did you bomb Belgrade?' he yelled, as nurses laughed. Inevitably, he then asked me if I was an English spy. I left with my arm in a crude sling, staggering past a teenager with half his face burnt off who was sobbing in a corner and stumbled through the surrounding forest to the main road, where I hitched a lift back into town with a passing truck driver.

Back in Moscow, a Russian friend told me that he and his family were moving to a small, remote town in Canada. 'But won't you be bored there?' I asked. He looked at me and sighed. 'Marc, to be absolutely honest, we are very much looking forward to a bit of boredom.' I suddenly felt very foolish. It was one thing to be a foreigner amid the turmoil and near-anarchy of post-Soviet Russia, but it was an entirely different experience for those who had seen their lives turned upside down within the space of a few short years. Back then, I had no ties at all to Russia. I could have packed up and left within a day and very few people would have even noticed. 'Boredom,' my friend repeated, taking a swig of beer, as if it were the name of an expensive holiday resort. Within a month, he and his family were gone. I never saw them again.

3

A Pact with The Devil

In under a decade, the Russian people had witnessed an attempted coup, the near collapse of the economy and an unprecedented crime wave. Amid the chaos, many craved a firmer hand. 'One cannot exclude the possibility of a fascist period in Russia,' Galina Starovoitova, a reformist politician and the co-leader of the Democratic Russia party, warned. 'We can see too many parallels between Russia's current situation and that of Germany after the Treaty of Versailles. A great nation is humiliated and many of its nationals live outside the country's borders. The disintegration of an empire has taken place at a time when many people still have an imperialistic mentality.'[1]

It was not just the rise of fascism that Starovoitova, an MP and adviser to Yeltsin in the early 1990s, was worried about. After the failure of the 1991 coup by Soviet hardliners, Vladimir Bukovsky, a well-known dissident and former political prisoner, had cautioned that it was too early to celebrate the defeat of the totalitarian state that had murdered and imprisoned tens of millions of its own people. 'Don't be fooled,' Bukovsky said during a speech[2] in Moscow. 'The dragon is not dead yet. It is mortally wounded, its spine is broken, but it still holds human souls and many countries in its claws.'

His words had little impact. When the Soviet Union collapsed a few months later, Russia's new authorities took no steps[3] to ensure that former servants of the communist regime could not return to power. Instead of disbanding or reforming the KGB, the dreaded Soviet secret police, they simply renamed it the FSB. Its archives, which contained damning files on informers and human rights abuses, remained closed to the public. Russia did not even undertake what would have been a hugely symbolic gesture by relocating the FSB from its vast headquarters on Lubyanka Square, where those who fell foul of the communist state were once tortured and executed.

There was nothing at all to stop former Soviet-era officials responsible for political persecution from assuming high-ranking posts in the new Russia. Vyacheslav Lebedev, a judge who had convicted pro-democracy dissidents, was appointed the head of the Supreme Court. In St Petersburg, Viktor Cherkesov, a notorious ex-KGB officer, was made the city's top security official. Even the coup plotters were amnestied by the Kremlin, despite initially being charged with high treason. One of them, General Valentin Varennikov, a diehard Stalinist, insisted on a trial, which he used to showcase his lack of remorse. 'I have no regrets about what I did, but I have a bitter feeling that we failed to save the country,' he said.[4] He was acquitted by the court, which accepted his defence that his actions were inspired by patriotism.

In Germany after World War Two, many people who had been members of the Nazi Party were banned from holding positions of influence, while in post-Soviet Eastern Europe, similar measures, known as lustration (the word derives from the Latin word for purification rituals, *lustratio*), were undertaken with regards to former communist officials.

Starovoitova wanted something similar for Russia. She twice proposed legislation that would have forbidden *all* ex-KGB employees, as well as Communist Party members implicated in human rights violations, from taking up government posts for five to ten years. 'The possibility of revenge by the totalitarian regime still remains, and in our society, there are still no institutions that guarantee against this,' she said. When critics of her proposal protested that such a law would amount to a witch hunt against Russians with ties to the fallen Soviet regime, Starovoitova replied: 'But do you want the witches to hunt us?'[5]

Yet parliament was packed with communists and nationalists and Starovoitova's legislation had no chance of being approved. Even Yeltsin, who had been a Communist Party member for almost 30 years, was sceptical about Starovoitova's proposals, which he feared could be used to undermine his own power. Still, Starovoitova would not give up. Even a discussion of lustration, she suggested, had the potential to bring about a vital change in public attitudes. 'Sometimes it's important to identify a goal,' she said. 'Moving towards it can be more important than reaching it.'

In 1996, Starovoitova attempted to stand for president and submitted 1.2 million signatures in support of her bid, a legal requirement under Russian election law. Yet officials claimed that many of the signatures were false, and barred her from the ballot. Years later, under Putin, the head of the Kremlin-loyal election committee, Ella Pamfilova, would routinely use the same tactics to block opposition figures from standing for office. A one-time democrat, Pamfilova had in the mid-1990s put her name to an open letter that was also signed by Starovoitova and other reformers warning of 'the threat of a new totalitarianism in our country'.[6] As Putin's election chief, Pamfilova would tell Russians that they had no need for democracy, 'in the western sense'.[7] Her dramatic transformation had taken a little over 20 years.

Starovoitova's concerns for Russia's future were prescient, but like many prophets, she did not live to see her worst fears come true. In November 1998, as she arrived at her apartment building on the embankment of the Griboyedov Canal in St Petersburg, she was shot three times in the head by two waiting killers, the gunfire ringing out in the darkened stairwell. Her aide, Ruslan Linkov, who had accompanied her home, was injured by the gunmen but survived. He managed to raise the alarm, but Starovoitova was dead before the ambulance arrived. She was just 52.

Assassinations had become a grim fact of life in Russia in the 1990s, but Starovoitova's murder was shocking even by contemporary standards. Her funeral drew a crowd of thousands. For many, her death signalled the end of any hope that Russia could transform into a normal democratic society. 'Russia is never going to be the same. I think Russia has lost its soul,' said Vitali Vitaliev, a writer who had known Starovoitova. 'Maybe we could have democracy, but we don't have it yet,' said Lada Uvarova, another mourner. 'If at the beginning of reforms there was an enthusiasm, an optimism, now something has changed. For older people, times are difficult, and they blame the situation on democracy.'[8]

The head of the FSB at the time was one Vladimir Putin, a former KGB officer who had previously served as St Petersburg's Deputy Mayor. There is no evidence that Putin was involved in Starovoitova's assassination, but her death was one of those moments on which history turns: if Starovoitova had succeeded in her bid to bar former KGB agents from taking office, Putin would never have come to power. After her murder, there was no more serious talk of lustration. 'If this law had been passed, we would be living in a different country,' her sister, Olga Starovoitova, said in 2015. The same, of course, holds true for Ukraine.

The prosecutor's office in St Petersburg opened a criminal case under Article 277 of the Russian Criminal Code, which specifically deals with the assassinations of politicians aimed at 'terminating' their political activities. Putin, however, disagreed: 'I do not have any elements from which I can conclude that this was a political murder,' he said.[9]

It was a stance that he and his handpicked security service chiefs would take over the following decades as the Kremlin's fiercest critics were poisoned or gunned down in cold blood. By the time of Russia's full-scale invasion of Ukraine, with Putin's main foes in exile, in prison or in their graves, they no longer seemed to care if the denials were plausible or not. Indeed, Starovoitova remains, to date, the only Russian pro-democracy figure to have been officially recognized as a victim of politically motivated violence.

A number of men, including a former Russian military intelligence officer and an ex-MP with ties to criminal groups, were later convicted of organizing and carrying out Starovoitova's murder. Yet no one has been brought to justice for ordering her assassination and no credible motive has been established, at least officially.

While contract killings were common in St Petersburg in the 1990s, critics said that the close ties between organized crime and the authorities meant that it was unlikely a politician as prominent as Starovoitova could have been targeted without at least the approval of senior officials. Starovoitova's sister, who died in 2021, said that she suspected other members of the Russian security services had also been involved. They had, she said, always loathed 'talkative women'. She did not believe, however, that Putin had given the order for her sister's murder. 'He didn't take such radical decisions back then,' she said. It was possible, she conceded, that the future Russian president had known about the assassination plot: 'But that it was his idea? It's hard for me to wrap my head around that,' she said.[10]

While the exact circumstances of Starovoitova's murder remain murky, what is clear is that she had represented another side of Russia, one that, unlike Putin and his revanchist allies in the security services, wished to live in peace with its neighbours. In 1991, on the day after Soviet Ukraine had voted in a referendum for independence from Moscow, Starovoitova, in her role as an advisor on interethnic issues for Yeltsin, visited the office of Kyiv's permanent representative in Moscow, Volodymyr Kryzhanivsky. She was carrying flowers. 'I handed him roses and congratulated him on the first day of Ukraine's independence,' she recalled later. 'He was amazed by this. They were probably expecting tanks more than roses at that moment.'[11]

Less than a year after Starovoitova's murder, an ailing Yeltsin appointed Putin as Prime Minister. Shortly afterwards, a series of explosions ripped through apartment blocks across Russia, killing hundreds. Amid suspicions that the blasts had been organized by the FSB to propel its former boss to the presidency, Putin blamed militants from Chechnya and sent troops back into the rebellious region. 'We are going to pursue terrorists everywhere. If they are in the airport, we will pursue them in the airport.

And if we capture them in the toilet, then we will waste them in the outhouse,' Putin vowed.[12] His popularity soared.

Three months later, on New Year's Eve, Yeltsin announced in a televised address that he was quitting as President. In mumbled comments that underlined just how fast he had declined since leading Russia out of the Soviet Union, he named Putin as his successor. I was in Britain for the holidays and watched as the new man in the Kremlin, tight-lipped and terse, spoke to the nation. In 1991, the Soviet hardliners who had tried unsuccessfully to resurrect the communist regime had been disorganized and inefficient. Nine years on, they had been avenged by Putin and his ruthless allies from the security services. The dragon, its wounds healed, would soon grow fat again on human suffering. And I would be there to witness it all.

Putin didn't exactly promise Russians 'a bit of boredom', but he did offer what was for many the next best thing: stability. The chaos of the 1990s had left deep scars on the Russian psyche and it wasn't only my friend and his family in Moscow who were seeking some relief from the unrelenting turmoil.

'In the nineties they killed people/ And everyone was running around completely naked/ There was no electricity anywhere/ Only fights over jeans and Coca-Cola,' went the lyrics to '90', a track by Monetochka, a popular singer-songwriter, that was released in 2018.[13] Still a teenager when the track was recorded, Monetochka was not even old enough to have witnessed the era's tribulations. 'Everybody in my generation gets told all these terrible stories about the 1990s by their parents, but for us these are kind of like fairy tales before bedtime,' she told an interviewer.[14]

In 1999, my stable income as an English teacher in Moscow, around $600 a month, had been enough to put me among Russia's top earners, officially at least. That would not last long. From 2000 to 2008, Russian gross domestic product (GDP) increased by 94 per cent, while GDP per capita doubled. Living standards soared, the rouble strengthened and foreign investment spiked. It was 'the most outstanding decade in Russian economic history' for almost a century, according to Sergei Guriev, a prominent Russian economist and critic of the Kremlin.[15] It also laid the foundations for Putin's long and brutal rule.

Putin was aided massively by rocketing global oil prices. Oil was the country's main export and the linchpin of its economy and it rose from $13 a barrel in 1998 to $97 by the end of his second term in 2008. Economic policies brought in during Putin's first term, including imposing a flat rate of income tax at 13 per cent, slashing red tape for small businesses and introducing civil service reforms also contributed to the country's upturn in fortunes. As Russians coasted on this unusual wave of economic prosperity, cheap loans, or *kredit*, were available at the drop of a hat and people who had never been abroad, suddenly found that they could afford to take foreign holidays. As for me, I suddenly felt a lot poorer. But at least I no longer had to feel awkward about being richer on an English teacher's salary than many of Russia's most qualified people.

Under Yeltsin's chaotic rule, for all its many failures, Russians were generally freer to say and do what they wanted than at any time during their country's long history. (Unless, of course, they happened to be a resident of Chechnya or impinged upon the profits of Kremlin-connected crooks). Yet the economic turmoil that accompanied Yeltsin's presidency meant that the very concepts of democracy and freedom of speech were linked with memories of deprivation and humiliation for decades. The logic, or so it ran, was that democracy, or at least the fatally flawed version of it that Russia had experienced under Yeltsin, had been given its chance and had blown it.

In March 2000, three months after Putin had taken power, Petr Aven, the head of Alfa, Russia's biggest and most successful private bank, urged the country's new leader to model his rule on that of Augusto Pinochet, the Chilean dictator. 'The only way ahead is for fast [neo]-liberal [economic] reforms, building public support for that path but also using totalitarian force to achieve that. Russia has no other choice,' Aven said. He added in the same interview 'I'm a supporter of Pinochet, not as a person but as a politician who produced results for his country. He was not corrupt. He supported his team of economists for 10 years. You need strength for that. I see that parallel here. There are similarities in the situation.'

While Pinochet's regime had killed and tortured thousands of people in the 1970s and 1980s, Aven said he was not advocating a return to the dark days of Soviet political repression. However, he said that Putin would need to use extrajudicial force to clamp down on crime and corruption. 'You can't always fight criminals by staying within the law. You can't always do it peacefully,' he said.[16]

For most Russians, the gradual return to authoritarianism under Putin was no price at all to pay for improved living standards. As the oil dollars flowed, Putin moved to bring national television under the Kremlin's control, scrapped direct elections for governors and promoted his friends from St Petersburg to positions of power or handed them control of state assets. In the years to come, almost every time I suggested to Russians who supported Putin that their leader was a dictator and a crook, if not a heartless killer, they invariably replied something along the lines of: 'We remember what it was like here in the 1990s!'

Following the unprecedented humiliations of the post-Soviet era, Putin also sought to restore a sense of national pride. Key to this was his decision to transform the annual Victory Day holiday to commemorate the defeat of Nazi Germany into a militarized, quasi-religious event. Almost every family in Russia had a relative who was killed in World War Two. No matter that the Soviet Union had signed a secret deal with the Nazis to carve up much of Eastern Europe: the 'sacred war' against Hitler's invading army was a uniting factor like few others. On occasion, this pride obscured the sacrifices made by others. 'Did Britain also fight the Nazis?' an acquaintance in Moscow once asked me. Conversely, it is true that Western countries often failed to fully recognize the massive losses suffered by the Soviet Union during the war, something that stirred resentment in Russia.

In the 1990s and during Putin's first two terms in office, Victory Day was celebrated with festivities, fireworks and families' quiet remembrance of their fallen relatives. My main memory of one alcohol-fuelled Victory Day celebration that I attended in Moscow in the early 2000s is of thousands of people wearing fake rabbit ears that had been handed out, as far as I recall, as an advertising stunt. 'What do rabbit ears have to do with the war?' I asked a friend. 'Who cares?' she replied and took a swig of beer.

All this changed in 2008, when Putin ordered the return of intercontinental ballistic missiles to the Victory Day parade on Red Square for the first time since the Soviet era. The Kremlin's display of its military hardware was largely dismissed in the West: after all, Russia was an energy superpower, raking in billions of dollars every year in sales of oil and gas to eager European markets. The possibility of Moscow actually doing anything with these weapons to harm its mutually lucrative business with the West was far-fetched and barely worth considering, at least in the eyes of American and European policymakers.

'If they wish to get out their old equipment and take it for a spin, they're more than welcome to do so,' a Pentagon spokesman said that year, as Russian tanks and ballistic missiles rumbled across Red Square.[17] Andy Vernon, the British defence attaché in Moscow, interpreted the display as Putin's way of announcing that Russia was back on the world stage. 'But we shouldn't take this as an aggressive act. Nor are we quaking in our boots. We are not returning to the Cold War,' he said.[18] Three months later, Russia sent troops into neighbouring Georgia. It was the first time since the Soviet era that Moscow had undertaken military action outside its own borders. It would not be the last. 'Putin's Plan is for Victory!' billboards in central Moscow had proclaimed in the run-up to the conflict.

As tensions with the West accelerated, Victory Day celebrations grew increasingly frenzied. It became common for schools and even nurseries to dress children up in Soviet military uniforms, while some parents decorated their baby strollers as tanks. Military outfits were also available for newborns: in 2016, a khaki onesie was on sale for 950 roubles (around £8 at the time). 'The buttons and the star are real, made out of metal, so we don't recommend leaving the child in the costume unsupervised,' the accompanying advert read.[19] The same year, a popular Victory Day video portrayed the 'ghost' of a young boy who had been killed while fighting the Nazis. 'Was it scary to die?' another child asked him. 'That's not important,' he replied. 'What's important is that we won.' On the following Victory Day, I stood watching on Tverskaya, the street that runs towards the Kremlin, as children were given free lessons on how to disembowel a stuffed dummy with bayonets. In 2020, two years before Putin launched his multipronged invasion of Ukraine, Karolina Chernikh, an 11-year-old girl, stood barefoot on a bed of nails for 75 minutes – one minute for every year since the end of the war. She wore a military uniform while carrying out her feat of endurance and listened to Red Army songs to keep her spirits up. 'I thought it was a worthy record in memory of my great-grandfathers and great-great-grandfathers who heroically fought on the front,' she said. 'From the forty-fifth minute, I wanted to get off the nails, but I could not allow myself to give in. Gathering my will, I endured, trying to comprehend the sacrifices that were made so that I could grow up healthy and happy.'[20]

As well as a willingness to use violence to maintain power, Putin also inherited from the Soviet regime a determination that Moscow should be feared by the West. It was a desire shared by millions of his fellow citizens, particularly those older Russians who were nostalgic for the communist era. In 2018, shortly after Kremlin agents had attempted to kill Sergei Skripal, the Russian double agent, in the small English city of Salisbury, I arrived home from a trip to Britain. We had recently moved to a new apartment block and the residents' comings and goings were watched over by elderly women who topped up their pensions by working as caretakers for a few days a week. The building had been constructed in the 1970s for employees of the Russian foreign ministry and for years the caretakers had been tasked with informing the KGB of any unusual (i.e. foreign) visitors. By the time we moved in, most of the residents had nothing to do with the government, but the caretakers, who worked and even slept in a tiny space at the entrance to the building, were as watchful as ever. As I dragged my suitcase through the entrance, the caretaker on duty greeted me and asked how my journey had been. We were on good terms, and I often entertained her with stories about my reporting trips to Russia's most distant regions.

'So, what do people in Britain think of our Putin? Are they afraid of him?' she asked, smiling. 'Not really,' I replied. 'Most of them just think he's a crazy dictator and feel sorry for you all that he's been your President for so long.' She frowned and picked up her newspaper. We did not speak again for a week or two. The exchange puzzled me: she was not a bad person, or at least I had seen no indications that she was, so why did she feel this need for foreigners to fear her country's ruthless leader? It would never even have occurred to me to ask Russians if they were scared of Theresa May, the British prime minister at the time (May and her government terrified me, it must be said, but that's a separate issue). Russia was in thrall to a semi-suppressed desire for revenge; for the loss of Moscow's superpower status; for the humiliations of the Yeltsin era, both domestically and internationally, and for the collapse of its Soviet empire.

Yet the overwhelming sense I got from travelling across Russia was one of apathy. Most people were utterly convinced that nothing depended upon them, a conviction the Kremlin did its very best to encourage. This indifference sometimes reached barely believable levels. Yevgeniya Chirikova, a well-known opposition figure during Putin's third term in office, told me once that she had been so uninterested in politics that she only discovered the Soviet Union had collapsed in 1998, seven years after the event. The break-up of the communist state was one of the major geopolitical occurrences of the twentieth century, but despite living on the outskirts of Moscow, its epicentre, it had completely failed to register with Chirikova. I initially assumed she was joking, or exaggerating, but it soon became apparent that she was serious.

'I only found out when my husband told me one of his colleagues had had problems on the border with Ukraine,' Chirikova told me. '"What border?" I asked. "It's the same country." My husband looked at me with these massive eyes,' she recalled. '"Not anymore, it's not," he said. "Since when!?" I asked him. And he told me all about it. I really hadn't paid any attention at the time.'[21]

If sufficiently provoked, Russians could rise up but the numbers at even the biggest protests were never really large enough to make a genuine difference. Human rights abuses and massive corruption scandals that would have threatened to bring down governments in the West were often met with a shrug by the majority of the population. That is, of course, if they had even heard about them. Most people cared about little beyond their immediate families and the everyday business of living. Sometimes, they didn't even care that much about those things. It was so easy for Putin to fill this vacuum with his own violent compulsions, welding the collective Russian psyche to his own.

Perhaps the most glaring example of this frightening indifference came during my visit to Russia's Black Earth Region, where environmental activists had raised concerns that a Kremlin-backed nickel mining project had caused dangerous heavy metals to surface. In one tiny village, an otherwise idyllic place called Yelan-Koleno, high levels of uranium had been detected in a well, the primary source of drinking water for most of the residents. 'Leave us in peace!' shouted an elderly woman in a headscarf, as environmental activists took fresh samples from the well. 'We've been drinking this water for years, and nothing has happened to us.' Curious about her reaction, I asked the woman, who refused to give her name, if she was really so unconcerned that her children and grandchildren were drinking contaminated water. 'So what? We don't decide anything here,' she told me, her tone a mixture of aggression and weariness. 'Everything is resolved there, in Moscow. What can we do?'

Oleg Orlov, the head of Memorial, a human rights group that sought to keep the memory of Stalin's victims alive, said at the start of Putin's third presidential term that Russians had 'agreed on a pact with the devil', trading relative prosperity for any say whatsoever in how their country was run. Orlov described the unholy deal as such: 'We will stay out of the social and political process and concentrate on our private lives – just don't touch us and leave us a small slice of the profits from your oil booty.'[22]

Everyone knows, of course, what you must inevitably forfeit, if you make a deal with the devil. Just months after the start of Russia's all-out war in Ukraine, Memorial was closed down by Moscow after failing to identify itself as a 'foreign agent' in social media posts. In court, a prosecutor accused the human rights group of making Russians 'repent for the Soviet past, instead of remembering our glorious history'. In early 2024, as I began writing this book, Orlov, aged 70, was sentenced to two and a half years in prison for speaking out against the war in Ukraine. As the Kremlin's missiles rained down on Ukrainian cities, Russia was enshrouded in a darkness that the veteran activist feared might never lift again.

'Those who led our country into the pit which it is now in represent the old, the decrepit, the obsolete,' Orlov said in court as he was sentenced. 'They have no sense of the future – only false images of the past, only mirages of imperial greatness. And they are pushing Russia backwards, back into the dystopia.'[23]

4

'He Is Reacting to Pictures in His Own Head'

When the threat of full-scale war in Ukraine first emerged, it was ill-defined, like an ominous figure in the darkness or a nagging fear, indistinct yet terrifying, that appears in the depths of a dream. It was hard to make out its contours, or what form it would take, when, or if, the murkiness lifted.

In February 2022, five days before the Kremlin's missiles began smashing into apartment blocks in Kyiv, I travelled to Taganrog, a port city in southwest Russia, on a reporting assignment for *The Times*. The city was close to Russia's border with eastern Ukraine's Donbas region, large swathes of which had been controlled by Moscow since 2014. As Russia massed its forces ahead of its all-out invasion, the Kremlin-backed authorities in the Donbas abruptly ordered tens of thousands of women and children to evacuate ahead of what they claimed was an impending Ukrainian attack. The refugees were now pouring into Taganrog.

Military analysts had said that such a huge build-up of Russian troops, along with the supplies of blood brought to newly established field camp hospitals, indicated that Putin had decided to proceed with an invasion. Yet I couldn't bring myself to believe that he was really preparing to try and seize Ukraine: as tensions soared, Putin had described the Russian and Ukrainian nations as 'one people'. Although his remarks were nothing more than a justification for his brutal war of conquest, there are deeply intertwined familial ties between the two countries. An estimated 11 million Russians have relatives in Ukraine:[1] it not only seemed unthinkable that Putin would sever them overnight, but that the Russian people would allow him to do so. I simply could not imagine Russian bombs falling on Kyiv or other Ukrainian cities: it would be like Britain firing cruise missiles into the heart of Dublin.

Yet there was also a sense that Putin had decided he would never have a better chance to challenge what he saw as the West's global dominance. In December 2021, the Russian foreign ministry had issued a sudden statement on 'security guarantees' from Nato. Under Moscow's explosive demands, Nato would be banned from making military deployments to member states that had joined the Western alliance after 1997. In practice, this would have meant Nato withdrawing troops and weapons from much of eastern Europe, including Poland, as well as the Baltic states of Estonia, Latvia and Lithuania. It would also have been forbidden to accept new members without Moscow's approval and would have to publicly renounce a pledge that Ukraine would one day be allowed to join the organization.[2]

It was, to all intents and purposes, an ultimatum, although Moscow did not outline what actions it would take if the West refused to buckle. Putin was, in essence, demanding the restoral of Russia's sphere of influence over European countries that had gained independence from Moscow after the collapse of the Soviet Union. 'What's Putin up to?' an editor in London asked me. 'He must know that Nato won't agree to this.' One month later, the United States and Nato formally rejected the Kremlin's demands. The clock was ticking, but no one really knew what would happen when time ran out.

'Come looking for the war?' the receptionist joked when I checked into my hotel in Taganrog. But the rows and rows of tanks and armoured vehicles massed at the nearby border were no laughing matter. Neither were the refugees: many of them were being packed onto trains and sent deeper into Russia, apparently at random. 'I'm not going to Nizhny Novgorod!' shouted one elderly woman, referring to a city to the east of Moscow, as insistent pro-Kremlin activists escorted her towards a waiting train. I never found out what happened to her because police moved in to clear the station of journalists. I later discovered that other Ukrainians who had been deported from their homes in the Donbas ended up in the far east of Russia, more than 5,000 miles away, on the coast of the Pacific Ocean. Others were relocated to Murmansk, a city that is north of the Arctic Circle.

In central Taganrog, I spoke to a young woman and her infant son who had been housed in an indoor sports hall along with dozens of other families. The arena was filled with hundreds of fold-out beds covered with shabby bedding and plastic disposable sheets. A huge Russian flag hung on a wall. 'We've been travelling all night and we're not going any further,' Yekaterina said, as she stroked the head of her six-month-old son. 'But we don't want to stay here either.' Closer to the border with Ukraine, around a dozen inflatable tents had been set up amid the flat Russian steppe to provide temporary shelter. 'I have no idea where they are sending us. Wherever they tell us, we'll go,' said a middle-aged woman. 'I just hope it's not for too long. We all want peace.'

But any lingering hopes that Putin would pull back from the abyss were about to be extinguished. The next afternoon, he announced an urgent meeting of his National Security Council at the Kremlin's St Catherine Hall. With just days left until war, Putin was now in full-on mad Tsar mode. During the coronavirus pandemic, which was just winding down, Putin had been mocked for sitting at the other end of absurdly long tables when he met with officials: now he was seated across a vast columned room from his ministers and top security chiefs, who waited like nervous schoolchildren outside the headmaster's office.

I was on the border with eastern Ukraine when the meeting began, watching as people continued to stream across into Russia. One woman was in a wheelchair, while a young boy hobbled through on crutches. The sun was just setting when Putin's distinctive tones came from a car radio. Everyone stopped to listen. One by one, Putin called his officials up to a podium to ask them if they supported the recognition of the two proxy Russian regions in eastern Ukraine. Sergei Naryshkin, the head of the foreign intelligence service and an alleged former KGB officer who had known Putin since the early 1980s, was clearly flustered and fumbled his lines. Putin smirked and issued a rebuke. 'Speak plainly,' he snapped, his voice echoing in the cavernous hall.[3]

Other officials were better prepared. 'We don't have a border with Ukraine, we have a border with America because they are the masters there,' said Viktor Zolotov, the thuggish chief of the Russian national guard. Zolotov also claimed, falsely, that Ukraine was preparing to build nuclear weapons to threaten Russia. In fact, Ukraine, which was left in possession of the third largest nuclear arsenal in the world following the collapse of the Soviet Union, had voluntarily surrendered its warheads in 1994 as part of international arms control efforts. In return, it had received guarantees of its security and sovereignty from Britain, the United States and Russia.[4]

As I drove back to Taganrog, I spotted a group of young Russian soldiers who were smoking in a muddy field next to dozens of tanks. I asked the taxi driver to stop and headed towards them. They looked at me as I trudged across the field. They were reluctant to say too much: when I asked them if they believed Putin's false portrayal of the government in Kyiv as 'Nazis', they shrugged. I got the impression that it wasn't something they had thought about too deeply, if at all. Yet, when I asked if they would be willing to fight in Ukraine, they nodded. They all appeared to be in their early twenties, which meant that they had not been born when I first arrived in Russia.

I often thought of those soldiers in the weeks and months to come. How many Ukrainians had they slaughtered before they were themselves killed in Putin's obscene war; a conflict whose roots they barely understood? Yet when I imagined the decaying bodies of Russian troops like them strewn across Ukraine's battlefields, I felt only numbness. It would have been wrong, I knew, to feel much pity, but the depths of my indifference troubled me, at least for a while. Later that evening, Putin addressed the nation. In reality, it was an hour-long rant about Ukraine during which he repeated his long-held claims that it was not a real country and that, by extension, it had no right to exist. After Putin had spoken, I messaged a good friend in Moscow. 'I think he's really going to do it,' I said. 'Do what?' came the reply. 'The whole thing. Bomb Kyiv and Kharkiv. A full-on invasion.' There was a pause before the reply came; when it arrived it was just one word, drawn from Russia's rich lexicon of obscenities: '*Pizdets*.'

The next day, I drove around hunting for Russian tanks. The ones I had seen in the field were gone. They were most likely already in Kremlin-controlled eastern Ukraine, awaiting the order to attack. Yet Russia was massing more tanks and troops near Belgorod, a city that was a nine-hour drive to the north. There were no direct flights, so I decided to fly there via Moscow the next morning. I bought a ticket and set my alarm clock. Instead, I was woken up by a message from Aeroflot, the Russian airline, telling me that my flight was cancelled. I immediately understood what that meant.

The invasion was underway. I walked downstairs to the hotel lobby, where staff were watching Putin announce the start of his 'special military operation' in Ukraine. As state television ramped up the rhetoric and tensions soared between Moscow and the West, I began to suspect that provincial Russia was not the best place for a British journalist to be. 'But it was ok for America to bomb Iraq?!' a hotel employee shouted at me when I expressed my disgust at Russia's actions. Around 60 miles down the coastline, Russia had already launched the carpet bombing of Mariupol, the Ukrainian port city that would soon be reduced to rubble. Later that afternoon, near the border with eastern Ukraine, as I tried my best to avoid a Russian military patrol, I was startled by the sound of a low-flying plane. I looked up but it was hidden by the clouds.

Putin had justified the war by claiming that Nato was planning to threaten Russia from Ukraine, even though Kyiv had received no clear indication on when it would be allowed to join the Western military alliance. He had also claimed that Moscow was acting to save ethnic Russians in eastern Ukraine's Donbas region from 'genocide'. Yet there had been no serious fighting there for years and the civilian death toll in the Kremlin-controlled areas of the Donbas in the year before Russia's February 2022 invasion was barely in double figures. The most recent deaths had come in October 2021, four months before Putin ordered in the tanks. When the invasion began, it was these very same Russian-speaking regions who bore the brunt of Russia's onslaught. Putin was killing the very people he had claimed to be saving, while also wiping their towns and cities from the face of the earth.

I took a walk around Taganrog to try and clear my head, setting off to the seafront to gaze for a few minutes at the calming waves. But it was impossible to think of anything else. Although thousands of anti-war protesters would take to the streets that evening in Moscow and other big cities, the mood in Taganrog was muted. Most people appeared not to have realized that Putin's decision would change Russia for a generation at least. As I ate in a café in the centre of town, I eavesdropped on the conversations around me. No one was talking about the war: at the table closest to me, two women were discussing the thorny issue of kitchen refurbishments. Mellow jazz played on the radio. When asked what they thought of the conflict, most locals repeated the Kremlin's line that the attacks were 'precision strikes' and that Russia had been forced to protect the Donbas from Ukraine's 'aggression'.

Later, a Ukrainian military source told me that Russia had been so confident of a swift victory that it had sent riot police across the border, apparently to carry out 'crowd control' in Kyiv. 'They were just in ordinary police trucks,' he said. 'We blew them all up. That was when we realized that we might have a chance.'

When I got back to my hotel room, I called Gleb Pavlovsky, a former Kremlin adviser who had played a key role in securing Putin in power. Dismissed for opposing Putin's return to the presidency for a third term in 2012, Pavlovsky was now deeply critical of the ex-KGB officer's rule. I asked him straight out: had Putin lost it?

Pavlovsky sighed. 'I'm not a doctor,' he said. '[But] I don't recognize Putin at all anymore. He has changed almost completely since the time when I worked in the Kremlin. He was inclined then to discuss things with advisers, and he was more open to alternative opinions. The previous Putin would not have done this. He was a very sane-thinking person. But this has all vanished now. He has an obsession about Ukraine that he didn't previously have, at least not to this degree. He is reacting now to the pictures in his own head.'

Like other people in Russia, Pavlovsky, who was born in Soviet Ukraine, had been sure that Putin was sabre-rattling, not planning to launch the biggest war in Europe since the defeat of Nazi Germany. 'I didn't believe that he would go through with this,' he told me. 'Besides everything else, it's a very serious blow to Russia's own security.' He sounded calm, despite his obvious shock at the images of Russian missiles hurtling into Kyiv, Kharkiv and Odesa, his hometown. Birds tweeted in the background as he spoke, a surreal soundtrack to the unfolding conflict. I pictured him sitting in a peaceful garden somewhere near Moscow.

I then called Tatiana Stanovaya, a Russian political analyst who specializes in the Kremlin. Over the years, she had provided me and other reporters with some of the sharpest insights into Putin's thinking: her words that afternoon only accentuated my concerns that he had slipped into madness. 'He has withdrawn into himself a lot during the past two years,' Stanovaya told me. 'He has become distanced from the bureaucratic machinery, from the establishment, from the elite. He spends a lot of time alone stewing in his own fears and thoughts.'

Over the following years, as Russia laid waste to Ukraine and Putin threatened nuclear war if the West came to its aid, this chilling image of the ageing Kremlin dictator in the grip of maniacal, obsessive visions was hard to shake. Yet, even before the war there had been worrying indications that Putin was not in the best place, psychologically. During the coronavirus pandemic, he had spent almost two years holed up in near-total isolation at his Novo-Ogaryovo residence near Moscow, as well as his Lake Valdai mansion. Before entering Novo-Ogaryovo, visitors were forced to walk through metal tunnels that sprayed them with disinfectant.[5] Some Russian officials who met Putin face to face were reportedly obliged to provide faecal samples several times a week to ensure they were not infected.[6] They were also forced to self-isolate for two weeks before they were allowed into his presence, with the result that many of them spent up to 150 days a year in hotel rooms, separated from their families for the sake of a few hours every month with Russia's paranoid dictator. Even World War Two veterans were made to self-isolate for 14 days before briefly shaking hands with Putin at the annual Victory Day parade on Red Square.[7]

During this period of extreme isolation, Putin's almost constant companion was Yuri Kovalchuk, a banking and media tycoon who had known him since the 1990s when they both owned property in the Ozero gated community near St Petersburg. According to Mikhail Zygar, a well-connected Russian journalist, Putin and Kovalchuk shared a world view that combined Orthodox Christian mysticism and anti-American conspiracy theories. As the virus swept across Russia, the two men spent hours discussing ways to 'restore Russia's greatness' and 'avenge the humiliations of the 1990s'.[8]

Another senior official who had Putin's ear prior to the war was Nikolai Patrushev, a former KGB officer who headed the Russian national security council. Patrushev, who had been friendly with Putin for decades, was another believer in a vast Western conspiracy to topple Mother Russia. In 2023, he told state media that the United States was plotting to invade Russia because Western elites wanted to relocate to Siberia following the eruption of a super volcano under Yellowstone National Park in Wyoming.[9] 'The death of all living things on the territory of North America is inevitable,' he said, with more than a touch of relish.[10]

It was also likely that Putin had begun to believe his own propaganda. For years, senior officials and state television had been telling Russians that their fates depended on Putin, that he was the only one capable of defending them from the West and ensuring prosperity. In 2020, Russia's parliament voted to 'renew' Putin's presidential term limits to allow him to stay in power until 2036, even holding a tightly controlled 'referendum' on the issue during the pandemic. 'Oil and gas are not our advantages. As you can see, both oil and gas can fall in price. Our strength is Putin, and we must protect him,' said Vyacheslav Volodin, the chairman of the Russian parliament.[11]

In reality, of course, Putin is an ageing divorcé who had a modest career in the KGB and is often unable to get his facts about Russian history straight, frequently mixing up dates and events when he deigns to lecture his subjects on their country's past. While Russia's leader once demonstrated his health and virility to the nation by riding horses bare-chested through the wilderness or swimming in Siberian rivers, as he approached his 70th birthday, state media was reduced to a parody of itself as it sought to maintain the president's tough-guy image. In 2021, with Putin confined to his residence near Moscow during the pandemic, national television aired a video that showed him stopping a pencil from falling off his office desk. 'Here is actual footage of how he caught a pencil that was rolling off the table. His reactions were wonderful, and he is clearly in great shape – his martial arts skills have not left him,' gushed Vladimir Solovyov, the presenter of a primetime television show devoted to the Russian leader.[12] Such fawning rhetoric had long become the new normal and it would have been surprising if Putin had not begun to suffer from delusions of grandeur.

There was no real way, of course, of determining Putin's state of mind, but only someone who had lost touch with reality to some degree would have launched a full-scale invasion of Ukraine. Forced to second-guess Putin's often muddled attempts at justifying the war, Russian officials couldn't even agree on exactly why their country was bombing Kyiv. Was Russia defending the motherland from attack by Nato? Protecting ethnic Russian speakers? Fighting a heroic battle against resurgent Nazism? Striking a blow against Western hegemony? Or ensuring that Russian children would never be exposed to 'Satanic LGBT-friendly policies'?

Almost two years into the war, Alexander Beglov, the governor of St Petersburg, Putin's hometown, claimed that Russian soldiers who had seen gender-neutral toilets in Ukraine, something that Kremlin officials routinely held up as an example of the West's 'perversions', were now more committed than ever to the war. 'There's no need to explain to these guys what values we stand for,' he said, after visiting injured Russian soldiers in hospital.[13] Later, Putin provided yet another explanation. 'That's how fate turned out,' he told war veterans in the Kremlin. 'This is how the Lord wanted it.'[14]

Back at the hotel in Taganrog, a colleague from French media told me that he had overheard an FSB officer enquiring about me at reception. 'He was asking about all the reporters, but he seemed especially interested in you,' he said. Overzealous FSB officials in regions far from Moscow had been one of the main issues facing Western journalists on reporting trips even before the war: they would now be even keener to make a name for themselves. It was time to get out of Taganrog. All civilian flights had been grounded and so I took the train back to Moscow, an 18-hour journey that I mostly spent scrolling through images of Ukrainian towns and cities on fire. I shared a cabin with a Russian woman who had emigrated to the United States in the 1990s but who had returned to resolve an inheritance issue. 'This war is a disgrace to Russia!' she shouted. 'Putin is insane!' She then stopped, abruptly, and said: 'Do you think anyone heard me?' I told her that the whole train probably had and she shrugged. 'Well, good,' she said. 'Let them listen!'

At least the train passengers got a dose of truth. The Kremlin had become adept at obscuring reality behind shifting layers of confusion and falsehood; by the time I left Russia, the power of Putin's propaganda machine was truly frightening. It was like nothing I had ever experienced or had ever expected to. Russians had already relinquished many of their democratic rights to Putin in exchange for his promise of economic stability – now millions appeared to be surrendering their sanity to him as well.

In Moscow, as I realized that my time in Russia was coming to an end, I went to visit a neighbour, a woman that we had known for many years. She had always supported Putin, but she had never seemed fanatical about it. We were chatting about my plans for returning to Britain when the news came on the television in the corner of her front room. Inevitably, the first item was the 'special military operation', as the Kremlin was calling its invasion of Ukraine. I had been determined not to get into a pointless argument about politics with her on what was quite likely to be the last time we would see each other. But when the presenter began talking about the 'liberation' of Ukraine from drug-addled nationalists and neo-Nazis, I thought that she might listen to me if I told her the truth: that Russia was not liberating anyone from anything and that, in fact, her country's missiles and troops had already killed thousands of Ukrainian civilians. That Putin's war was not making her country stronger or more secure and that the searing hatred of everything Russian that it was instilling in Ukrainians would last for generations. That the greatest threat to her security and the security of her family was not Nato, or Ukraine, but Putin and his willingness to sacrifice countless Russians in his senseless and obscene war, one that had already taken the world closer to nuclear conflict than it had been for 60 years.

Maybe, I thought, she just needed someone to tell her these things and the Kremlin's spell would be broken. After all, tens of millions of Russians have friends and relatives in Ukraine. This was not some far-off country they knew almost nothing about. How could she – how could anyone in Russia – believe such things?

My words had an instant effect, but not the one I was hoping for. My neighbour's eyes flashed with sudden fury and her voice seemed to drop a tone. 'There's nothing good in Ukraine,' she growled. It was as if she was possessed by a demon. Seconds later, she reverted to the mild-mannered woman I had known for years. This kind of craziness, I feared, was infectious. If we stayed for much longer, would we also succumb? I had a terrible vision of myself, seated in front of a television screen, muttering obscenities about Ukraine and its 'Western puppet masters'. Later that day, I passed the State Duma, the Russian parliament, for one last time. A nationalist activist stood outside with a sign that read, 'For the army! For the motherland! For Putin!' I took a deep breath: it was definitely time to leave.

'HE IS REACTING TO PICTURES IN HIS OWN HEAD'

Many people in Russia were deeply opposed to the invasion. Yet the Kremlin's ruthless crackdown – over 5,500 protesters were arrested across Russia in the first four days of the war[15] – meant that the numbers at rallies soon dwindled. Leading opposition figures were seized and given long prison sentences for speaking out against the invasion, while other dissidents fled the country while they could. Supporters of the war had also begun denouncing their fellow citizens to the police for comments that 'discredited the Russian army', a crime under a new law that had been hurriedly passed following the start of the invasion. Police had been called to nightclubs and cafes, while schoolchildren had informed on their teachers. An eerie silence descended upon Moscow. One day, in the early days of the invasion, I witnessed two friends sizing each other up, trying to gauge each other's opinions, without giving too much away. 'Oh, you are against this madness too!' one of them eventually blurted out with relief. 'Of course!' came the reply. It was depressing, infuriating and uplifting, all at once.

The strength of Russian propaganda is that while not everyone is fooled all of the time, or even watches state television regularly, it is so ubiquitous that it is still capable of poisoning people's minds and crippling their capacity for rational thought. Indeed, it is not unheard of for Russians to insist that they distrust state television while repeating its arguments almost word for word. Propaganda spreads its awful malaise through social media, radio, books and the conversations people overhear on the metro. It is also massively aided by the desire of many Russians not to draw undue attention to themselves for their views, a survival tactic that has been handed down through the generations from repressive regime to repressive regime. And who, really, can blame them, given that the consequences, from summary executions to long prison sentences, have frequently been so severe?

Ilya Yashin, an opposition politician who was arrested shortly after the start of the invasion for condemning the Kremlin's war crimes, wrote in a message passed from his cell how a fellow inmate named Vasily had told him that Ukraine was 'full of Nazis'. When

Yashin asked him where he had got the idea from, Vasily told him: 'From the telly'. When Yashin questioned if he really believed what he saw on state television, Vasily indignantly replied: 'What am I, a fool? The telly's full of lies!'[16] When faced with such logic, all analysis goes out of the window. The Kremlin's propaganda not only deluded Russians: it also disorientated them.

People often ask me whether Russians can still access Western or opposition media and, if so, why do they continue to believe Putin's propaganda? The answer is that very few Western news websites have so far been banned or blocked and alternative sources of information in Russian are available on the Telegram messaging app, which is extremely popular in Russia. Blocked opposition websites are also accessible to anyone who installs a private virtual network (VPN), a computer programme that disguises an internet user's location. Yet, as in most countries, ordinary Russians tend to trust their national media during times of upheaval.

'I get up and turn on the telly before work,' Yelena, a middle-aged woman, told me. 'They tell me we are fighting Nazis in Ukraine. I don't have time to look into that too deeply, you know?' It was, in essence, an abdication of logic and reason and, perhaps, the most depressing explanation of all. Russians like Yelena were simply too busy scraping together a living, or indifferent, or both, to verify for themselves the Kremlin's absurd propaganda. 'I don't like it when they lie to me, but I'm also tired of the truth,' Kino, the Russian rock group, had sung shortly before the collapse of the Soviet Union. The sentiment was more apt than ever.[17]

At a luxury shopping centre near Red Square, customers shrugged off the potential impact of Western sanctions. 'I can do without an iPhone,' said Igor, a well-dressed older man with an earring. 'But things will blow over soon. It will just take a bit of time, and everything will be back to normal again.' When I asked him what he thought about Russian missiles slamming into Ukrainian cities, he looked at me like I was an idiot. 'These are all fake videos,' he said. 'I only believe our media. We are only hitting military targets.'

There were also those who simply trusted that Putin knew best. 'This isn't for us to decide. Who are we after all?' one woman told opposition media after her teenage grandson was jailed for opposing the war.[18] Others were far more enthusiastic. 'Our troops don't shoot Ukrainian civilians', a man in his twenties told me in Moscow, shortly before I left, echoing Putin's allegations that the massacres by his soldiers were staged by Western intelligence services to discredit Russia. 'But I wish they did. We should annihilate all of those *khokhly* scum,' he added, using a derogatory term for Ukrainians. As American and European companies withdrew from Russia in protest against the invasion, anti-Western feelings rose. 'Here's our response to American sanctions! We aren't afraid of you! We'll get by without your nice trendy things!' one Russian man shouted as he smashed up an iPad with a hammer in an online video.[19]

Miraculously, the Ukrainian Cultural Center in central Moscow, just a few minutes from our home, was still functioning. Inside, the monument to Taras Shevchenko, Ukraine's national poet, was still in place and the country's blue and yellow flag still flew outside the building. Nationalist activists had set fire to it after the annexation of Crimea by Russia in 2014, but there had been no such incidents for several years. The young woman who was on duty that day deflected my questions about the war with a smile.

'Why are you talking about such things when we have all this beautiful art here?' she said, gesturing at an exhibition of paintings by Ukrainian artists. 'A young man gave me a flower today and you are talking about war? Why?' I was unsure how to reply. Was she in shock? In denial? Worried about saying too much?

A few days after my visit, the centre was closed down and the Ukrainian flag removed from the building's exterior. It was later transformed into a pro-Kremlin venue that hosted events promoting Putin's view that Ukraine was simply a wayward region of Russia that needed to be brought back into the fold, by any means necessary. One event was called: 'One faith – one people.'

National television played a huge role in shoring up support for the war in Ukraine, but it wasn't the only factor: as Russia went to war, many people simply rallied around the flag, governed by the logic of 'my country, right or wrong'. Yet, of all my Russian friends, not a single one supported the invasion of Ukraine. A few days after the unsettling encounter with my neighbour, I went to a bar near my flat in Moscow with Grisha, a talented poet who was also preparing to leave the country. Grisha and I had made it a tradition to meet every year on 5 March and drink to the anniversary of Joseph Stalin's death. Over the years, the Soviet tyrant's ignoble passing, soaked in his own urine and surrounded by his political rivals, had become a symbol of hope for Russians who opposed Putin. In 2016, on the 63rd anniversary of Stalin's demise, a poster depicting his death mask appeared overnight at a bus stop near Moscow's Paveletsky train station. 'That one died, this one will, too,' it read. No one was in any doubt who 'this one' referred to. The poster was quickly removed, but not before images of it had time to go viral online.[20]

As Grisha and I met that evening at a bar close to a statue of Bulat Okudzhava, the singer-songwriter whose music had inspired the Soviet dissident movement, we both realized that this could be the last time for many years that we would be able to toast Stalin's death again. In Russia, at least. We soon got talking, as you do, to a group of ageing football hooligans. They were in turns defensive and defiant about the invasion of Ukraine but utterly convinced that it was necessary to get behind their troops. 'I hated Putin before the war and I'll hate him again after it,' one confessed as he swigged imported beer. 'But while our guys are fighting in Ukraine, I'll give him all my support.'

Inevitably, Grisha and I got into a row with them. As the beers flowed, I told them everything I thought about Putin and his war and why it was not only evil, but catastrophic for their country's future. One of the men attempted to shut me up, reaching across the table to try and silence me, but the oldest of them knocked back his hand. 'Let him speak,' he said, sternly. 'I haven't heard this stuff before.'

But such talk was already dangerous in Russia. I spent the next day nursing a terrible hangover and dreading a visit from the security services. What if someone had filmed me speaking and then posted the video to one of the pro-war social media accounts that had sprung up in the early weeks of the conflict? I'd heard Soviet dissidents talk about how they once lived in terror of the unexpected knock on the door at midnight. It wasn't something I had ever thought I would one day experience for myself.

When I had recovered from my hangover, I went to my local bookshop, the biggest in Moscow. For as long as I could remember, Dom Knigi (The House of Books) had contained a wide selection of English language books, including many critical of Putin. Now, they were gone. 'They've all sold out,' a shop assistant told me, unconvincingly. It was a minor detail in the grand scheme of things, but also one that testified to the total censorship that was already being put into force.

In south Moscow, the staff of a local newspaper called Zhyolud had found an inventive way to make their feelings clear. 'Nothing is happening,' its headline read in huge black letters on a white background. Underneath, there was an image of yellow crime-scene tape and the words, dripping with bitter sarcasm: 'Move along. A special operation is under way. No one is impoverished. The rouble is rising. The economy is growing.' Olga Sidelnikova, the newspaper's editor, told me that she had felt compelled to do something to get the attention of locals. 'It would have been strange to just put out the paper as usual,' she said.[21]

But even these tactics of vicious compliance were now increasingly risky. As the invasion approached the end of its third week, Putin delivered a speech that underlined the depths of his hatred for those Russians who opposed his revanchist crusade in Ukraine. 'The Russian people will always be able to distinguish true patriots from scum and traitors and simply spit them out like a fly that accidentally flew into their mouths,' he snarled into the camera. 'Such a natural and necessary self-purification of society will only strengthen our country.'[22]

In the 1990s, pro-democracy reformers such as Galina Starovoitova had unsuccessfully sought a moral and judicial cleansing of Russia to ensure that the terror of the Soviet regime could never return in any form. Now, Putin, swollen with fury, was undertaking his own purge.

5

FALSE HOPES

Things had not always been like this in Russia. Upon coming to power in 2000, Putin did not immediately plunge the country into violent nationalism and it would be many years before he was seen, at least in the West, as the smirking personification of evil. Yes, he was a vicious crook who cared little about human life, but Russia was not the Soviet Union and Putin was not yet a fully-fledged dictator.

Russia's vast oil and gas reserves also meant that Western political and business leaders were willing to make allowances for Putin's ruthlessness. In Moscow, tourists from Europe and the United States felt no guilt about buying the kitschy, Putin-themed souvenirs that were on sale everywhere. Some of them even went home with Stalin t-shirts.

Putin's first foreign visit upon becoming President was in April 2000 to London, where Tony Blair, the British prime minister, hailed him as a reformer, despite Russian atrocities in Chechnya. 'It's my job as Prime Minister to like Mr Putin,'[1] Blair told Anna Politkovskaya, a Russian investigative journalist, according to her column in *Novaya Gazeta*, an independent Russian newspaper.[2] In an echo of Galina Starovoitova's murder, Politkovskaya was later shot dead by assassins outside her apartment. The assassination took place on Putin's 54th birthday. As with the Starovoitova killing, the person who ordered her murder has yet to be identified.

In 2001, President George W. Bush invited Putin to his ranch in Texas. 'I looked the man in the eye. I found him to be very straightforward and trustworthy,' Bush said. 'I was able to get a sense of his soul.'[3] It seems, however, that Bush did not stop to consider that Putin was an ex-KGB agent who had been trained to cultivate useful contacts and gain their trust. In 2003, Sir Paul McCartney visited Putin for tea at the Kremlin before performing on Red Square. A stern-faced Putin was in the crowd for the concert, his black briefcase containing the codes for Russia's nuclear weapons alongside him. Unpunctual as ever, the Russian leader missed the first few songs, including 'Back In the USSR.'[4]

That same year, Putin headed to Britain to meet Queen Elizabeth II. As he stepped off his private jet onto a red carpet, Putin was greeted by Prince Charles, the future king, before being whisked into central London. His motorcade was welcomed by the queen, Blair and mounted cavalry troops in silver helmets, while a military band struck up the Russian national anthem. Putin and his wife, Lyudmila, were then taken to Buckingham Palace in an open, horse-drawn carriage. It was the first ceremonial state visit to Britain by a Russian leader since 1874. Not coincidentally, it came as BP, the British energy giant, sank $6.7 billion into the Russian oil industry. The deal was the largest single investment by a foreign company in post-Soviet Russia.[5] Although Blair had not entirely ignored Russian human rights abuses in Chechnya, his critics accused him of caring far more about lucrative energy ties with Moscow. 'Diplomats who witnessed Blair's sessions with Putin were distinctly underwhelmed by the purely formal tone of British objections,' read an article in *The Times*.[6]

Indeed, just weeks before Putin jetted off to London to meet the queen, the Council of Europe had issued a damning report accusing Russian troops of war crimes, including rape and torture, against Chechen civilians.[7] In one of hundreds of documented cases, Russian soldiers without identifying insignia stormed into a private home in Chechnya's Vedensky District and abducted Sirajdi Zumaev, a local schoolteacher. He was executed next to a tree, where his family discovered his lifeless body at dawn.[8]

Less than two weeks later, Putin, wearing a dinner suit, joined the royal family at Buckingham Palace for a banquet in his honour. 'Russia has established itself as our partner and our friend,' the queen told him. 'My message to you, Mr President, is therefore one of admiration, respect and support.'[9]

The West's pragmatic approach towards Putin was summed up by Bill Browder, an American-born British businessman whose Hermitage Capital Management was for a time the largest foreign investor in Russia. Although he is now one of Putin's biggest foreign critics, Browder was for many years a vocal cheerleader for Moscow. 'There are unpleasant aspects to the system of governance – you can't have pluses without minuses. But the pluses in Russia far outweigh the minuses, and as they get richer hopefully, they can have a less autocratic system,' he said during Putin's second term. 'I see myself as Russia's true believer. This is a bump in the road; there are a lot of bumps in the road. One would be unrealistic to expect a smooth transition after 70 years of communism, but I'm optimistic.'[10]

His comments came after Putin had also closed the last independent television station, TVS, while the liberal opposition had been purged from parliament in elections that were described as 'unfair' by Western vote monitors. Browder had also supported the jailing by Putin of Mikhail Khodorkovsky, Russia's richest man, on fraud charges that were widely seen as revenge for his open criticism of Kremlin corruption. [Browder has since admitted that he was wrong to do so]. Even a ban on entering Russia that was imposed on Browder in 2005 had failed to dampen his enthusiasm: he initially saw it as revenge by a business rival and hoped, in vain, that he would be allowed back into the country.

Inevitably, Browder's optimism gave way to disillusionment and anger. 'I thought [Putin] wanted to act in Russia's national interests and restore the nation's glory,' he later said. 'In fact, his plan was to embezzle as much money as he could.'[11]

In 2009, Sergei Magnitsky, a lawyer for Browder's Hermitage Capital company, was arrested after investigating massive tax fraud by interior ministry officials. Less than a year later, he died in prison. The Kremlin's own human rights council, back when it still had teeth, ruled that Magnitsky had been beaten by prison guards and denied medical treatment.

'I made a vow to his memory, to his family, to myself that I was going to devote all of my time, all of my energy, and all of my resources to go after the people who killed him, [to] make sure they faced justice,' Browder recalled later.[12]

In 2012, after lobbying by Browder and Russian opposition politicians, the United States enacted the Magnitsky Act, a piece of landmark legislation that allowed Washington to sanction officials involved in the lawyer's death. It was later expanded to include government officials anywhere who were judged to be guilty of human rights abuses.

In hindsight, Browder's optimism for Russia's future appears remarkably naive. Yet, despite the war in Chechnya, the murders of investigative journalists such as Politkovskaya and massive corruption, there really were some tentative grounds for hope, something that has traditionally been in short supply in Russia. For years, Western journalists in Moscow were faced with the challenge of explaining to readers whose knowledge of Russia was based on Soviet stereotypes that while Putin's system was by no means a democracy, the modern-day Kremlin preferred smoke and mirrors, twinned with selective violence when necessary, to the sledgehammers of the communist regime that had preceded it. Ironically, we had just begun to get something of this complicated truth across, when Putin reverted to type and unleashed a campaign of political repression that had not been seen since the darkest days of Stalinist terror.

But this was all in the future. In 2008, after serving two presidential terms, the limit under the constitution, Putin shifted to the role of Prime Minister and handed the keys to the Kremlin to Dmitry Medvedev, his long-time ally and Chairman of the state-run energy giant, Gazprom. No one was under any illusion that Putin was going to retire to the countryside to count his money, but some Russians initially allowed themselves to believe that Medvedev was the leader they had been waiting for. A fan of Western rock music with an enthusiasm for iPhones and other American technology that saw him dubbed Russia's 'chief blogger', Medvedev was widely viewed as a breath of fresh air. Although he later transformed into one of Moscow's biggest hawks, peppering his foul-mouthed tirades about Ukraine and the West with threats of nuclear apocalypse, his promises to root out corruption and end Russia's 'legal nihilism' were initially welcomed by many liberal opposition figures.

'Freedom is better than unfreedom,' Medvedev said upon taking office. 'Everyone needs freedom – this is an axiom.' In a keynote essay entitled 'Forward, Russia!' Medvedev also warned that influential groups of corrupt officials would try to prevent his efforts to modernize Russia. He gave the first interview of his presidency to *Novaya Gazeta*, the opposition newspaper where Politkovskaya, the journalist who was killed on Putin's birthday, had worked. 'You never sucked up to anyone,' Medvedev told its editor, Dmitry Muratov.[13]

Medvedev's time in office also saw an attempt to fix worsening relations with the United States and its Western allies. In 2007, Putin had delivered a furious speech at the Munich Security Conference in which he accused Washington of attempting to try and build a world where there is 'one master, one sovereign'.[14] Later that year, Putin told a rally of flag-waving supporters in Moscow that his critics were 'jackals' who were being paid by Western countries to destabilize Russia.[15] This was his harshest rhetoric yet against the pro-democracy opposition.

Yet, in March 2009, ten months after Medvedev had become President and less than a year after Russia had sent troops into neighbouring Georgia, Hillary Clinton, the US secretary of state, and Sergei Lavrov, the Russian foreign minister, met in Geneva to announce that Moscow and Washington were determined to improve relations. A smiling Clinton and Lavrov even pressed a red button emblazoned with what the Americans thought was the Russian for 'reset'. In fact, the word – *'peregruzka'* – meant 'overload'.[16] Despite the gaffe, it was a positive sign and tensions thawed between the two nuclear superpowers.

'I really thought that Medvedev could become an independent politician and carry out the political reforms he had written about. He captured a genuine feeling of hope,' Dmitry Gudkov, an opposition politician, told me a few years later in Moscow, after it had become painfully clear that the Kremlin's 'chief blogger' was not liberal Russia's long-awaited saviour. Like almost every major opposition figure who is not dead or in prison, Gudkov is now in exile, unable to return home for fear of arrest, or worse.

Was Gudkov idealistic? Yes. Misguided? Yes. Could I blame him? Not really. After all, the very fact that Putin still appeared to respect the constitution was surely evidence that he was not yet confident enough to take on the mantle of a modern-day tsar. Putin's opponents might not have been empowered by Medvedev, but they had been emboldened. It was during this period that Alexei Navalny, the lawyer who later became Putin's biggest domestic foe, rose to prominence. His popular blog, 'The Final Battle between Good and Neutrality,' detailed jaw-dropping evidence of government corruption and quickly turned him into the opposition's undisputed leader. He also came up with the nickname that clung to Putin's ruling United Russia party for years: 'The Party of Crooks and Thieves.'[17]

Navalny posed a threat to Putin like no other. Brave and charismatic, he had a talent for hitting the Russian leader where it hurt, sprinkling his exposés of Kremlin corruption with references to pop culture and off-beat humour. For millions of young Russians, he was the political leader they had been waiting for all their lives. He later established an impressive network of supporters from St Petersburg to Vladivostok, while the Moscow headquarters of his FBK anti-corruption foundation was the buzzing hub of his bid to bring down Putin.

'I want to become President,' Navalny said in 2013. 'I want to change life in our country. I want to change the system of governance. I don't want the 140 million people who live here and who have oil and gas running out of the ground to live in hopeless poverty, but I want them to live normal lives, like in a European country.'[18]

Not everyone in Russia, it turned out, had agreed to a pact with the devil. 'Urban, educated Russians declared that the everyday freedoms so generously bestowed on them by the Putin epoch – the freedom to drink, eat, travel, sleep, read, watch television and stick their fingers up their noses – were insufficient to feel a part of Europe. They also needed political freedoms,' wrote Stanislav Belkovsky, a Russian political analyst.[19] The mood under Medvedev was encapsulated by the opening of a new independent online television channel called TV Dozhd, or TV Rain, that set up shop in 2010 in a former chocolate factory close to Red Square.

Its slogan? 'The Optimistic Channel.'

Gudkov wasn't the only one feeling good about the future at the beginning of Medvedev's presidency. I had first met T, my future wife, during my time in Voronezh and we had kept in touch after I moved back to Moscow. We eventually started living together in the Russian capital in 2002, renting a tiny flat in a leafy district a short bus ride from the city centre. Three years later, we got married at a registry office and celebrated at one of the sushi restaurants that were popping up all over the city. T was – and is – funny, smart and beautiful. She was also like no one else I had ever met. The youngest of two children in a Soviet military family, she was born in a hospital close to Buchenwald, the former Nazi concentration camp, while her father, a Russian army officer, was stationed in East Germany. Her entry into the world was marked by the dull tolling of the death camp's commemorative bells. Not long afterwards, the army transferred the family to Chita, a city in eastern Siberia. When they arrived, it was so cold that a neighbour who had invited them for dinner told her husband to 'chop up' some soup they were storing on the open-air balcony. He dutifully picked up his axe and hacked out a slab of icy borscht.

A few years later, the family was on the move again, this time to Sosnovy Bor, a military town a few hours from the Mongolian border that was so secret it did not even feature on maps. In 2011, Medvedev and Kim Jong Il, the North Korean dictator, met there for talks. Sosnovy Bor may have been 3,500 miles east of Moscow and sealed off from the outside world by a pine tree forest and barbed wire fence but living standards there for an officer's family were far better than in most other places in the Soviet Union. The family's fridge was well-stocked with caviar, while they also had access to bananas and pineapples – both rarities in the Soviet Union at the time. 'It was only when I went to visit a friend's house that I realized not everyone was living like this,' T told me later. 'Her family had almost no food in the house. Only sour cream and bread.'

Initially, T and I lived in a series of nondescript flats outside the city centre. However, one winter morning early in 2006, we packed our possessions into an old, beat-up van and drove to our new home in the heart of the Russian capital. The flat was on Starokonyushenny Lane, just off the Old Arbat, a pedestrianized street famous throughout Russia for its theatres and distinctive nineteenth-century architecture. It had an out-of-tune grand piano, a windowsill that was so large you could sleep on it and an ornate façade that dated from before the Bolshevik revolution in 1917. The landlord, an elderly professor of astrophysics, visited once every three months to collect the rent. He also told us stories of how, as a child, his kickabouts in the nearby streets had been interrupted by Stalin's motorcade as it made its way to the nearby Kremlin. Our neighbours were Soviet film stars. Walking home from Red Square one afternoon amid temperatures of minus 30 degrees Celsius, I marvelled at the twists of fortune that had brought me to Moscow. We stayed in that flat for 12 years – it is still the longest I have lived in any one place.

At the time of our move to the Old Arbat, I was making a living by teaching English to private students. Back then, it was extremely easy to get a business visa to stay in Russia all year round. For a few hundred pounds, there were numerous companies who would arrange everything quickly and without fuss, even if not everything was entirely above board. One year, when I received my visa, I discovered that I had been listed as 'a member of the crew'. Luckily, no one asked me to fly any planes. Most of my students were rich businessmen and I would go to their houses for lessons. Although they were already able to speak English fairly well, they were keen to practise their conversational skills in a no-pressure environment. One student was the owner of a nationwide chain of shops. Twice a week, his bodyguards would pick me up outside a metro station in the west of the city and drive me to his home, a huge property in Rublyovka, a district that is home to Russia's business and political elite. It was not long after Putin had been appointed President by Yeltsin when he casually told me that he had heard a businessman acquaintance shouting down a telephone at Russia's newly installed leader: 'Vova, just be quiet and do what we say, ok?' the businessman said, at least according to my well-connected student. ('Vova', not 'Vlad', is short for 'Vladimir' in Russian.)

I had no way of knowing if this story was true, of course. Just as I had no way of verifying the account of a taxi driver who swore blind that a friend of a friend had driven elite sex workers to the Kremlin during a visit to Russia by Silvio Berlusconi, the Italian leader. Or what to make of the self-proclaimed psychic with offices near Red Square who confided in me that high-level officials often consulted her, 'especially before taking important decisions'. Or the friend whose acquaintance had apparently witnessed the christening of Putin's out-of-wedlock children with Alina Kabaeva, the Olympic gymnast whose rumoured love affair with the Russian leader was both an open secret and a taboo topic for Russian media?

Moscow pulsed with rumours about Putin and his elite companions. And no wonder, Putin was so secretive about his personal life that Russians were more familiar with the names and faces of the children of American presidents than their own leader's offspring. Indeed, Putin is so paranoid about his private life that he has still not acknowledged the identities of his two adult daughters, who now go by the names of Maria Vorontsova and Katerina Tikhonova. Western governments, however, have had no such qualms: both women have been sanctioned by Britain and the United States over their alleged roles in holding Putin's assets.

In 2009, our daughter was born in a maternity ward in Moscow. Back then, it was unusual for fathers to attend births in Russia and the ambulance driver who arrived to take us to the hospital that evening looked at me suspiciously. 'Is he coming, too?' she asked T. Around 12 hours later, M arrived, immediately being wrapped in swaddling blankets by a jolly midwife. I was now tied to Russia for ever. Accordingly, my thinking about the country shifted. I now had an undeniable stake in its future. It was my daughter's homeland and I wanted the best possible version of it for her. My attitudes towards Putin and his regime hardened almost overnight. I had previously been opposed to the Kremlin's plundering of Russia's natural resources on an intellectual and moral level, but now, things were personal.

Issues that I had paid little attention to suddenly came into focus. For a while, I grew particularly angry about the use of harmful chemicals to clear snow from the streets. These substances were so toxic they could ruin your shoes and burn dogs' paws, but they were preferred to salt or sand because someone in Moscow City Hall was raking in massive kickbacks on state procurement orders. I loved winter in Moscow, but I dreaded the chemicals. Council workers walked around the city, emptying sacks of toxic substances onto the pavement. Sometimes, they wouldn't even bother to spread them evenly: it was common to see piles of them outside the entrances to flats or next to children's playgrounds. Someone told me once that one of the toxins used to melt snow in Moscow was also used in lethal injections in the United States: I wasn't sure how true that was, but it certainly didn't make me feel any better. As I pushed M through the frozen streets of Moscow in her bright orange pram, her cheeks rosy with the cold, I nervously eyed the heaps of chemicals and scrapped off any that had stuck to my boots when we got home.

When our daughter started school, I insisted that she take a packed lunch every day. The reason? I didn't want her eating the pre-cooked meals that were supplied to schools across Moscow by Concord, a catering company owned by Yevgeny Prigozhin, the Russian tycoon who was then known as 'Putin's chef'. Besides being Moscow's richest school dinner man, Prigozhin was also the head of the Wagner Group, a shadowy organization of Kremlin-backed mercenaries who did Putin's dirty work in Africa, Syria and eastern Ukraine. A former convict who had served almost a decade in prison for violent street robberies, Prigozhin was released from prison in 1990, a year before the Soviet Union's collapse. He immediately got into the catering business, starting off with hotdog stands before eventually opening New Island, an up-market restaurant on a floating boat in St Petersburg, Putin's hometown.

When he became President, Putin often took foreign visitors to New Island, including George W. Bush in 2002. 'Vladimir Putin saw how I built up my business from nothing,' Prigozhin once said. 'He saw how I wasn't above personally bringing plates.'[20] Over the following two decades, Prigozhin would do far more for Putin than serve food to him and his VIP guests. Besides the Wagner Group, he also established an internet 'troll factory' in St Petersburg where dozens of employees posed as American citizens to try and spread discord throughout the United States. In 2018, Prigozhin was indicted by a grand jury in America on charges of meddling in the internal politics of the United States, including the 2016 presidential election that brought Donald Trump to power.[21]

Back then, though, my major concern was that Prigozhin had been given a lucrative state contract to supply meals to Moscow's schools and nurseries. Opposition figures had linked the meals to a mass outbreak of dysentery among nursery children; some of the children had even been admitted to intensive care. Unsurprisingly, state media was barred from covering the topic and parents who complained were threatened with violence. A journalist at Tass, the Russian state news agency, told me that she had been dismissed after trying to report on concerns about the quality of the food provided to schools by Concord in the months before the children fell ill. 'Perhaps, if my report hadn't been hushed up, then this outbreak of dysentery wouldn't have happened,' she said.[22]

So, packed lunches it was. 'Remember – don't eat Prigozhin's food!' was our morning mantra as we dropped M off at school. Yet Prigozhin was still a relatively obscure figure back then and most Russians had no idea that he even existed. My attempts to explain to the parents of our daughter's classmates that their children were being fed five days a week by a violent, election-meddling mercenary chief were usually met with bewildered looks. It was surreal back then and the memory of it remains so: was that really me, standing at my daughter's school gates in Moscow, ranting to no discernible effect about a crazed Russian chef with his own private army of cold-blooded killers? I made no secret of my dislike of Putin and what he was doing to my daughter's country. Now, after the evisceration of all the dissenting voices, it barely seems believable that I was once able to sit in the local playground, debating politics with fellow parents. Some felt the same way about Putin and there was very little fear back then about saying so openly.

Besides becoming a father, I had also become mildly obsessed with Russia's football culture, digging deep into the histories of teams such as FC Dynamo Moscow, the club of the Soviet secret police, as well as the corruption that plagued the modern game. I met with football hooligans, players and club owners. Many were bemused by my interest in their national sport and even more puzzled by my spiel that 'Football mirrors society and society mirrors football.'

Yevgeni Giner, the cigar-smoking businessman who owned CSKA Moscow, the Russian army side, advised me against reporting on corruption. 'Dostoevsky, Tolstoy, Dickens. They didn't write about [corruption] scandals, did they?' he told me when I interviewed him in his office.[23] In 2007, I sold a book on Russian football culture to a British publisher. It was the first time I had ever seen my name in print. Russian football also defined my relationship with alcohol. After suffering a three-day hangover following an interview/drinking session with Spartak Moscow hooligans, I swore off alcohol for ever. I did not touch a drop for the next 12 years, only relenting in 2018, when Russia hosted the FIFA World Cup and I was unable to resist the lure of matchday beers in the Moscow sun.

I didn't want to write about football for ever, though. Under Medvedev's ambitious drive to modernize Russia, a Soviet-era news agency called RIA Novosti was given an overhaul. Svetlana Mironyuk, the agency's first female editor-in-chief, was tasked with making it a rival to Reuters and other Western news agencies. It was a huge ask, but Mironyuk gave it a go. RIA's English-language service recruited editors with experience at the BBC and Agence France-Presse, the Paris-based news agency. Its online magazine, *Russia Profile*, hired young journalists who later went on to become respected correspondents for the *Guardian*, Reuters, and the *Daily Telegraph*.

In late 2010, after a period editing for RIA, I became its first ever full-time English-language correspondent. The agency was housed in a huge, monolithic Soviet building not too far from Red Square that immediately made me think of George Orwell's Ministry of Truth. Founded in June 1941, just days after Nazi Germany launched its surprise attack on Stalin's Soviet Union, it was initially known as the Soviet Information Bureau – or Sovinformburo. By the time I arrived, the agency was undergoing a huge facelift: its newsroom had been gutted and refurbished and state-of-the-art computers replaced typewriters and fax machines. It was an extraordinary time to work at what had once been the bastion of Soviet news.

RIA was very different from RT, also known as Russia Today, the Kremlin-backed television channel whose journalists were adept at reporting on discontent in the West but remained silent about Russia's many problems. At RIA, we interviewed opposition figures and criticized the Kremlin, without a hint of censorship. I was even allowed to write a weekly column, which I often used to take potshots at Putin.

'For me, Russia Is Like A Big Prison,' read the headline for my RIA interview with Yekaterina Samutsevich, a member of the Pussy Riot protest group that had been jailed for protesting in Moscow's biggest Orthodox cathedral. Another article, penned by a Russian colleague, was little more than an undiluted rant against the Young Guard, a pro-Putin youth movement, that fantasized about 'packing the whole lot into a bus and throwing it off a bridge'.[24] The agency's abrupt transformation took some officials by surprise: when I grilled Alexander Sidyakin, a hard-line MP who was one of the authors of a 'foreign agent' law that Putin used to muzzle dissent, he raised a quizzical eyebrow. 'Are you sure you are from RIA Novosti?' he asked.

6

HE WHO SOBS WITH JOY

Despite the toxic snow and the potentially lethal school dinners, I still enjoyed living in Russia. The country had given me some purpose, an identity, even, and I sometimes wondered what would have happened to me had I remained in London, unemployed and with few real prospects. In Moscow, I liked walking along the banks of the frozen river in winter, then observing every spring as it thawed and huge ice floes drifted through the heart of the city. In the summers, often long and hot, we sometimes rented a cottage in the countryside, exploring the nearby forest and then drinking tea or wine late into the night, the sound of nightingales drifting in through the windows.

From our flat, we had a view of the imposing towers and turrets of the nearby Stalin-era foreign ministry. When our daughter was small, I told her that it was home to a government office that controlled how many cartoons children were allowed to watch a day. 'The government says that's enough,' I would tell her, gesturing towards the ministry, as I switched off the DVD player. It was lazy parenting, I admit. But it's also the only time the Russian foreign ministry ever made my life easier.

We shared our lives with our cat, Vitya, who I had picked up one evening during an after-hours party at Moscow's Museum of Modern Art in the spring of 2001. He lived with us for almost two decades, dying just before the outbreak of the coronavirus pandemic. At the time of his death, the dark joke in Russia was that there was not a single cat alive who had not been born under Putin. I'd hoped Vitya would outlast the ex-KGB man, but it was not to be.

For a journalist, Russia was possibly the most interesting country on the planet, especially if you were able to get outside Moscow and travel around its vast territory. In the Altai region, a remote and thinly populated area close to Mongolia where people still believed in shamanic magic, I drove for hours through its arid, lunar-like wilderness, weaving past the herds of goats and free-roaming horses that often blocked the roads, to tiny villages with names like Kosh-Agach (Last Tree), where ethnic Kazakh locals pumped me for titbits of information about life in the distant capital.

In Yakutia, a vast, frozen region also known as Sakha that is some 5,000 miles east of Moscow, I visited fishermen on the frozen Lena river amid temperatures that fell as low as minus 47 degrees Celsius. They transported their portable huts to the river when it froze over and left them there until the spring. 'Is this your hobby?' I asked one ruddy-cheeked enthusiast as he sat tracking fish on an underwater camera that he had lowered into a hole in the ice. 'No, it's an obsession,' he laughed, as wood crackled in his stove, the smoke rising into the frigid air through a metal chimney. On another reporting trip, I visited a facility in Yakutia that was used to store the amazingly well-preserved remains of Ice-Age animals that had been dug up from the permafrost. As I looked on, a staff member reached into a freezer box and pulled out a 28,000-year-old cave lion cub that had been nicknamed Sparta. The cub's fur, skeleton, internal organs and even its whiskers were intact. It looked as if it was sleeping. I felt truly privileged to have seen it.

Another winter, while travelling around the Russian Arctic, I stumbled upon a vast, abandoned Soviet-era train station: a reminder of the fallen communist regime. Built during the 1930s at the foot of the imposing Khibiny Mountains, the station's marble columns had been battered by the elements since it was abandoned after the Soviet Union's collapse. I clambered over a huge mound of snow to get a better look, almost injuring myself when I slipped. As an icy wind whipped through the deserted waiting rooms, I imagined I could hear the ghostly conversations of long-dead Soviet citizens, unaware of what the future held. 'A bad peace is better than a good war,' someone had scrawled onto a wall. On my trips home to Britain, I often felt like the android in Blade Runner, the science-fiction film, whose most famous line is: 'I've seen things you people wouldn't believe.'

I remained sceptical though about the idea of some mysterious Russian soul, inexplicable to outsiders, that was pushed by besotted Westerners and some locals alike. It would also be inaccurate to say that I loved Russia: I have always been unsure how one goes about loving an entire country, Britain included. Yet, it is a strange and rare experience to lose yourself so completely in a foreign culture, especially one that had been so inaccessible for so many years. I became as familiar with the music of Russian rock groups as I was with the albums of my favourite Western musicians. I still hadn't formally studied Russian, so I made the odd mistake or two, but I could say everything I wanted to and I understood everything that I heard or read. I liked speaking Russian so much that I dreamt in the language, holding long and bizarre conversations in the phantasmagorical Moscow of my own imagining. On occasion, back in the real world, I would forget, at least for a few disorientating seconds, the English translations for everyday words in Russian, floundering as I searched for the correct term. I also began to find myself using 'nu', a Russian interjection that can mean 'er' or 'well', in my everyday English speech, often without realizing. 'It's, *nu*, very cold here today,' I would tell my parents on the phone, eliciting laughter from my wife. Later, when the simmering hatred boiled over and the missiles began to fly, I sometimes wished I could switch off my knowledge of the language to filter out the ugliness, at least for a while. But there was no escape.

The brief optimism that had inspired many Russians when Medvedev took office quickly dissipated as it became clear that his words about freedom and the rule of law were just that – words. Less than a year before his term in office expired, Medvedev confessed that while he wanted to run for re-election, the issue of whether he would actually do so was not quite as simple. Although he never came out and said it bluntly, it was obvious that his decision depended on Putin. At times, perhaps hopeful that genuine democratic change might allow him to remain in office, Medvedev appeared to openly encourage Putin's opponents to up the stakes. During a private meeting with leading cultural and public figures in Moscow, he hailed them as 'the best people in our city' and urged them to 'take power!'

But it was all a lie. That autumn, Medvedev announced that he would step down at the end of his term in office in favour of Putin and assume the post of Prime Minister. Under the constitution, Putin had been barred from serving two *consecutive* terms, but there was, the Kremlin argued, nothing to stop him taking up the position of Head of State again later. There was also, of course, nothing technically to stop Putin and Medvedev from running against each other. But Putin would brook no further challenges to his authority. He wanted his old job back – this time for life.

In December 2011, just months after Medvedev's announcement that he would not stand for a second term, large protests broke out in Moscow over vote fraud in favour of Putin's ruling party in parliamentary elections. Vote rigging was nothing new in Russia, but the explosion of high-speed internet meant that people could now see it for themselves, often in real time. When Putin came to power in 2000, just over 1 per cent of Russians were online; by 2011, this had risen to almost 50 per cent of the country or some 51 million people.[1] Amid rising anger over video after video of ballot box stuffing, tens of thousands of people took to the streets, packing the squares of central Moscow on several occasions, even as temperatures plunged to minus 25 degrees Celsius. 'We are the power here!' demonstrators chanted.

For a brief moment, it seemed to many in the Russian opposition movement as if Putin's time was up. Even as a foreigner, those few brief weeks in Moscow when the Kremlin lost the initiative were exhilarating. 'We have to take this chance to change our country. We'll regret it if we don't,' a protester told me. I often thought about his words over the coming years.

But while these were the biggest protests in Russia since the break-up of the Soviet Union, they never reached the critical mass necessary to topple Putin. The organizers of the rallies were also unwilling to force a confrontation with the Kremlin. At a pivotal moment, they agreed with the authorities to move the initial protest from its original site of Revolution Square, smack bang between Red Square and the State Duma, to Bolotnaya Square, a location that was still in central Moscow, but far enough away from the Kremlin as to drastically reduce its impact. It was, by any standards, a ridiculous situation: Russia's protesters were furious about Putin's hijacking of the elections, yet they were also willing to be told where exactly they should go to express their dissent. Significantly, Alexei Navalny, the uncompromising opposition leader, was serving a short jail sentence and was not involved in discussions with the authorities about the protest site.

After agreeing to relocate their rally, around 100,000 people gathered on Bolotnaya Square, waving white balloons and wearing the white ribbons that had become the symbol of their nascent protest movement. Faced for the first time with large numbers of middle-class protesters, the Kremlin ordered police to go softly: there was not a single arrest that day. Protesters even applauded officers for their restraint. As state television tried to downplay the scale of the protests, RIA Novosti published drone footage that showed massive crowds, including on a city bridge that some feared might collapse under the sheer weight of demonstrators. Yet, Bolotnaya translates, roughly, as Swampy and, accordingly, the protest movement sank.

The vast majority of the protesters were willing to make some noise and even brave the freezing cold, but ultimately, they were not prepared to put their freedom or their lives on the line to force the Kremlin to hold fair elections. It wasn't hard to understand their reluctance. Russians had fresh and very raw memories of the hardships that followed the collapse of the Soviet Union – who could be certain that a revolution to topple Putin would not see a repeat of the poverty of the 1990s?

It was a way of thinking that was brought home to me most vividly by a wintertime visit to Yakutia, the enormous frozen region in north-east Russia. Would people here, I wondered as I stepped off the plane into a biting cold after a seven-hour flight, have any interest in the protests in the capital? Contacting opposition activists proved impossible: the numbers for the handful of contacts I had been given rang and rang, without reply. Later the same evening, I took a drive out into the snow-covered countryside, the stars sharp in the brittle Siberian sky. 'Lots of people here have never even been to Moscow and for them the anti-Putin protests were a kind of faraway show,' said my driver, Leonid, a talkative man in midlife, as we skidded along the icy roads. 'We don't know those guys leading the protests. Who knows what they want? People here need stability. Their lives depend on it.' Nationwide wintertime power and heating failures had been routine under Yeltsin, leaving vast swathes of Siberia to freeze. Now, all that was largely a thing of the past: as we drove back into the city, we passed rows and rows of tower blocks, hypnotic glows emanating from countless windows. What were a few stolen votes compared to a guarantee of warmth and electricity?

Yet, I like to think that if Russians had been able to see into the future, if they had been possessed of the knowledge that the stakes were so much higher than rigged parliamentary polls, they would have risen up, as one, and driven Putin and his allies from power. But, in truth, I am not sure that they would: apathy was too deeply entrenched, even back then. Within months of the protests, the arrests of opposition leaders, a vicious state television smear campaign and the realization that Putin was not going to go away so easily meant that the rallies eventually lost momentum without securing any meaningful change. Putin had survived and Russia's opposition movement would never be so strong, or united, again. Yet even the Kremlin's biggest critics had no idea of the nightmares that lay ahead.

Although the result of the March 2012 rubber-stamp elections that handed Putin a new six-year term in office were never in any doubt, he was overcome by apparent tears of joy at a victory rally in Moscow. The elections themselves were tightly controlled and marred by massive vote fraud, but the protests and Medvedev's popularity meant that Putin had come as close to losing power as he ever would. His relief was clear to see.

'I promised you we would win. We have won. Glory to Russia!' Putin shouted, standing next to Medvedev. State television, wary of shattering Putin's tough guy image, did not mention the tears that streamed down his face. Pro-Kremlin bloggers argued that Putin had not given way to emotion – God forbid! – and that the 'tears' on his face were simply the result of driving rain and a heavy wind. But then why were Medvedev's cheeks dry?[2]

My column for RIA that week was called 'He Who Sobs with Joy.' In it, I noted that Putin could now stay in power until at least 2024. It read: 'That's a long time for anyone to be in charge, even if he was the most benign, gracious, and purest leader on the planet. I'm not sure who that title might apply to, but it certainly isn't He Who Sobs with Joy.'[3] By this time, I was no longer even surprised that RIA was letting me publish such things.

I was determined to make the most of my time reporting for a Russian news agency. After all, Ryszard Kapuściński, often described as the greatest journalist of the twentieth century, had managed to produce his highly acclaimed books while reporting for the communist-era Polish Press Agency. Why not try and make use of the advantages that working for RIA gave me and arrange visits to what remained of President George W. Bush's 'axis of evil'?

In the space of six months in 2011 and 2012, I made reporting trips to both Iran and North Korea. They weren't easy to arrange; in order to secure a press visa for North Korea, I was obliged to make multiple visits to the embassy in Moscow, where diplomats wearing Kim badges loaded me down with literature about Juche, the national ideology. Our flat was soon overflowing with North Korean propaganda. Yet it was far easier for me to get permission to report from both countries than if I had been working for a Western media outlet. Besides giving me a rare close-up look at two of the world's most repressive regimes, the trips also provided me with a sneak preview of the dystopian future that awaited Russia.

In Tehran, I attended an Islamic Revolution Day rally, where massed ranks of the Islamic Revolutionary Guard Corps pumped their fists into the air as President Ahmadinejad railed against Israel and the West. Later that week, I was allowed to visit a nuclear facility in the Iranian capital: Ahmadinejad was there again, this time to insert his country's first domestically produced nuclear fuel rods into a reactor. In south Tehran, I visited an arts centre and met Iranian artists, rappers and heavy-metal kids. The smell of hashish was heavy in the air. When I asked one man, his long hair swept up in a headband, if he was worried about war with the United States, he smiled beatifically and said, in English, 'peace man'. It was a side of Iranian life that I had not expected to see.

In North Korea, although my Russian colleague was fluent in Korean, we were forbidden to speak to ordinary people and were forced to rely on our guides to explain anything that seemed puzzling. They were remarkably inventive. In Pyongyang, when we visited a new state-of-the art university that was entirely devoid of students, our guides insisted they were all 'at lunch'. In reality, in the aftermath of the Arab Spring uprisings, the regime had sent all the students to work in the fields or on construction sites over fears that this passion for revolution might be infectious. Even in the capital, electricity shortages meant that it was common to see locals sitting under the few working streetlamps with books in their hands. When we asked what books North Koreans enjoyed, our guides told us they were almost entirely uninterested in foreign authors. 'Foreign writers only write about love. And our people require more serious reading matter,' one said. Not that they had much choice: the only books I saw on sale that week were either dedicated to Kim Il Sung and Kim Jong Il, the North Korean dictators, or had been written by them.

Our flight back to Russia was via Beijing, where we had a day-long stopover. After the suffocating intensity of North Korea, even the Chinese capital felt like a breath of freedom. When we finally got back, Moscow seemed like a utopian paradise, at least for a day or two. It could never have occurred to me, or indeed to any of the Russian friends whom I told about my trips, that just over a decade later, Iran and North Korea, along with Belarus, would be the Kremlin's biggest allies in a total war against Ukraine.

I left RIA in early 2013 and began freelancing on a regular basis for American and British media. Looking back now, armed with the knowledge of what came later, my feelings about my work at the agency are conflicted. It was a unique experience, and I have no doubt that it was a genuine attempt to create a Western-style news agency. I also took satisfaction in being able to criticize Putin while on the Kremlin's payroll. Yet in hindsight, I now believe that it was a mistake to work for RIA. Back then, before the war in Ukraine and the horrors that preceded it, I was not yet possessed of the instinctive distrust and loathing for the Russian state that is second nature to so many of its intelligentsia, those members of the country's dissident class who have been persecuted, locked up and killed by the Kremlin throughout the decades. I thought, at least for a while, that Russia could change – they did not. I was wrong.

I would never determine for sure why the Kremlin had allowed RIA's English-language service to be so critical, not to mention disrespectful, of Putin. We realized, of course, that such mockery and criticism was no real threat to the Kremlin. Yet, it was a puzzle as to why they had paid us to produce such content. How did it benefit the Russian state? Russia later attempted to influence presidential elections in the United States through a massive disinformation campaign – had it really been unwilling or unable to control the output of a state news agency located just a short walk from Red Square?

I have heard rumours that the RIA English-language website was allowed to function without censorship because the Kremlin was keen to convince Western investors that there was such a thing as freedom of speech in Russia. That is one possible reason. If it is true, we were being used and all our clever criticism of Putin was playing right into the Kremlin's hands. But I think there is another explanation: Russia had yet to be entirely consumed by the ultranationalist and ultra-conservative ideologies that came to obsess Putin from his third term onwards. There was still some space left to breathe, especially for those of us writing in English, but what was left of the oxygen was running out and any hope of normal relations with the West was being sacrificed on the altar of Putin's growing paranoia and desire for confrontation.

'Western values, from liberalism to the recognition of the rights of sexual minorities, from Catholicism and Protestantism to comfortable jails for murderers, provoke in us suspicion, astonishment and alienation,' wrote Evgeny Bazhanov, the rector of the Russian foreign ministry's diplomatic academy, in an essay for its in-house magazine that I picked up while receiving my first foreign media accreditation after leaving RIA.[4] I had grown used to this sort of thing from state television, or the 'zombie box' as it was now being called by the opposition, but to see it laid out so starkly for future Russian diplomats was proof that such rhetoric was not just for propaganda purposes. Putin was rapidly reshaping Russia and there was no room left for even the most moderate of the pro-Western stances from the Yeltsin era.

In December 2013, RIA Novosti was disbanded by presidential decree. It was replaced by a news agency called Rossiya Segodnya, which translates as Russia Today, but was separate from the Kremlin-funded media outlet of the same name. In place of Svetlana Mironyuk, RIA's relatively liberal Editor-in-Chief, Rossiya Segodnya was headed by Dmitry Kiselyov, a state television presenter who had become notorious for his rabidly pro-Kremlin and anti-Western views. He had also called for gay people to be banned from giving blood and their hearts burnt after their deaths to prevent them being used for transplants. Later, he would also boast on air that Russia was the only country that could reduce the United States to 'radioactive ash'.[5] It was no surprise then when he emerged as one of the most vocal cheerleaders for the Kremlin's war in Ukraine.

Writing about the crackdown on RIA, the BBC noted that the news agency had 'reflected the views of the opposition and covered difficult topics for the Kremlin'.[6] Sergei Markov, a former Kremlin adviser, said its closure had likely been triggered by the pro-opposition views of many of its columnists.[7] It was startling to realize that I may have played a role in the demise of one of Russia's oldest news agencies. Inevitably, RIA's English-language service summed things up the best, calling the move 'the latest in a series of shifts in Russia's news landscape, which appear to point toward a tightening of state control in the already heavily regulated media sector.'[8] It was one of its final articles. On his first visit to the RIA newsroom, Kiselyov informed its staff that those who wanted to stay on would be tasked with 'creating values' and 'loving' Mother Russia.[9] 'Objectivity is a myth,' he said.[10]

Yet, Kiselyov hadn't always thought like this. In 1999, the year before Putin came to power, he had spoken about the need for journalists to ensure that they did not present their audiences with distorted images of the world. 'People will, of course, swallow anything,' he said, in a training video for Russian journalists that was co-produced by the BBC.[11] 'But if we keep lowering the bar and dropping our morals, we will one day find ourselves splashing in the mud like pigs ... until we are unable to sink any lower.'[12]

For liberal Russians, Kiselyov's comments on the importance of media freedoms were both a stark illustration of how much his views appeared to have altered since the Yeltsin era, as well as a prophecy that appeared to have come to pass. But Russia still had a long way to fall. The sickness that had gripped the country would now grow progressively worse, its symptoms becoming more terrible with every passing year.

7

'Putin *Khuilo*!'

It was gone 10 p.m. and the sun was still high in the sky when the Arctic fisherman, fuelled by cheap vodka and the disorientating euphoria of the polar day, began shouting about war. 'It's all around us!' he yelled, as he lay slumped against the wall of a fishing hut close to the icy shores of the Barents Sea. 'War! It's everywhere!' He then looked up, as if seeing me for the first time. 'Crimea is ours, right? Our Crimea!' He sat up and slammed a fist on the table, almost toppling a vodka bottle. 'What do you think of Obama?' he demanded.

I didn't have time to answer before another fisherman picked up a huge, serrated knife from the table. He had already shown me the knife, which he used for gutting fish, while raving bizarrely about the British royal family, druids and blood sacrifices, a thread I had struggled to follow. Now, the conversation had taken a far more dangerous turn. I cursed silently. I was on a travel-guide assignment in Russia's far northern Murmansk region and getting drawn into a debate about Ukraine with drunk pro-Putin fishermen was the last thing I needed.

'There are no such things as borders,' he told me, apropos of nothing. 'But Crimea is Russian, right? And the Donbas, of course.' He stared at me, waiting for a reply. I was still considering my response and the blood-stained blade being waved just inches from my eyes when someone knocked at the front door. 'Has anyone seen my puppies?' asked an elderly woman, popping her head into the hut. I took the chance to make my excuses and leave, hurrying out while they were distracted by talk of wayward dogs.

I had grown wearily accustomed to such things. Ever since November 2013 and the start of protests in Kyiv against President Yanukovych, a thuggish, corrupt leader who was under Putin's sway,[1] everyone in Russia, it sometimes seemed, wanted to talk to me about Ukraine. Or, as was more often the case, talk *at* me. It was exhausting, frustrating and often illogical. I hadn't seen Russians so animated about anything since I first arrived in the country.

These fishermen were eking out a living in a ramshackle Arctic village with minimal infrastructure, yet their thoughts were consumed by Crimea, a sun-kissed Ukrainian peninsula in the Black Sea, around 2,000 miles to the south. What difference could it possibly make to their lives who Crimea belonged to, I thought, as I picked my way along the edge of a bay, where rotting fishing boats lay half-submerged, like the skeletal remains of sea monsters. I was only a few hundred metres away when the shouting began again, the words carried to me by an Arctic wind: 'Crimea is ours!'

Although Yanukovych came to power during elections that were ruled transparent by Western monitors, he angered millions of Ukrainians in 2013 by reneging on a pledge to sign an association deal with the European Union (EU) that would have taken their country out of the Kremlin's orbit. His abrupt policy reversal came after a meeting with Putin and undisguised pressure from Moscow. 'They stole our dream, our dream of living in a normal country,' Vitali Klitschko, the world heavyweight boxing champion and future Mayor of Kyiv, told furious protesters.

The protests that erupted on Kyiv's Maidan Nezalezhnosti, its central square, may have been triggered by the row over the EU, but they quickly accelerated into a more general show of anger against entrenched corruption, human rights abuses and Russian influence. Yanukovych did not go peacefully – over 100 protesters were shot dead before he finally fled Ukraine for Russia in February 2014, whisked out of the country by the Kremlin's special forces. Putin was incensed: he had never particularly liked Yanukovych, but support for the protesters by American and European officials had convinced him that the West's ultimate goal was to foment revolution in Russia. Six years earlier, in 2008, Putin had reportedly told Bush: 'Ukraine is not even a state.'[2] Now, he would try and tear it apart. His first moves came in Crimea.

A picturesque Black Sea peninsula that has over the centuries been home to Goths, Greeks, Genoese, Tatars and Slavs, Crimea was seized by Catherine the Great, the Russian tsarina, from the Ottoman Empire in the eighteenth century. Seven decades later, the British cavalry rode into the 'valley of death' during the Crimean War, an event that was immortalized in verse by Alfred, Lord Tennyson. Crimea was also where William Howard Russell of *The Times* wrote what is widely considered to be the world's first modern war reporting. As I covered Russia's invasion of Ukraine, I often wondered what my predecessor would have made of twenty-first-century warfare, with its advanced combat drones and hypersonic missiles.

In 1954, Nikita Khrushchev, the Soviet leader, transferred Crimea to Ukraine from Russia, a move that had few tangible consequences while both countries were part of the Soviet Union. After the collapse of the communist state in 1991, Crimea became an autonomous republic within independent Ukraine. Yet, up until 2014, few people in Russia cared very much that Crimea was Ukrainian. The peninsula was a popular holiday resort for Russians and Ukrainians alike and it was only radical nationalist groups who called for its 'return to the Motherland'. Even Putin, speaking in 2008, had stated unequivocally that the Kremlin recognized Crimea as part of Ukraine. 'Crimea is not disputed territory,' he told ARD, the German broadcaster.[3]

The revolution in Ukraine changed all that. Despite tensions after the collapse of the Soviet Union, Sevastopol, Crimea's main port, had been home to Russia's Black Sea Fleet since the eighteenth century. Four years before he was toppled, Yanukovych had signed a deal with Moscow allowing it to remain in Crimea until at least 2042.[4] After the Maidan revolution, Putin warned,

Nato's naval forces were poised to replace the Black Sea Fleet in Sevastopol, creating what he called a threat to Russia's national security. This was something he said he could not permit.[5]

Within days of Yanukovych's hurried departure from Ukraine, Putin deployed troops without identifying insignia who became known as 'little green men', to take control of strategic facilities in Crimea. Just weeks later, in March 2014, the Kremlin staged a sham referendum in Crimea, at which it claimed that 97 per cent of voters, with a turnout of over 80 per cent, had voted to split from Ukraine and join Russia. It was the biggest landgrab in Europe since the end of World War Two. Although there was significant support for the move in Crimea, which had an ethnic Russian majority, a free and fair vote was impossible when carried out at the barrel of a gun. It was also highly unlikely that ethnic Ukrainians and Crimean Tatars, who together made up over 35 per cent of Crimea's population, would have voted for Russian rule in the numbers claimed by the Kremlin. In any case, the referendum only contained two options: joining Russia or declaring *de facto* independence – there was no opportunity to remain in Ukraine. Indeed, Russia's very own Human Rights Council posted a report that estimated turnout at between 30 per cent and 50 per cent, with just over half in favour of Kremlin rule. It was quickly removed.[6]

Just four days later, Russia's rubber-stamp parliament approved the 'results' of the referendum and voted to annex Crimea. Ilya Ponomarev, an opposition politician who now lives in Ukraine, was the only MP to vote against the move. The atmosphere in parliament that day was so fevered, he told me, that a pro-Putin MP named Alexei Mitrofanov had attempted to prevent him from recording his opposition. 'Mitrofanov tried to grab my hand as I reached for the [voting] button in parliament,' Ponomarev said. 'He was shouting "don't do it – we will be punished! They will say that we saw that you were going to vote against it, but we didn't prevent you!"'[7] Putin portrayed his move to annex Crimea as a fightback against what he said were attempts by Western countries to impose a global dominance after the break-up of the Soviet Union. Moscow had clashed with the West over the bombing of Yugoslavia, the US-led invasion of Iraq in 2003 and the recognition of Kosovo against the objections of Serbia, a major ally, but its protests had largely been rhetorical. Now, in Crimea, Putin was determined to show that Russia could stand up for its interests.

'[In the West,] they have come to believe in their exclusivity and exceptionalism, that they can decide the destinies of the world, that only they can ever be right. They act as they please,' he said in a speech at the Kremlin.[8] His words were lapped up by the Russian public.

Three out of every four Russians had been opposed to Moscow interfering in Ukraine's internal affairs after Yanukovych was toppled, according to VTsIOM, the state pollster.[9] Yet the seizure of Crimea triggered a wave of euphoria that sent Putin's approval ratings rocketing to unprecedented heights. 'Crimea is ours!' chanted enormous crowds at rallies and concerts. Even Navalny, the opposition leader, said that while Crimea had been seized illegally by Russia, he would not commit to automatically returning it to Ukraine in the unlikely event that he became President. 'Is Crimea a sausage sandwich that can be passed backwards and forwards? I don't think so,' he said, absurdly. He later reversed his stance.[10]

Aggressive anti-Western rhetoric and warnings of looming nuclear war quickly became the new norm. The Russian foreign ministry repeatedly warned its citizens against travelling abroad, where it alleged that US special services were 'hunting' for them. Irina Yarovaya, a leading MP with Putin's ruling party, spoke out against the study of foreign languages in schools, claiming it hurt Russia's traditions,[11] while a pro-Kremlin youth group laser beamed a racist image of Obama eating a banana onto a building opposite the American embassy.

The West's reaction to the Kremlin's annexation of Crimea was restricted to relatively weak economic sanctions against Moscow, a decision that critics said only encouraged Putin to believe that Europe and the United States lacked the will to prevent his aggression in Ukraine. Could Western countries have done more? In essence, that depended on whether they were prepared to confront Russia militarily over Crimea, a move that Moscow had lost no time in warning could lead to a nuclear conflict. A decade later, in 2024, on the second anniversary of Russia's full-scale invasion, I put the question to General Viktor Muzhenko, who was the commander-in-chief of Ukraine's armed forces from 2014 to 2019. Muzhenko, who took over as Ukraine's top general just months after the annexation of Crimea, suggested that a show of strength by the West would have been enough to stop Putin in his tracks.

'I think that Russia could have been deterred if [Nato] had moved troops up to Ukraine's borders and deployed warships to the Black Sea,' he told me, in Kyiv, after yet another air raid alert. 'Russia was acting very cautiously in Crimea at the time. Its forces would go forward, then stop and wait and see if there was any resistance. When there wasn't, only then would they advance. If the West had taken more decisive steps back then, then it's likely that we would not be at war today.'

After the annexation of Crimea, Putin sent more forces into eastern Ukraine's Donbas region to support a nascent separatist movement, once again without declaring Russian involvement. Many people in the Russian-speaking Donbas were furious that Yanukovych, who hailed from the coal-mining region, had been deposed, but there appeared to be little genuine support for the separatist gunmen and the Kremlin agents who arrived to help them seize control of city halls. 'I've never seen this lot before and the ones I do recognize are alcoholics and junkies,' a local told me when I visited Donetsk, the epicentre of the turmoil.

As Russia sought to carve up Ukraine, the country's football ultras – fanatical fans with a passion for matchday punch-ups – united against the threat from the Kremlin. They quickly came up with an insanely catchy, wildly obscene chant about the Russian leader. 'Putin – *Khuilo*! La, la, la, la, la, la!' bellowed fans at a stadium in Kharkiv, a Russian-speaking city in northeastern Ukraine that spring. The chant is perhaps best translated as 'Putin is a fucking dickhead, la, la, la, la, la, la,' although it loses something of its wanton obscenity in its English-language rendering. Online footage of the chant went viral.[12]

In May 2014, I attended the Ukrainian cup final in Poltava, a city far from the unfolding conflict in the east of the country. The match was between Dynamo Kyiv and Shakhtar Donetsk, Ukraine's two biggest teams. But all footballing rivalries were forgotten that day as the fans combined in a show of unity. 'Putin!' chanted the Dynamo Kyiv fans from one side of the stadium, '*Khuilo!*' roared the Shakhtar Donetsk fans in response. The deafening call and response chants went on for most of the game.

That summer, Ukraine's newly appointed Foreign Minister, Andrii Deshchytsia, was filmed uttering the phrase to the delight of an angry crowd that had gathered outside the Russian embassy in Kyiv. 'Yeah, yeah, Putin is a fucking dickhead,' said Deshchytsia.[13] The X-rated slur had entered mainstream Ukrainian culture. On a reporting trip to Kyiv, I bought a tote bag with 'Putin-*Khuilo*' emblazoned on it and took it back to Moscow. Trains were still running between the two countries and I had a nervous moment when a Russian border guard asked me to open my bag: fortunately, he took a cursory look at my crumpled, smelly clothes and walked on. Needless to say, I did not use the *Khuilo* bag to do my daily shopping in Moscow.

After the start of Russia's all-out invasion in 2022, the *khuilo* insult was transformed into something akin to Ukraine's unofficial logo. It was plastered on banners, scrawled onto sandbags and displayed on car stickers and t-shirts. One night, after a missile attack in southern Ukraine, amid a blackout, locals began roaring the insult, the words '*Putin – khuilo!*' echoing across the pitch-black courtyards. And then, as the chanting died away, a lone voice piped up. '*Voistinu khuilo!*' – 'Verily a fucking dickhead!'

Was Putin aware of all this? As far as we know, the Kremlin dictator does not browse the internet and so he is unlikely to have stumbled upon any of the numerous videos of the chant online. It is also doubtful that any Russian official would have been brave enough to draw his attention to it. 'Vladimir Vladimirovich, the Ukrainians are calling you a *khuilo*,' is not something that it is easy to imagine a Kremlin aide uttering. Yet the chant was so widespread that it was unthinkable that Putin was entirely ignorant of it. If so, were his feelings hurt? We can only hope so.

A year after the annexation of Crimea, I visited Sevastopol and Simferopol, its two biggest cities, to report on how the Kremlin's rule had changed life on the peninsula for those residents who had resisted the Russian takeover. According to Russian law, anyone residing legally on the territory of Crimea on 18 March 2014 automatically became a citizen of Russia. Those who objected were given a month to file a refusal. Having done so, they immediately became foreigners in the land of their own birth, without the automatic right to work, receive state medical care or even reside permanently in Crimea. One woman I spoke to, who asked to be identified only as Ella, told me that after she had refused the Kremlin's unsolicited offer of citizenship, she found herself entangled in the maze of Russia's notorious bureaucracy as she tried to secure a residency permit to remain in Crimea. One of the documents she was obliged to provide was a signed and stamped form from a state-approved psychiatrist testifying to the applicant's mental health. She shook her head with understandable exasperation. 'Excuse me, but why should I have to prove my mental wellbeing so as to remain living in Crimea? I've been here for over 30 years!'[14]

The Kremlin had claimed to be protecting the residents of Crimea from Ukrainian 'neo-Nazis', but it was Putin's forces who brought a Gestapo-style terror to the Black Sea peninsula. Everywhere I went, I heard stories of violence against Crimea's Tatar population. A mainly Muslim ethnic group, around 200,000 Crimean Tatars had been forcibly deported to Central Asia by Stalin in 1944. Entire villages were crammed into trains; many villagers did not survive the long journey or the harsh conditions that awaited them in exile. In the 1990s, thousands finally returned to their homeland, by then in an independent

Ukraine. They were, understandably, some of the biggest critics of Russian rule in Crimea, a stance that has seen them pay a terrible price. While the Kremlin escalated its attacks on the opposition in Moscow after the full-scale invasion of Ukraine in 2022, its harshest clampdown first came against the Crimean Tatars who had dared to oppose Putin.

As Russian forces took control of Simferopol in March 2014, Rishat Ametov, a Crimean Tatar who had staged a one-man protest against Kremlin rule, was bundled into a car in broad daylight by three men wearing paramilitary uniforms. Almost two weeks later, Ametov, a 39-year-old father of three young children, was found dead in a nearby forest. His hands were handcuffed, his head wrapped in duct tape and a sharp object had reportedly been thrust into one of his eyes. He was the first victim of a brutal campaign of political repression in Crimea. The entire abduction was filmed by a bystander and uploaded to YouTube.[15] The video clearly shows the faces of the men who forced Ametov into the car; they were later identified by Ukrainian prosecutors as two pro-Moscow locals and a former member of the Russian armed forces.

On the first anniversary of Ametov's abduction, I met his elder brother, Refat, at a Crimean Tatar restaurant in Simferopol. The owner took us into a backroom so that we could talk without being disturbed. Softly spoken, Refat was consumed by grief, as well as anger, over the way his brother's killers had been allowed to walk free.

'My brother was a law-abiding man. This is very important to understand. He just wanted to express his opposition to what was going on and to demonstrate that this is the Crimean Tatars' homeland and we have every right to be here,' Refat told me. He realized though, that justice would not come for years, if ever. 'No one will ever face charges over my brother's death. The investigators are covering up for the men who abducted him,' he told me.

After speaking to Ametov's brother, I headed to the tiny Tatar village of Sary-Su, around an hour's drive from Simferopol. The village, whose name means 'Yellow Water' in the Tatar language, had been built from scratch after the Crimean Tatars returned in the 1990s. The houses, school and mosque had been constructed on empty fields, creating a sense of community after years in exile. When I arrived in the village, it was into an atmosphere of fear and suspicion. Two young men, Islyam Dzhepparov, aged 18, and Dzhevdet Islyamov, 23, had recently been seized by men in black uniforms and pushed into a Volkswagen van with tinted windows. They had not been seen since. The missing men were the son and nephew of Abdureshit Dzhepparov, a Crimean Tatar political activist opposed to Kremlin rule. He met me at the entrance to his home and we went inside to talk. The windows were drawn shut to keep out the sun, accentuating the gloom.

'The investigator in the case told me that their disappearance had something to do with my activities,' Dzhepparov said. 'He told me to think about that. I told him I was willing to do whatever it takes – go to prison, wear an electronic bracelet – if only the boys would be set free. He just shrugged and said he'd report this to his superiors.'

He spoke slowly and carefully, weighing up each word for its possible consequences. I felt next to useless: it was important to document Russia's brutality in Crimea, but there was almost next to no chance that my reporting would lead to his son and nephew's release. Just before I left him, Dzhepparov told me: 'Every time I hear a noise, or some knocking, I jump up, because I think, perhaps it's my son.'[16]

Over the following years, dozens of Crimean Tatar men were arrested and convicted by Russia on trumped-up terrorism charges. Prison sentences of 15 years and longer were common, as was torture. To date, no one has been charged by Russian occupying forces over the abduction and murder of Reshat Ametov. More than a decade on, Dzhepparov's son and nephew are still missing, just two more victims of Putin's hatred of Ukraine.

8

'No More Time for Truth-Seeking'

Russian state media's coverage of events in Ukraine was hysterical, relentless and dripping with pure venom. In July 2014, Channel One, Russia's main television station, broadcast a report claiming that Ukrainian soldiers had crucified a 3-year-old boy on Lenin Square in Sloviansk, a town in the Russian-speaking east of the country. The report was also picked up by RT, the Kremlin's English-language media outlet, whose headline read: 'Kiev army now literally crucify babies in towns, forces mothers to watch.' It soon emerged that the story, unsurprisingly, was fake. Russian opposition journalists who travelled to Sloviansk were unable to find anyone who had witnessed the purported atrocity. What was more, the town didn't even have a Lenin Square.[1]

When around 50,000 people gathered in central Moscow in the spring of 2014 to protest against Russia's actions in Ukraine, I witnessed a journalist from NTV, a Kremlin-controlled television channel, filming her stand-up for the cameras in front of an almost empty street. Just a handful of misguided radicals, she informed viewers, had turned up for the demonstration. When she had finished, I asked her why she had lied. She looked at me with an expression that was somewhere between pity and scorn. 'You do your job, and I'll do mine, right?' she said, before walking away. It was a succinct and accurate description of Kremlin propaganda: these people knew they were lying and they knew the damage they were doing but they did it anyway, spreading dangerous lies for money and a modicum of fame. Others believed themselves to be warriors in an information war with the West, a conflict in which truth was a regrettable casualty. 'There is no more time for truth-seeking,' the editors of one media outlet in Moscow told staff after the annexation of Crimea. 'Our country is back in the Cold War era.'[2]

Less than a week after the 'crucified boy' report, when Malaysia Airlines flight MH17 plummeted to the ground in eastern Ukraine with the death of all 298 people on board, Kremlin propaganda churned out a stream of outlandish conspiracy theories. Instead of the truth, which was that pro-Moscow forces with links to the Kremlin's security services had shot down the plane with a Russian-supplied surface-to-air missile, state television and other outlets suggested that the aircraft had been targeted because the Ukrainians mistook it for Putin's presidential jet, or the airliner was already full of dead bodies or a bomb had exploded on board or… the list went on. The Rossiya 1 channel even suggested that the United States was blaming Moscow for the plane's destruction as revenge for Putin's failure to turn up on time for a meeting with President Obama on the sidelines of a G20 summit.

A court in The Hague later sentenced three men in absentia to life in prison over the downing of MH17. One of them, Igor Girkin, was an ex-FSB officer who had played a major role in the annexation of Crimea. When I spoke to him in 2020 after he had been formally charged by international investigators, he admitted 'moral responsibility' for the deaths of the MH17 passengers but insisted that pro-Moscow forces under his control had not launched the fateful missile. I then asked him if that comment could be construed as an admission that the regular Russian army itself was to blame: 'People can interpret this as they like,' Girkin said. Then, he hung up. In 2025, the United Nations aviation council ruled that Russia was responsible for the downing of the plane, saying it had failed to 'refrain from resorting to the use of weapons against civil aircraft in flight'. The Kremlin called the UN ruling 'biased'.[3]

The impact of this constant stream of crude but effective Kremlin propaganda on regular viewers was as predictable as it was disturbing. Inflammatory broadcasts helped to whip up unprecedented levels of hatred, plunging tens of millions of Russian television viewers into what one academic in Moscow described as a 'trance-like state'.[4]

I could barely have a five-minute conversation with my mother-in-law before she steered the conversation towards Ukrainian 'Nazis' and the 'evil' West. I had once enjoyed listening to her stories of life in East Germany or deepest Siberia, but I now dreaded speaking to her. She had once urged T and I to leave Russia and set up home in Britain. 'What are you doing here? Nothing good will ever happen in Russia,' she had told us. Slightly over a decade later, her ability to reason having been deliberately and methodically warped by Kremlin propaganda, she was virulently anti-Western and fervently pro-Putin. As the only Westerner she knew, I swiftly became the target of my mother-in-law's rage. In her eyes, I was the living embodiment of what the Kremlin had begun referring to as the 'Anglo-Saxon world', a derogatory moniker for Britain and the United States. Not long after Russia's annexation of Crimea, we stopped speaking entirely and, as she consumed state media's foulness like a drug, I grew in her mind into a grotesque, almost demonic figure.

As my mother-in-law's opinions on the West came full circle, she also tried to make my wife promise that our daughter would never live in England. When asked why, she replied: 'They drink a lot there.' She had, it turned out, watched a state television report about under-age drinking in Britain that made no mention at all of Russia's well-documented problems with alcoholism. I felt sorry for her, and a renewed hatred for the Kremlin's propaganda agents, those highly paid individuals who have become frighteningly adept at twisting minds in pursuit of Putin's murderous ambitions. What hope did an elderly woman living alone on a pitiful pension in the Russian provinces have against the Kremlin's propaganda machine?

My mother-in-law wasn't the only Russian who had been driven out of her mind, of course. 'Nationally televised broadcasts have scared people and led to increased hostility in society,' Lev Gudkov, the head of the independent Levada Center pollster told me in 2015. 'We have seen a drastic change in the collective consciousness of the Russian people over the last year or so.'

The damaging lies pushed by state media after the annexation of Crimea were merely the first threads in the Kremlin's vast tapestry of deceitfulness: by 2022, and the start of Putin's 'special military operation' in Ukraine, Russian state television was transformed into an almost non-stop propaganda machine, broadcasting chilling rhetoric about Ukraine and the West for 16 hours a day.[5]

For weeks ahead of the invasion, Russian officials had been assuring the world that Moscow had no intention of waging full-scale war. State media had even mocked those who were rightly concerned about Russia's massive troop build-up on Ukraine's borders. Echoing the official line, ordinary Russians also dismissed Western warnings about an imminent attack as propaganda aimed at discrediting the Kremlin. 'It's utter rubbish. I've never heard anything so stupid in my life,' said Galina, a middle-aged woman, when I spoke to her outside a popular café in central Moscow. 'Why would we attack Kyiv? What for? No one wants war.' She looked at me. 'It's you Western journalists who are stirring things up.'

Yet all these denials were forgotten the instant that Putin announced he was sending in the tanks, sucked into the memory hole of Kremlin propaganda. State television offered no justification or explanation as to why Russia had lied about its intentions. Indeed, such was its hypnotic power that few viewers even posed the question, at least publicly. Instead, state media alleged without evidence that the West had been planning to use Ukraine as a platform for a nuclear attack on Russia. 'The aim of Russia's special operation in Ukraine is to prevent a global war. Russia's actions are, in essence, anti-war,' a state television presenter announced.[6]

One of Putin's top propaganda agents was Olga Skabeyeva, the host of the *60 Minutes* current affairs show on the Rossiya 1 television channel.[7] With a screen presence that was somewhere between Hannibal Lecter and the Wicked Witch of the West, Skabeyeva, whose critics called her Putin's 'iron doll', was arguably state television's biggest hawk. Just one week after the start of the invasion of Ukraine she called for Russia to carry out a special operation to 'demilitarize' Nato and launch nuclear strikes on Western countries, and declared: 'God is with us. And with Ukraine – the devil.' When Yevgeny Popov, her husband and co-host, who was also an MP, warned there would be no one left alive on the planet after a nuclear war, Skabeyeva grinned and said: 'We'll start from scratch.'[8]

Some analysts have argued that such broadcasts are aimed as much at intimidating Western policymakers as the Russian people. That may be so: yet they still serve to poison the public mood and normalize, in as much as it is possible, the concept of nuclear war. In 2024, according to research by the Levada Center, Moscow's only independent pollster, four out of ten Russians said that the Kremlin would be justified in using a nuclear bomb during the war in Ukraine.[9] A previous Levada poll had found that levels of support were greatest among those who relied on state television for most of their information.[10]

'My dad watches two televisions and listens to the radio at the same time,' Irina, a photographer in Moscow, told me. 'If I say anything against the war, he screams at me that I am an "enemy of the people". I'd like to think that this insanity is temporary, but I suspect that it is untreatable.' Another woman told me that her elderly mother had tried to convince her that Western countries had all but stopped producing toilet paper due to the economic costs of supporting Ukraine. 'My mum told me that she had seen a woman at the post office sending a parcel of toilet paper to her "poor" relatives in the West,' Lyudmila said. 'It later turned out that she hadn't seen this herself but had heard about it on state television.' She rolled her eyes, still unable to believe quite how effectively Putin's propaganda had twisted her mother's mind.

It was impossible to watch these frenzied propaganda broadcasts in one sitting: instead, I consumed them in 15-minute doses, submerging myself in their bilious, suffocating rage before coming up for air, a little part of my mind defiled for ever each time. Eventually, after my departure from Moscow, having overdosed on apocalyptic state media rhetoric, I snapped and called Popov. Did he realize, I asked him, that he and his wife's broadcasts made them appear unhinged? It was, in retrospect, a pointless question, but I felt the need to ask it nevertheless. Popov, never one to miss an opportunity for a vitriolic rant, pounced.

'Your opinion means nothing. If it looks crazy or strange, well, we, the Russian people, don't give a damn what you think about our country in the West,' he said. He then accused me of being personally responsible for the death that week of a teenager in occupied Crimea who was reportedly killed by a Western-supplied Ukrainian missile. 'You approve [in your articles] of the killing of Russian citizens!' he snapped. This wasn't true and, by the way, I asked, had he even read my articles?

'Thank God, I can't pay anymore for a subscription to *The Times*, because you don't accept payments from Russia. But I found another way to read it and now I just steal your articles,' Popov told me, laughing. He then ended the call with a cheery 'Bye! Call again!' Like the reporter who had advised me to let her do her job and get on with my own, Popov's work was over and it was, he seemed to think, nothing personal.

Vladimir Solovyov, another notorious state television presenter, told a theatre audience in Moscow in 2008 that any Russian leader who went to war with Ukraine would be 'a criminal'. An invasion, he said, would be 'the worst crime that you could think of'.[11] Fourteen years later in 2022, he called for nuclear attacks on Ukraine and its Western allies, including the United States, which he urged the Kremlin to submerge in a 'radioactive tsunami'.[12] He also accused Ukraine and its western allies of being 'servants of the Prince of Darkness'.[13]

Solovyov was not the only one of the Kremlin's propaganda agents whose views had undergone a dramatic reversal. In the early 2000s, Dmitry Kiselyov, the state television presenter who took over at RIA Novosti when the Kremlin purged it of anyone who sought to produce objective journalism, was an outspoken admirer of Ukraine. Although his broadcasts are now full of descriptions of Ukraine as a 'Nazi state' and calls for violence against its people, from 2000 to 2006, he worked in Kyiv, heading the ICTV channel's news service. A former colleague told me that he had started weekly meetings with the phrase 'we are all working for the good of Ukraine'.

'I care about Ukraine, as if I am part of it,' he told an interviewer in Kyiv in 2000, smiling warmly as he spoke. 'I've begun to feel more Ukrainian. I feel like I belong [here.]'[14] This was not especially surprising: Kiselyov's grandfather, he revealed, had been born in western Ukraine. 'People here love their country, and that's not something I can say about Russia,' he said in another interview.[15]

When I spoke to Kiselyov's former colleagues in Kyiv, they suggested that his switch to the dark side was motivated entirely by money and career progression. 'He is a highly professional mercenary without the slightest empathy for anyone,' said Dmytro Polyukhovych, a journalist who worked with Kiselyov at ICTV. 'If he was tasked by Moscow to promote the idea of Ukrainian–Russian friendship and democratic values to the masses, he would do it no less talentedly. For now, his task is to promote the hatred of Ukraine and Ukrainians. And so that's what he does.'

Had Russian television not pumped vast funds into its sprawling propaganda machine, then my mother-in-law and I would likely be on speaking terms today. It's a minor issue, of course, when compared to the colossal suffering that Putin's lies and disinformation have brought about in Ukraine, as well as in Russia itself. But all the same, I hope that the Kremlin's propaganda agents one day receive the punishment that they deserve. In this life, or the next.

Still, at least my mother-in-law hadn't tried to kill me. The wave of unbridled nationalism and paranoia that was unleashed by the confrontation with Ukraine and the West had already proven the trigger for a number of senseless murders. In 2015, just months apart, a retired Russian army officer battered a merchant seaman to death after becoming convinced that he was a spy because he made frequent work-related trips abroad, while a pensioner stabbed to death 'an American agent' – in reality a guest in his home who had unwisely joked about knowing Obama. Predictably, vodka was involved in both cases.[16]

That same year, a Kremlin ban on most Western food imports in retaliation for sanctions over Crimea prompted surreal scenes of bulldozers flattening piles of French cheese and workers hurling packages of Spanish ham into furnaces. Around 600 tonnes of food were burned or crushed within the first two weeks of the ban. In one bizarre incident, three frozen Hungarian geese were seized by grim-faced Russian officials from a tiny grocery store in Apastovo, a village about 500 miles east of Moscow. Under Putin's decree, the destruction of contraband Western food had to be filmed to prevent officials confiscating the products for their own use. Accordingly, the geese were taken to a landfill site, where witnesses stated their names and addresses for a cameraman. The vacuum-packed geese, weighing 3.6 kilograms each, and garnished with vegetables and seasoning were then placed on the ground in a neat row by an official. On order, a bulldozer rumbled forwards and began rolling over the geese repeatedly as the officials and witnesses looked on. The entire operation lasted half a day and involved at least ten people, including police and agriculture inspectors.[17] Russia's agricultural watchdog said later that the three geese should have been incinerated, rather than crushed, and that the officials responsible would be punished. It was too late, though, to prevent widespread mockery. One former Kremlin adviser compared the scenes to a Monty Python sketch. 'What's wrong with these people? They read the death sentence to three frozen geese,' an opposition supporter wrote on social media.[18]

In Moscow, I was watching the bizarre video of the 'execution' when our daughter, now aged six, came into the room. 'Why are they crushing those geese?' she asked. I struggled to come up with an adequate answer to her question. How exactly, I wondered, did one explain away, in child-friendly terms, the whirlwind of xenophobia and paranoia that had gripped Russia since Putin had returned to the Kremlin for a third term?

At the time, this orgy of culinary destruction seemed merely disgusting: now, I wonder if it was not the moment when Putin lost all touch with reality, his isolation in the Kremlin and years of unlimited power finally tipping him over into madness. Not long before the food imports ban, Angela Merkel, the German chancellor, was reported to have described Putin as living 'in another world' and out of 'touch with reality'.[19] Still, I occasionally let myself fantasize that Putin and his inner circle couldn't really be serious about the path they were leading Russia along. That, perhaps, it was all a grotesque joke, a sophisticated intellectual trick and that, before long, Putin and his sidekicks would tear off their metaphorical masks and laugh at us all. 'You didn't really think we believed in all this craziness, right?'

Not too long after the incident with the geese, I interviewed an opposition politician at a café on the Old Arbat street near our flat. A few seconds after we arrived, a woman walked in and sat down next to us. It was the middle of the afternoon and the weather was good. The few other guests were sitting outside. The woman glanced at us, took out her phone and placed it on the table. When we had finished speaking, we left. She walked out seconds later. I was never too sure if the Kremlin cared enough about what Western journalists wrote to keep tabs on us, but this was blatant. 'She was recording our conversation, right?' I said to the opposition politician. He shrugged. 'Of course,' he said, as if it was the most natural thing in the world. We said our goodbyes and I decided to follow the woman, curious about where she would go next. Without even bothering to look back, she walked straight into the nearest police station.

A few weeks later, I went to the foreign ministry to pick up my new press accreditation card. Tensions between Russia and the West were at their highest since the Cold War and I hadn't been sure that Moscow would allow me to continue reporting. I needn't have worried: 'So I guess you'll be here until the end?' a foreign ministry employee said as she handed me my new card. 'The end of what?' I asked, but she just smiled and I didn't repeat the question. I still wonder what she meant.

9

MAKING THE GATE WIDER FOR FASCISM

On the second day of Russia's all-out war in Ukraine, Putin stared blankly into a camera and urged Kyiv's military to side with his invading army. 'Take power into your own hands,' he said. 'It will be easier for us to come to an agreement with you, than with this gang of drug addicts and neo-Nazis that has entrenched itself in Kyiv.'[1]

I was still near Russia's border with eastern Ukraine and watched the Kremlin dictator's snarling speech on my laptop in the hotel lobby. The hotel receptionist glanced over, as if to challenge me to dispute her leader's lies. We had already clashed over the war and I didn't feel like getting into another row with her, especially with FSB officers prowling around. In any case, if she hadn't worked out for herself by now that Ukraine was not ruled by Nazis, let alone drug fiends, then at this point there wasn't much that I could realistically say to change her mind.

The Kremlin had been pushing the idea of 'Nazi Ukraine' on its people since the 2014 Maidan revolution in Kyiv that brought an end to Russian influence in the country. It was a claim that had no basis in reality and began to look even more bizarre in 2019 when Ukraine elected Volodymyr Zelensky, a Russian-speaking Jew, as its President. Zelensky's great-grandparents died when German troops burned down their village, while the Ukrainian leader had also described Nazi ideology as 'inhuman'.[2] Yet, Putin was confident enough in the power of his propaganda machine to feel that he could sell his people the idea of invading Ukraine as a rerun of World War Two, with his forces in the role of the Red Army, saving Europe from fascism.

The Kremlin's lies were not simply pulled from thin air. Unlike the laughable propaganda of most twentieth-century dictatorships, Russian state media has become adept at seizing on tiny slices of reality and magnifying them to grotesque proportions, until they block out the truth. In the case of Ukraine, it is a fact that there were a number of very vocal far-right groups in the country before the war, including some who played a key role during the Maidan uprising. Although a coalition of ultra-nationalist parties had secured just 2 per cent of the vote at the 2019 parliamentary elections, they were extremely visible and human rights groups were concerned about their growing influence.

In 2018, hundreds of members of an ultra-nationalist organization called the National Militia marched through central Kyiv wearing camouflage gear. Their show of strength culminated at a torch-illuminated fortress, where they swore oaths of allegiance to Andriy Biletsky, a far-right politician. Later that year, I joined National Militia vigilantes as they searched for illegal loggers in a snowy forest near Kyiv. 'There's nothing inherently wrong with national socialism as a political idea,' Oleksiy, a militia member, told me as they moved stealthily through moonlit trees frosted with ice. 'I don't know why everyone always associates it immediately with concentration camps.'[3]

A minority of soldiers within the Ukrainian army also held far-right or even neo-Nazi views. Azov, a well-known military unit with ultra-nationalist roots, was the most notorious of Kyiv's forces. Yet, even before the start of Russia's invasion in 2022, its ideologies had been diluted by an influx of recruits who were attracted primarily by its reputation as an effective fighting unit.

Four years before Putin ordered missile strikes on Kyiv, I shared a train cabin heading from Mariupol to the Ukrainian capital with an Azov medic. We got talking and he told me about his passion for American hip-hop. When I asked him how he squared his love of Black music with Azov's far-right philosophies, he laughed. 'I don't even think about that,' he said. 'They are just the best at fighting Russians. That's why I joined them. No other reason.'

It was true that western Ukraine, in particular, had an unhealthy reverence for Stepan Bandera, a nationalist leader whose insurgent fighters collaborated for a time with Nazi Germany in a bid to achieve independence from the Soviet Union. Nationalist fighters loyal to Bandera slaughtered up to 100,000 Polish civilians during a campaign of ethnic cleansing in 1943–45, albeit while he was in captivity in Germany. Yet, despite the statues of Bandera in the west of the country and an annual nationwide commemoration of his birth, it would be inaccurate to say that his legacy had exerted a significant influence on Ukrainian government policy. Many Ukrainians who admired Bandera did so exclusively, although perhaps unwisely, because they were inspired by his attempt to free their country from Moscow's yoke. Indeed, the number of Ukrainians with a positive attitude towards Bandera soared from under 30 per cent before the annexation of Crimea to 74 per cent following Russia's full-scale invasion of their country in 2022, according to an opinion poll.[4]

If Ukraine had a problem with far-right radicals, then this was also true of Russia, to an even greater degree. Vladimir Zhirinovsky's Liberal Democratic Party of Russia, with its openly fascist policies, was Russia's third biggest political force, while the Kremlin's invading troops included men who made no secret of their neo-Nazi affiliations. Dmitry Utkin, the second-in-command of the Wagner Group, a Kremlin-backed mercenary organization that played a major role in the invasion of Ukraine, signed off his letters with the SS lightning bolts of Hitler's death squad.[5] He also sported Nazi tattoos.[6] Rusich, a neo-fascist, neo-pagan paramilitary unit that was affiliated with Wagner, was even more explicit. One of its leaders, Alexei Milchakov, had posed with a swastika,[7] while he had also posted photographs of himself holding the severed ears of Ukrainian soldiers on social media. In an interview, Milchakov freely admitted to being a Nazi and spoke of the 'great smell of burning human flesh'.[8] In August 2024, Rusich uploaded a video to the internet showing a Ukrainian soldier's head on a spike.⁹ It also asked allied Russian units to provide it with a captured Ukrainian prisoner of war, preferably a dark-skinned Crimean Tatar, 'for a ritual sacrifice to Slavic gods' at the autumnal equinox.¹⁰ Shortly afterwards, the FSB reportedly deployed the unit to Russia's border with Finland.¹¹

During one of my trips to wartime Ukraine, I obtained a copy of a propaganda newspaper that had been printed by Russian occupying forces in the Kherson region. The newspaper had used a photograph of a group of skinheads holding up a swastika and giving the Nazi salute as 'evidence' that Ukraine was infested with fascists. I recognized the image immediately: it was from a far-right/nationalist rally in Moscow that I had covered in 2012. The photograph was still freely available on the website of Reuters, the international news agency.¹² Russia's peddlers of propaganda were not just evil, they were also extremely lazy.

Putin's argument that the invasion of Ukraine was necessary to 'denazify' Russia's neighbour was absurd: it was as if France had launched a military attack on London in the 1970s over the existence of the National Front, the far-right movement that received almost 200,000 votes at the 1979 UK general election.¹³

Why then was Putin able to get away with portraying Ukraine as a Nazi regime? In part, it's because for many of his citizens, the words 'Nazi' or 'fascist' often signify little more than anti-Soviet or anti-Russian. School history books focus on Hitler's horrendous crimes against the Soviet people, with the slaughter of millions of Jews in concentration camps reduced to almost a footnote. There is little meaningful examination of the actual ideology that defines and underpins fascism or Nazism. This is understandable and perhaps even deliberate, given that Putin's Russia ticks many of the boxes for a typical fascist state, from the militarization of education to the idea of a messianic national leader who restored the nation's long-lost glories.

This can lead to some bizarre and disturbing contradictions. In 2015, I visited Volgograd, the city in southern Russia formerly known as Stalingrad, for an event to commemorate the 70th anniversary of the Soviet defeat of Nazi Germany, known as

Victory Day in Russia. This sprawling city on the Volga River was where Hitler's forces suffered a decisive loss during over six months of savage combat that killed around half a million Red Army soldiers. It is one of Russia's 'Hero Cities' and there are reminders of the battle almost everywhere you look. As I chatted to Viktor, a veteran of the Battle of Stalingrad who was in full uniform for the day, he informed me with a grimace that Russia was once again in mortal danger. This time, he told me, it was not the Nazis but a 'Zionist plot' that sought the destruction of the Motherland. I was still wondering about this when I got in a taxi to take me to Mamayev Kurgan, a vast memorial complex to fallen Soviet soldiers. After a few minutes of pleasantries, the driver told me that Jews and gypsies were 'the parasites of the Earth'. They were, he said, entirely responsible for Russia's many economic and social problems. It was, I replied, a very good thing indeed that the Soviet Union had defeated fascism. He nodded vigorously in agreement and wished me a happy Victory Day.

Anti-Putin activists in Moscow once joked, bitterly: 'When Putin hears the slogan "fascism shall not pass", he gives the order to make the gate a little wider.' In 2022, the joke stopped being funny. One month after the start of the invasion of Ukraine, Anna Krechetova, an anti-war protester, was arrested in Moscow and convicted of holding up a sign that a court ruled had 'discredited' the Russian army. The words on her sign? 'Fascism shall not pass.'[14]

Even as the Kremlin railed against the 'Nazi regime' in Ukraine, Russia was rapidly transforming into a fascist state that mimicked, consciously or unconsciously, the aesthetics of Hitler's rule. The letter Z, which does not exist in Russia's Cyrillic alphabet, quickly became the symbol of the Kremlin's war in Ukraine. It was daubed on tanks and armoured vehicles and written on the walls of destroyed Ukrainian homes by marauding Russian troops.

The Russian defence ministry said the Z symbol stood for '*Za Pobedu*,' or 'For Victory,' but some analysts suggested Moscow was playing catch-up and that it had initially been a simple abbreviation for *Zapad* (West), a military designation among its invading troops. In any case, it was soon everywhere, a malevolent symbol of war and destruction that appeared to have been dredged up from the darkest recesses of the national consciousness. Among opponents of the war, it soon became known as a zwastika, with one online meme suggesting that it was the lovechild of the infamous Nazi symbol and the Soviet Union's hammer and sickle. Others joked that it was half a swastika, with the missing half having been stolen by Russia's notoriously kleptocratic officials. In Kazan, a city in central Russia, terminally ill children were lined up in the shape of a massive Z on the grounds of a hospice, while equipment at Russia's Baikonur spaceport in Kazakhstan was also marked with the pro-war symbol. At a sporting event in Doha, a Russian gymnast named Ivan Kuliak wore a t-shirt decorated with a large Z as he stood on the podium next to a Ukrainian athlete.[15]

The association between the Z symbol and the Nazis wasn't entirely inaccurate. In the weeks after the start of the invasion anti-war Russians began posting to social media an extract from a Soviet-era cartoon called *The Treasures of Sunken Ships*. The 1973 cartoon[16] tells the story of a group of children who are on holiday at a Soviet youth camp on the Black Sea coast. During their adventures the children explore the seabed for treasure in a submersible. They discover a sunken vessel and the submersible's robotic arm wipes away seaweed to reveal the designation Z-29. 'Fascist destroyer,' one of the children says, in hushed tones. 'Nazi destroyers were designated by the letter "Z".' It is unlikely that Russian officials were unaware of this fact, but perhaps they simply didn't care.

'One nation. One President. One victory,' Leonid Slutsky, a prominent pro-Kremlin politician, declared in 2022, in an echo of Nazi Germany's 'Ein Volk, Ein Reich, Ein Führer!' ('One People, One Realm, One Leader!').[17] Shortly before I left Moscow, I went shopping on the Old Arbat street near our flat. As I passed a souvenir shop, I noticed that its window display was a mixture of black

Z shirts mixed randomly with a set of dolls depicting characters from *Masha and the Bear*, a massively popular Russian cartoon. I wasn't a big fan of the series, much preferring the sly wit and style of Soviet-era animated films, but it was entertaining enough.

The juxtaposition of the dolls and the symbol of Putin's maniacal war made me feel nauseous. The glass-eyed dolls were wrapped in cellophane that immediately made me think of body bags. 'Why would you do that?' I asked a shop assistant, gesturing at the display. She shrugged. 'What's the problem?' she replied, genuinely puzzled. Apparently, neither she or any of her colleagues had considered how inappropriate it was to place t-shirts that symbolized the bloody invasion of a neighbouring country next to children's dolls. When I pointed this out, perhaps more forcefully than was wise, given the mounting crackdown on anti-war dissent, the shop assistant looked at me like I was mad. She turned away and attended to a customer. I wondered if the shop was selling many of the t-shirts. At that stage in the war, although the Z symbol had been draped on buildings across the city, I had yet to see anyone apart from pro-Kremlin politicians and celebrities wearing one.

Within weeks of the start of the invasion, Ukrainians took to calling Russians *Rashisti,* a portmanteau of *Rasha* (Russia) and *fashisti* (fascists). For Russians who had grown up with stories of the Soviet Union's war against Nazi Germany, the insult was as close to the bone as possible. 'It's so painful to hear the word Rashisti,' a friend in Moscow who had been on anti-war protests told me. 'But I understand why the Ukrainians use it – the Russian army really is acting like fascists.'

Russia's invasion of Ukraine got its own soundtrack with the emergence of Shaman, a blond pop star whose best-known song, 'Ya Russkiy' (I'm Russian), contained the lines 'I'm Russian, to spite the whole world.'[18] In a video for another song called 'Mi' (We), Shaman, clad in black leather, marched around Red Square in his big black boots as he belted out a paean to the Russian nation. 'God is with us! For ever united in our blood!' he sang, sporting an armband in the colours of the Russian flag.[19] 'If we didn't know the context, then it would seem that this is a parody of the Hitler Youth,' said Marat Gelman, a former Kremlin adviser and art expert who had long been critical of Putin.[20] The video was released on 20 April 2023 – the 134th anniversary of Hitler's birth.

While hundreds of Russian musicians were forced to flee the country after speaking out against the invasion of Ukraine, Shaman, whose real name is Yaroslav Dronov, rode a wave of aggressive nationalism to stardom. He appeared alongside Putin at mass pro-war rallies on Red Square and state media promoted his music with a relentless passion. After the release of 'We', Channel One, Russia's main television station, told viewers that the song was the harbinger of a future when the concept of individuality would be suppressed entirely for the glory of the Russian state. 'There will no longer be any "I",' a presenter declared. 'There will only be "We" – this gives us strength.'[21] It was unclear if the presenter, or indeed Shaman, had read *We* by Yevgeny Zamyatin, the early Soviet novel about a totalitarian state where people are known by numbers, rather than names. In 2025, Shaman played in Pyongyang in front of Kim Jong Un, holding up the North Korean and Russian flags.

Shaman's music may have represented everything I hated about Putin's regime, but it was irritatingly catchy: I often found myself humming his 'I'm Russian' track after my departure from Moscow. The song was a foul earworm that crawled around my head for weeks. I eventually managed to flush it out with the music of exiled Russian groups opposed to the war. One song, 'Eto Proidyot' ('This Will Pass'), by Pornofilmy, a punk group, was especially effective: its lyrics describe Putin as 'alone in the morgue, yesterday's dictator, now just a dead old man'.[22] That was the kind of music I wanted to hear played on Red Square, not Shaman's totalitarian beats.

Predictably, the song was banned by the Kremlin as extremist and Vladimir Kotlyarov, the group's singer and lyricist, was designated a foreign agent and charged with 'discrediting the Russian army'. Like most other Russian musicians opposed to Putin,

Kotlyarov and his bandmates fled the country after the 2022 invasion began. 'I didn't want to share with Russia, with that huge empire of evil, even the possibility of victory over the peaceful country of Ukraine,' he told me, when I met him in Tbilisi, the capital of Georgia, where the group had set up home. 'This song was banned because it became popular. Lots of people in Russia think the same way. It was important to me that it reflected the spirit of the times and the mood of the people. That's what was important and not that some old madman might be offended by it.'

In April 2022, approximately six weeks after Putin had ordered tanks into Ukraine, I met Maria Butina, a Russian MP and one of the biggest supporters of the invasion, at a plush Italian restaurant near Red Square. A former gun rights activist from Siberia, Butina made international headlines in 2018 when she was convicted by a court in the United States of conspiring to infiltrate Republican Party circles on behalf of the Kremlin. Her case became a cause célèbre for Moscow, which alleged the charges were politically motivated and aimed at undermining a summit between Putin and President Trump. She served 15 months in an American prison before returning to Moscow, where she was handed her own television show on RT, the Kremlin-funded television channel. On one show, she visited Navalny at the prison camp where the opposition leader was incarcerated, openly mocking him and favourably comparing the conditions at the penal facility with her own cell in the United States.[23] Having proven her loyalty, Butina was made an MP with Putin's ruling United Russia party. She didn't even have to go through the trouble of getting elected: another MP simply relinquished his own seat so she could take it.[24]

This is standard Kremlin procedure: Putin may be ruthless towards his enemies, but he is loyal to those who stay loyal to him. Andrei Lugovoi, the former KGB officer who Britain accused of murdering Alexander Litvinenko, a former Russian agent, by spiking his tea with a radioactive substance in London in 2006, was also made an MP. [Lugovoi denies the allegation]. Anna Chapman, a flame-haired Russian operative who was arrested in America and then freed as part of a spy swap in Vienna in 2010, was subsequently handed her own television show after Putin vowed that she and her comrades would 'work in worthy places' and have 'bright, interesting lives'.[25]

Since the war began, Butina had become one of the most vocal supporters of the Kremlin's campaign to 'denazify' Ukraine. In a video shared on social media on the morning of the invasion, she drew a white Z on her jacket and then looked into the camera. 'Work, brothers,' she said, addressing the country's soldiers. 'We are with you, for ever.'

Like most public officials in Russia, Butina held very little real power. Putin had turned parliament into a slavish body whose only real function was to rubber-stamp Kremlin policy. Indeed, in 2005, the Kremlin-loyal parliamentary chairman, Boris Gryzlov, reportedly declared, without irony: 'Parliament is not a place for discussion.'[26] Yet, I was still curious to meet Butina. I wanted to look into her eyes, although not for too long, and gauge for myself if she genuinely believed the things she was saying or if she was saying them merely to further her rise up the bloody rungs of Russia's political ladder. It would be, I reasoned, a unique chance to study up-close the nature of Russian officialdom during wartime.

Butina arrived late for the interview. She was accompanied by an assistant who I assumed also doubled as a bodyguard. Italian pop played on the radio. It was still early in the day and we were the restaurant's first customers. At this point, I was one of the few British or American journalists left in Russia and I was aware that I was in a precarious position. Moscow had recently approved a law banning media outlets from reporting 'fake news' about the actions of the Russian army in Ukraine: a move that made it a crime punishable by up to 15 years in prison to report the truth. An official had confirmed that the law would also apply to foreign reporters. Most of my colleagues had left Russia after it was introduced, but I stayed on for a few more months, reluctant to uproot my family. I had begun using a pseudonym for articles on the war that would have been illegal under the new law, but that clearly wasn't an option for face-to-face meetings with Russian officials.

Our meeting came just five days after the Russian foreign ministry had accused Western journalists of seeking to frame Moscow for the killing of hundreds of Ukrainian civilians in Bucha, the small town near Kyiv that had become a byword for the Kremlin's war crimes. Despite satellite imagery, witness testimony and video evidence showing that Russian troops were responsible, Putin had claimed that the atrocities in Bucha were staged by Ukraine and Western intelligence to discredit Moscow. 'I accuse the Western media, and above all the American media, not just of spreading fakes and disinformation, but of complicity in the crime in the town of Bucha. Your newspapers, your columnists, your television are complicit in this punitive act,' said Maria Zakharova, the Russian foreign ministry's spokeswoman.[27] Perhaps, it occurred to me, my decision to stay on in Moscow had been a huge mistake and one that I would soon come to regret.

That very morning, as I sat drinking tea with Butina, Russian missiles were levelling Mariupol, the Ukrainian port city. Butina insisted, however, that Russia was not targeting civilians and accused Ukrainian 'neo-Nazis' of the killings in Bucha. She also suggested that Ukrainian forces were bombing Mariupol themselves. Why they should have begun to do this only *after* the start of Russia's invasion, she would not or could not explain.

I asked Butina to define a Nazi. 'For us, a Nazi is anyone who discriminates against another nation,' she told me. She then claimed that the Russian language had been banned in Ukraine, repeating a popular Kremlin trope that can easily be disproven by a trip to any Ukrainian city. In fact, many of the Ukrainian troops on the frontlines are Russian speakers, including members of Azov. Later, when I asked a group of Ukrainian soldiers if they would have a problem speaking Russian to me, one of them laughed and replied: 'That's fine. I might have a problem speaking *Ukrainian* to you, though.' That didn't make him any less

Ukrainian, of course, or diminish his determination to fight back Russia's invading army.

As we spoke, Butina casually compared Zelensky to Hitler. 'If someone could have told the Jews what was going to happen and stopped Hitler, would you have done it?' she said. When I asked her if she really saw parallels between the Ukrainian president and the leader of the genocidal Third Reich, she replied 'Absolutely'. Russia's full-scale war was still in its earlier stages and such rhetoric was relatively new. Did she really believe this? It appeared so. After I had processed her comment, I told her that when Putin spoke about 'Nazi Ukraine', most people in the West thought he was stark raving mad. And, indeed, for Russian officials to compare Zelensky and his government to Hitler made zero sense. Even if ethnic Russians were being discriminated against in Ukraine, as Putin falsely claimed, that didn't mean that Zelensky was a Nazi. Even if Moscow thought that Ukraine was ruled by a far-right government, which again was untrue, for Putin to call them Nazis made it sound as if he was cosplaying World War Two.

To me, this seemed like pretty basic stuff, but apparently it was the first time that anyone had actually pointed it out to Butina. She considered my words. 'This is probably the most useful interview I have ever had,' she said, eventually. 'I was trying to kind of understand the Western mind. I'm actually going to talk to my colleagues in the foreign affairs committee and say that we probably should think about this.'

Was Butina mocking me? I wasn't sure. She appeared to be sincere, but surely it shouldn't have taken a British journalist to point these things out to her. Butina, incredibly, may have kept her word: a few weeks later, Russian opposition media reported that Kremlin officials were also having doubts about the 'denazification' term.[28] It wasn't only Western reporters who were puzzled by it, it seemed. Secret polling by the Kremlin's spin doctors had revealed that many Russians were unable to explain precisely what it even meant. Some even found it hard to pronounce. But the fixation on Ukrainian 'Nazis' was clearly coming from the very top: the term remained a staple of Russian propaganda.

Butina wasn't the only Russian official to compare Zelensky to Hitler. Sergei Lavrov, the Russian foreign minister, later claimed that there was no contradiction in equating Zelensky with the leader of the Nazi Party, because 'Hitler also had Jewish blood.'[29] As for Putin, he appeared to be obsessed with the very nature of Zelensky's Jewishness. 'I have a lot of Jewish friends. They say that Zelensky is not Jewish and that he is a disgrace to the Jewish people,' he said, apparently not noticing the glaring contradiction.[30]

Although keen to list alleged human rights abuses by Ukrainian forces against ethnic Russians, Butina was apparently unaware of what was going on within her own country. Just weeks before our conversation, Adam Delimkhanov, a Chechen MP with Putin's ruling party, had vowed to hunt down Abubakar Yangulbaev, an anti-torture lawyer, and his entire family and decapitate them all. The lawyer's father, Saidi, was a former federal judge. His mother, Zarema, had already been abducted from the family home by masked men claiming to be Chechen police.

'Know that day and night, not sparing our lives, property and offspring, we will pursue you until we cut off your heads and kill you,' Delimkhanov said in an online video.[31] He also warned that he would behead anyone who translated his Chechen language comments into Russian.[32] When I asked Butina about the incident, she told me she knew nothing about it. 'I can google it,' she said. When I later sent her online links to the Chechen MP's threats, she wrote back: 'What do you want from me?'

Perhaps she really didn't know. When I asked Butina during our conversation in the Italian restaurant how many people had been killed in hostilities in the so-called Donetsk People's Republic (DPR), a Kremlin-controlled territory in eastern Ukraine, in the eight years of fighting before the start of Russia's full-scale invasion in February 2022, she replied 'hundreds... of thousands.' Grimacing theatrically, she added: 'This is our pain.'

MAKING THE GATE WIDER FOR FASCISM

It was another bizarre moment among many. Ukraine's alleged genocide of ethnic Russians in eastern Ukraine was one of the reasons cited by Putin for his full-scale invasion, yet Butina, despite her very vocal enthusiasm for the Kremlin's 'special military operation', apparently lacked even basic knowledge of the situation there. According to the DPR's own statistics, the total number of deaths in the territory that it controlled between 2014 and the beginning of the war in 2022 was not 'hundreds of thousands' but 5,038, including soldiers.[33] Overall, in the wider Donbas region, the death toll, including Ukrainian troops, was 14,400 according to the United Nations.[34] The vast majority of the fatalities came in 2014 and 2015 at the height of the conflict.[35]

In 2021, the year before Putin sent in tanks to 'save' Russian speakers, the number of civilian deaths attributed to the conflict in the Kremlin-controlled areas of the Donetsk region was just seven, again according to its own figures.[36] In 2020, the figure was five.[37] Most of the deaths are believed to have been caused by uncleared landmines. This was the reality of what Putin described as a 'genocide'.

These were not statistics that I had to dig up from some obscure resource: they were updated every month on the Kremlin-controlled territory's website, presumably with the knowledge of its overlords in Moscow. Yet, Butina was ignorant of even the most basic realities of the conflict. I dreaded to imagine what was going on in her head and I wondered if she still believed that the Ukrainian army was crucifying children.

Butina spoke English during our conversation. I sensed that she felt we were getting on well, perhaps even, in her mind, finding some common ground. As if the issue of the Kremlin's savage war in Ukraine was just a minor disagreement between us that could be cleared up by a civilized chat. As if her work on legislation tightening restrictions on Western media was nothing personal. But her words were hollow, an unconvincing simulacrum of language that served only to highlight a great emptiness. 'I am a peacebuilder,' she said, absurdly, at one point and took a sip of green tea.

I never met Butina again, although a few days later she invited me to 'grab some coffee and chat just for pleasure'. I made my excuses. She would have been a useful source to cultivate, and I was grimly fascinated by her apparent ability to assimilate the Kremlin's propaganda so faithfully, but I fear I would not have been able to remain civil for long had I taken up her offer. It would have been truly obscene to sit in a café with a Russian MP 'for pleasure', while the Kremlin's missiles were destroying lives in Mariupol. Friends suggested that Butina may have been trying to recruit me, but I don't think that was the case. I think she genuinely enjoyed talking to Western journalists, if only to practise her English. After all, she must have realized that she would not have many more chances to do that in the kind of Russia she was helping to usher in.

When I eventually left Russia and travelled to Ukraine to report from the war zone, I sent Butina vivid photographs of the destruction that had been caused by her country's army: blocks of flats cleaved in half by Russian missiles; urban landscapes twisted out of shape by the Kremlin's firepower; children's playgrounds torn apart by bombs. From Dnipro, a city in central Ukraine, I sent her a video of the tangled remains of a house that had been destroyed by a powerful Russian missile, killing four members of a family, including two young children. The father was fighting at the front. I asked a small boy standing at a makeshift shrine to the family if he had known them. He burst into tears. Yet Butina continued to insist that all this misery was the result of Ukraine's armed forces bombing its own towns and cities, including those areas that were controlled by the government in Kyiv. 'Moscow misses you,' she added as an afterthought. 'I sometimes miss Moscow,' I replied. It was true: but the city I remembered was likely gone for ever.

10

MADMAN FOR HIRE

When Galina Starovoitova, the reformist politician who was assassinated in St Petersburg, had warned of looming fascism in Russia, it wasn't Putin that she had in mind. The ex-KGB officer had given no indication that he had serious political ambitions, and no one could have guessed what the future held. Instead, when Starovoitova drew attention to the similarities between Russia in the 1990s and the conditions in post-war Germany that led to the rise of Adolf Hitler, the focus of her concern was an ultranationalist politician named Vladimir Zhirinovsky.

One of Russia's most recognizable public figures, Zhirinovsky, with his extreme anti-Western rhetoric, was for years the Kremlin's rabid attack dog, a snarling, barely coherent political leader who hurled nuclear threats around with the same kind of enthusiasm that some other politicians usually reserve for kissing babies. He seemed to represent the fringes of Russian politics and few took him seriously. Yet, with the full-scale invasion of Ukraine, Zhirinovsky's ideas entered the mainstream: his rabid nationalism now seems less like a grotesque anomaly than a blueprint.

A self-proclaimed man of the people, Zhirinovsky burst onto the political scene in the early 1990s, winning the support of millions of Russians with his promises to restore Moscow's former glories. He spoke of expanding Russian borders so that the country's conquering soldiers could 'wash their boots in the warm waters of the Indian Ocean', seizing Alaska from the United States and using Moscow's vast nuclear arsenal to destroy Western countries. Despite his Jewish roots, he accused Jews of provoking the Holocaust, bringing Russia to ruin and selling Russian women into prostitution in the West. He was the living embodiment of all that was rotten in the Russian national consciousness, a symbol of the malign desires that had been simmering since the collapse of the Soviet Union.

In 1993, his misleadingly named Liberal Democratic Party of Russia (LDPR) shocked the world when it gained the largest number of seats in parliament, taking 23 per cent of the vote at that year's State Duma elections. In a BBC documentary that aired in 1994, Zhirinovsky claimed that he had only entered politics because he had no talent for music or sport and was not interested in stamp collecting or discos.[1] The truth was a lot murkier: there are allegations that his party, which began life in 1989 as the Liberal Democratic Party of the Soviet Union, was created by the KGB to oppose pro-Western reformers.

Alexander Lebed, a gruff Russian general, described Zhirinovsky as 'the Lord God's monkey', while the LDPR leader's own aides compared him to Russia's 'holy fools' – the individuals whose madness, often feigned, allowed them to speak truth to the tsars. Yet there was little that was holy about Zhirinovsky, whose passion for political controversy was reportedly matched by his appetite for sexual abuse. In the late 1990s, he is alleged to have raped vulnerable young men and women that his bodyguards rounded up and brought to his cottage in the southwest of Moscow. 'He asked if I had lice and started examining my teeth. He made me do things I didn't want to do,' Alexei, who was 18 at the time, told an opposition newspaper.[2] In 2014, at a press conference in Moscow, Zhirinovsky ordered his aides to rape a pregnant journalist whose questions had irritated him. They did not carry out the attack, but the journalist was hospitalized for shock.

Predictably, in later years, Zhirinovsky was thrilled to be compared to Donald 'grab-them-by-the-pussy' Trump. Unlike Trump, however, he would not face legal charges over either the rape threat or his alleged sexual assaults. Fortunately, despite promising free vodka, polygamy and to clone famous Russians such as Pyotr Tchaikovsky, if elected President, Zhirinovsky never again came close to taking power. Instead, from the 2000s onwards, he acted as a vital cog in Putin's carefully constructed political system, one of the tame 'opposition' figures whose role it was to allow voters to let off steam and provide the illusion of a functioning democracy. His LDPR took third or fourth place in parliamentary polls, while Zhirinovsky's hardcore supporters allowed him to claim up to 9 per cent of the vote in presidential elections. Most Russians, however, saw him as a joke or a showman, acting out the role of an anti-Western demagogue for the Kremlin's spin doctors.

His LDPR party received more than £20 million a year from the Russian state, a sum that was equivalent to 97 per cent of its funds. 'We get 152 roubles [£1.75 at the time] from the government for every vote we receive at elections,' Zhirinovsky boasted.[3] One year, he stood on Red Square handing out 1,000-rouble notes (worth around £12 at the time) to a crowd he addressed mockingly as serfs and riff-raff. 'Children, invalids, who else is there?' he asked, as people stretched out their hands for the cash.[4]

I wasn't so sure that Zhirinovsky was simply playing a part. Even if this was true at the dawn of his bizarre political career, the irrationality that he deployed as a vote-winning strategy later appears to have consumed him entirely, like an ageing actor whose personality has merged so much with his on-screen persona that it is impossible to say where one begins and the other ends. I once had the chance to observe Zhirinovsky up close at a roundtable discussion in Moscow: if he was indeed acting, then he had missed his calling. There were around a dozen speakers at the event, but I kept my eyes on Zhirinovsky, even when no one else appeared to be paying attention to him.

He was a symphony of gestures, twitches and random movements that I simply couldn't believe were staged. First it was his nose – a tiny tremor that signalled displeasure at something or other. Then, he picked up a pen, stared at it, placed it back on the table and grimaced. Another twitch, another scowl, both his hands moving now, picking up objects, examining them and putting them back down. More frowning, a snarl, a half-laugh. A semi-audible comment, perhaps an obscenity? All of this in less than 30 seconds. He made to stand up but sat back down. He looked around, wild-eyed. It was exhausting watching him and I couldn't imagine what it must be like to be inside his head. There were suggestions that Zhirinovsky may have suffered from Tourette's syndrome; if so, this was clearly not the extent of his psychological troubles.

Years later, I interviewed Zhirinovsky at his office in the State Duma, the Russian parliament, where his party had a whole floor to itself that appeared to be staffed entirely by young men in suits. The LDPR had just pulled off an unexpected election victory in governor elections in Russia's far-eastern region and Zhirinovsky was revelling in the limelight. One of his aides, a seemingly affable man named Alexander, met me at the State Duma ahead of the interview.

'So, what are you going to write?' Alexander asked. I shrugged. What was there to write about Zhirinovsky? 'That he is an ultra-nationalist who has urged the Kremlin to drop nuclear weapons on Western countries and Ukraine.' Alexander looked at me aghast. 'Vladimir Volfovich?' he said, using Zhirinovsky's first name and patronymic. 'He's never done that.'

It was my turn to be astonished. 'What do you mean?' I replied. 'These are well-documented facts.' I reached into my pocket for my phone. 'Shall I find some examples for you?' It wasn't hard. Earlier that year Zhirinovsky had proposed dropping a nuclear weapon on the Ukrainian president's residence. 'A small bomb. Not a big Hiroshima, a small one,' he said on state television. 'Radiation will be minimal.'

Alexander sighed. 'Ok,' he said, after a slight pause. 'Yes, ok he said all this. But it's Zhirinovsky, you know?' I reminded Alexander, although I was sure he hadn't forgotten, that his boss was the leader of Russia's third biggest political party and had once been the deputy chairman of the Russian parliament. Was he saying that Zhirinovsky was… unhinged? A political clown?

Alexander didn't reply. Instead, he led me into the room where the interview was to take place. After Zhirinovsky arrived, he looked at me with wide eyes and exclaimed: 'At last! I've been waiting for you for 30 years! Now they've finally allowed you to come and see me.' I nodded. We didn't have much time and there didn't seem to be much I could reply to that.

Instead, I asked him about his habit of urging nuclear attacks on foreign capitals. Zhirinovsky looked at me as if I had just enquired why he never bathed. 'Me?' he said. 'Call for nuclear attacks? I've never done that!' I started to protest, but Alexander, who had remained in the room, interrupted me. 'Vladimir Volfovich has never done that,' he said.

I looked at Zhirinovsky and then back at Alexander. They both waited for me to say something. I began listing the countries that Zhirinovsky had said should be targeted with nuclear weapons, but he didn't reply. He clearly wasn't interested in talking about Armageddon that afternoon. And, anyway, I reasoned, it had been at least a few weeks since he had ranted about atomic war. Maybe he'd forgotten.

'Nato is preparing an attack on our country,' Zhirinovsky said. 'But we must not allow another 22nd June 1941,' he said, referring to the date on which Nazi Germany launched its surprise invasion of the Soviet Union. 'If I am in the Kremlin instead of Putin, we would carry out strikes on June 20th and not wait until the 22nd.' He gave no evidence to support the claim and I didn't think much of it: Zhirinovsky had no real power and such views were still on the fringe of Russian politics. It was also the kind of thing he had been saying for years; his supporters lapped up such rhetoric.

As I was leaving, Zhirinovsky's aides handed me two bags. 'Some political literature,' they said and ushered me out of the door. When I was on the street, I opened the bags to discover the following: an alarm clock with Zhirinovsky's face on it; a bottle of Zhirinovsky's own brand vodka; Zhirinovsky toilet water, a Zhirinovsky wristwatch, a Zhirinovsky mug and a statuette in honour of the 25th anniversary of the founding of the LDPR.

There was also, as promised, some literature. I walked home in a daze. I had known Zhirinovsky was a borderline case, and perhaps even psychotic, but I hadn't expected to come out of an interview in parliament with one of Russia's top politicians with the feeling that I had spent my afternoon at the local asylum. I never met Zhirinovsky again and I would be lying if I said this is something I regret. I continued to speak to him occasionally on the phone, however. In 2020, with Joe Biden ahead in the opinion polls against Trump, he told me: 'I'd like to take part in Biden's funeral. Just let us know the date.'

Just two months before Putin ordered tanks into Ukraine, Zhirinovsky gave a speech in parliament where he appeared to predict that Russia would go to war on 22 February 2022. 'This will not be a peaceful year,' Zhirinovsky said. 'This will be the year when Russia finally becomes a great country again and everyone must shut up and respect our country.'[5] At the time, no one had paid any attention. Zhirinovsky was always making outrageous predictions or threatening war and few journalists were inclined to monitor his numerous wild-eyed rants.

I only found out about his prophecy as I was driving through the countryside in Russia's Rostov region, close to the border with eastern Ukraine, searching for Putin's tanks ahead of the looming invasion. In the end, Zhirinovsky's prediction was only off by around 48 hours. One of the justifications that Putin gave for the invasion was an alleged plan by Nato to destroy Mother Russia. Like Zhirinovsky, he gave no evidence to back up his claim and I wondered how often the two men had spoken on the topic.

It is unlikely we will ever know. Just weeks after the start of Russia's invasion, Zhirinovsky died in hospital of complications related to coronavirus. He had been in and out of a coma and it was unclear if he had been lucid enough to follow escalating events. In any case, he did not live long enough to act as a cheerleader for the full-scale war in Ukraine that he had craved, nor for Russia's final rift with the West.

It was as if the demons that had possessed him for so long, sustaining his life force with their malevolence, had finally taken leave of his soul, leaving behind an empty husk. Zhirinovsky's unchained spirits flew free and the shadows rose swiftly all over Russia, as hatreds multiplied like a virus and the genocidal war in Ukraine gave millions a new reason to live. Politically, it no longer mattered if he was dead or alive: his dark, violent fantasies had transmuted into official Kremlin policy. Zhirinovsky was now Russia, and Russia – a terrifyingly large proportion of it at least – was now Zhirinovsky. There could be no going back from this kind of madness.

11

'He Was Killed by The Hatred Poured Into The Air'

It was a chilly afternoon in February 2015 when I spotted Boris Nemtsov, a Russian opposition leader, while taking my daughter to drumming lessons in central Moscow. He was with a woman I didn't recognize and they were laughing about something on the other side of the street. I had interviewed Nemtsov on a number of occasions, but I wasn't sure that he would identify me immediately if I crossed over to say hello. I felt for a moment as if I should say something to my daughter like 'look, that man could have been President of Russia', but I got distracted and then he was no longer to be seen and the moment was gone. I'm not sure that a five-year-old child would have cared, anyway. But it was the truth: Yeltsin had at one time considered naming Nemtsov, a former deputy prime minister, as his successor, before settling eventually on Putin, a decision that would have catastrophic consequences for Ukraine and the rest of Europe, not to mention Russia itself.

Nemtsov had been in opposition ever since Putin came to power, leading protest marches, authoring in-depth reports on corruption and speaking out relentlessly against the Kremlin's covert military intervention in eastern Ukraine. 'He's fucking nuts, Vladimir Putin, you should know,' he once told a Russian journalist.[1] It was a typical Nemtsov statement: brash, uncensored and to hell with the consequences. A video of his comments went viral. In March 2014, after the Kremlin annexed Crimea and sent troops into eastern Ukraine, Nemtsov spoke at a peace march in central Moscow. His comments were eerily prophetic. '[Putin] wants to use the annexation of Crimea to rule us for ever, until Russia itself dies,' he said. 'What will he get? Ukraine as an enemy for ever, an Iron Curtain and sanctions.'[2]

I thought briefly about all this before we entered the drumming centre and then forgot about it. The following night, just as I was about to go to bed, I received an urgent email. I had to read it three times before the news sank in. Nemtsov had been shot dead near Red Square. Initially, as would so often be the case over the following years when I read early reports of horrendous events in Russia and Ukraine, I hoped that there had been some mistake. But the message was correct. 'They killed Nemtsov,' I said, aloud, even though my wife and daughter were already asleep. Images of his corpse in a black body bag on a bridge close to the Kremlin soon followed.

After giving an interview to opposition media to drum up support for a rally against Russia's actions in Ukraine, Nemtsov had gone to meet his girlfriend, a Ukrainian woman named Anna Durytska. They ate a late meal at a restaurant on Red Square that overlooks the Kremlin and then walked in the direction of Nemtsov's nearby apartment. As they crossed the Bolshoi Moskvoretsky Bridge, Nemtsov was shot six times at close range by a gunman armed with a 9-millimetre pistol. He died almost instantly. The assassin leapt into a waiting car with no number plates, which then sped off into the late-night traffic. Durytska was unharmed, but did not see the killer's face. It later emerged that at least a dozen surveillance cameras that were installed on or near the bridge had failed to film the attack due to 'technical reasons'.

Nemtsov's murder within sight of the Kremlin's walls, one of the most heavily protected and monitored areas in Russia, was a grim landmark. Other journalists and opposition figures had been killed since Putin had come to power, but none of them had been household names like Nemtsov. 'We are in a new political reality now, one which we as yet don't fully understand. It is a dark forest, and anyone who criticizes Putin is in danger,' Ilya

Yashin, one of Nemtsov's closest friends and political allies, told me, a few days after the murder.

Following the seizure of Crimea, Putin had made some of his harshest comments about opposition figures, calling them Western-backed 'national traitors' whose actions were aimed at bringing Russia to its knees.[3] His critics noted with alarm that the expression had also been used by Adolf Hitler, something that Putin, as a fluent German speaker, was likely to have known. Rumours spread that the Kremlin had drawn up a 'kill list' and that more assassinations would follow. Putin had been shaken by the toppling of Yanukovych in Ukraine and was determined not to share the same fate.

Predictably, the Kremlin's security forces refused to consider the possibility that Nemtsov had been assassinated as revenge for his political activities. Instead, they put forward a range of unlikely theories, including that he may have been targeted over a love affair gone sour, a business dispute, or as a 'sacrificial victim' in a Western plot to destabilize Russia. It was a repeat of state media's attempts to confuse the narrative in the aftermath of the destruction of MH17 over eastern Ukraine. It cannot be ruled out, of course, that investigators were deliberately mocking Nemtsov's family, friends and supporters with their torrent of lies.

More than two years later, five ethnic Chechens were convicted of Nemtsov's murder. The gunman was named by investigators as Zaur Dadayev, a lieutenant in an elite Russian interior ministry battalion called Sever that was based in Chechnya. The battalion was headed by the brother of Adam Delimkhanov, the pro-Putin MP whose threats to decapitate a human rights lawyer and his family had somehow failed to attract Butina's attention. Dadayev told the court that he had been tortured into confessing to the murder, but his testimony was rejected.[4]

Investigators said the men had been paid 15 million roubles (£190,000 in 2015) by Ruslan Mukhudinov, a Chechen army driver, to carry out the assassination. It was never explained, however, where a poorly paid driver in the Russian army would have been able to find such a sum. Investigators also claimed that Mukhudinov

'HE WAS KILLED BY THE HATRED POURED INTO THE AIR'

had ordered the hit on Nemtsov because he had been enraged by the opposition leader's condemnation of a deadly attack by Islamist terrorists on the offices of the *Charlie Hebdo* satirical magazine in Paris in 2015.[5] Nemtsov's allies rubbished the purported motive – his comments had been made on the website of a liberal radio station in Moscow and had attracted little attention. Nemtsov was not a nationalist, nor was he known for an anti-Islam stance. He seemed an unlikely target for a fanatical Islamist gunman.

Nemtsov's friends and family also said it was impossible that Mukhudinov, who is still at large, had been acting alone. Like Dadayev, he was also a member of the Sever battalion, but as a driver for an officer called Ruslan Geremeyev, who was in turn the nephew of a Russian senator. A witness at the murder trial testified that Geremeyev had been in charge of the suspects, while he was also seen with them before and after Nemtsov's assassination.[6]

Opposition figures argued that in any normal country, Geremeyev would at the very least have been interviewed by police as a potential witness. However, investigators who travelled to Chechnya to interview Geremeyev claimed that they were unable to track him down. In their official report, they said that they had visited his home[7] 'but no one opened the door'.[8] Apparently not wishing to make a fuss, the investigators shrugged, turned away and left Chechnya. It was an unusual, perhaps unique display of sensitivity by the Kremlin's security forces. In 2019, Geremeyev was sanctioned by the United States over his alleged involvement in 'extrajudicial killings' on behalf of Ramzan Kadyrov, the Kremlin-backed leader of Chechnya.[9]

'I believe my father's murder was politically motivated, and because of this it will not be completely solved and far from everyone who is guilty will be punished. At least while Putin is Russia's President,' Nemtsov's adult daughter, Zhanna, told me after fleeing Russia for her safety.

In the summer of 2024, Tamerlan Eskerkhanov, one of the men convicted of Nemtsov's murder was granted early release in exchange for serving in Ukraine. He was reportedly sent to guard a metal factory in the ruins of Mariupol, the Ukrainian port city that had been destroyed by Russian bombs, and allowed to travel home to Chechnya on holidays.[10]

Eskerkhanov was just one of tens of thousands of convicts, including serial killers and rapists, who had been released from Russian prisons to fight in Ukraine, receiving presidential pardons in exchange for six months at the front. Once they arrived home, many simply carried on killing – by mid-2024, over 100 Russians had been murdered by convicts back from Ukraine, media reports said. Among their victims was Russia's former teacher of the year, hacked to death with an axe by a convicted murderer who had spent fewer than three years behind bars before Putin set him free to kill Ukrainians.[11]

Another to be released was Nikolai Ogolobyak, who was sentenced to 20 years in prison in 2010 over the ritual murders of four teenage girls. Ogolobyak and his underage accomplices fried and ate the girls' hearts and tongues and stabbed one of them 666 times as a sacrifice to the devil.[12] His release came as Putin and other Russian officials depicted the war in Ukraine as a fight against what they called 'Satanic' Western values. Dmitry Zelensky, who killed a 27-year-old woman and then put her remains through a meat grinder, was also pardoned by Putin after fighting in Ukraine. As public anger grew, Dmitry Peskov, the Kremlin spokesman, said convicts had the right to 'atone for their crimes with blood on the battlefield'.[13]

Chechnya was officially a part of Russia, but in reality it was the personal fiefdom of Ramzan Kadyrov, a former separatist fighter who had switched sides to Moscow. In return for maintaining a shaky peace, Kadyrov, who was installed as Chechnya's leader in 2007 after the death of his father in a bombing at Grozny's main stadium, was allowed to rule the mainly Muslim republic as he saw fit. Human rights abuses, including secret prisons, were rife and Kadyrov also imposed his own version of Islamic law on Chechnya, including a de facto ban on the sale of alcohol and forcing women to wear headscarves.[14] He also ordered the construction of expensive vanity projects, including the largest mosque in eastern Europe in Grozny, the republic's biggest city. When asked where the funding was coming from,[15] Kadyrov replied: 'Allah gives it [to us].'[16] A hint to the real source of the cash, and Kadyrov's personal power, was in the name of Grozny's main street: Putin Avenue. 'My idol is [Vladimir] Putin. I want him to be the president as long as he lives. I love him very much, as a man loves a man,' Kadyrov said.[17]

Kadyrov was only 30 when he became the president of Chechnya; his enemies swiftly came to grisly ends. In 2006 and 2008, gunmen assassinated two of his rivals for power in Moscow. One of them, a former Chechen lawmaker named Ruslan Yamadayev was killed in a drive-by shooting just outside the British embassy. 'If you're a leader, people should fear you,' Kadyrov said in between the two killings.[18] In 2009, Umar Israilov, one of Kadyrov's former bodyguards, was gunned down as he walked out of a grocery shop in Vienna. Before his death, Israilov had filed a complaint against Russia in the European Court of Human Rights in which he accused Kadyrov of personally torturing him in Chechnya. In 2011, I attended a press conference in Grozny, the Chechen capital, where Kadyrov was quizzed about the assassination by an Austrian journalist. After initial bemusement when he appeared to confuse Austria and Australia ('I don't know anything about what goes on in Australia'), the Chechen leader shrugged and said: 'If I had wanted him dead, I could have killed him here in Chechnya and no one would have known about it.'[19]

Opposition politicians from Moscow were too terrified to visit Chechnya and independent vote monitors were at risk of abduction, torture and murder. At elections, the Kadyrov regime sought to outdo other regions to prove its loyalty to the Kremlin, routinely reporting over 95 per cent of the vote for Putin or his ruling party. When I visited Grozny, I asked Akhmad, a young man, if he really believed that his fellow Chechens would support in such great numbers a leader whose army had waged a savage war against their republic? I didn't expect him to risk his life by revealing his scepticism, but it was a question that needed to be asked. He looked at me askew, as if I had just asked him why the sun rose in the morning. 'Putin saved Chechnya,' he told me.

His friends, all fellow teens and early-twentysomethings, nodded their heads enthusiastically. But hadn't Putin overseen massive air strikes on Chechen towns and cities? 'No, no, no,' Akhmad and his buddies responded, still smiling. 'That's not right. Who told you this?' He appeared to be genuinely confused. 'He's a foreigner,' one of them whispered, and they looked at me with sudden understanding. 'Putin saved us, don't you know?' Akhmad repeated. This had been the official line in Chechnya ever since Kadyrov had come to power and I heard it over and over again during my stay in the city. 'The kids have been brainwashed,' said one local, who asked to remain anonymous. 'That's all they get taught in school nowadays.'

Following Nemtsov's assassination, in place of the rally that he had been planning against Putin's covert war in Ukraine, tens of thousands of opposition supporters gathered in central Moscow for a memorial march. 'Russia without Putin!' they chanted, angry and frightened in equal measure, as they walked slowly through the heart of Moscow on a cloudy afternoon, past Red Square and the onion domes of St Basil's Cathedral onto the bridge where Nemtsov had been gunned down in cold blood. Others held up placards with a play on Nemtsov's first name so that they read: 'Fight!'

But the battle was being fought on unequal terms. Nemtsov's murder was the starkest evidence yet that Russia was locked in an increasingly vicious battle for its future. Who would triumph? Would it be Putin and his allies, supported almost unquestioningly by millions of Russians fed a steady diet of hate speech on national television? Or would it be those Russians who wanted something better for their country, if not for themselves, then for their children? 'There is always hope, even when there is none,'

'HE WAS KILLED BY THE HATRED POURED INTO THE AIR'

an opposition supporter told me, as I joined the sombre crowd. But it was increasingly hard to remain optimistic.

'I know who killed Boris Nemtsov,' read a post on Facebook that went viral among opposition supporters. 'He was killed by the hatred poured into the air. He was killed by those who draw Obama with fangs. He was killed by those who hate darkies, yids, Ukrainians, and especially their neighbours. But physical death is not so important. We all die eventually. But take your children away [from Russia]. So that they do not become infected. Save not your bodies, but your souls. There is no need to be afraid of death. Be afraid, instead, of death before you die.'[20]

It was pertinent advice and many Russians began to make plans to leave the country. Some even went through with them, relocating to western Europe or the Baltic states of Latvia and Lithuania. Ilya Ponomarev, the opposition MP who had voted against the annexation of Crimea, moved to Kyiv. This was not on the scale of the exodus that occurred after the invasion of Ukraine in 2022, but there was definitely a sense that it was worth getting out now, before Putin's assault on dissent accelerated further. Even those Russians who felt they were too old to build a new life in the West were making plans for their children to get out. A successful businessman that I had become friendly with told me that he had sent his children to schools in Europe because he did not want them to grow up in Putin's Russia.

'I understand that life is easier in the West,' he said, as we sat in his comfortable home in central Moscow. 'But for many middle-aged people with the means to emigrate it's hard to pack a suitcase and move abroad. We send our children to study in London or Paris so that they will at least speak the language. This is our investment for the future because things are only going to deteriorate here.' The only hope, he suggested, lay with the elite, whose luxury overseas assets and jet-setting lifestyles were threatened by the Kremlin's confrontation with the West. 'I have some small hope left that these people might be able to influence Putin,' he said. 'They didn't sign up for this nightmare.'

At the time, it seemed like a reasonable idea: many of the Russian elite appeared to have no genuine ideological convictions: they were interested in power and wealth and ensuring that their children and grandchildren could live comfortable lives in America or Europe, far away from the Kremlin's repressive machine. Indeed, even Putin had once seemed more interested in plundering Russia's natural resources than a rerun of the Cold War, but history was moving fast now and the Kremlin dictator, his lust for material wealth almost sated, was falling under the spell of new obsessions.

Just before Nemtsov's assassination, around 35,000 people had marched through central Moscow at an 'anti-Maidan' rally. Among them were men who claimed to be Cossacks, armed with long leather whips, ultra-right nationalists and radical Orthodox Christian activists. Also in attendance was a bizarre motorcycle gang called the Night Wolves, a Kremlin-backed group whose leather-clad members often hung out with Putin. Alexander Zaladantsov, their leader, was a heavily tattooed biker whose nickname was 'The Surgeon', a reference to his past as a doctor specializing in post-traumatic face surgery.

'We will defend Putin and Russia by any means necessary,' he told me, when I spoke to him after a press conference at TASS, the Russian state news agency. He then launched into a rant about the 'eternal greatness' of Joseph Stalin. 'You in the West will never understand. Even now he frightens you,' he said, meeting my incredulous gaze.

Not long before the anti-Maidan march, NTV, a Kremlin-controlled television channel, had aired a death threat against Olga Romanova, a well-known opposition journalist who was also the head of the prisoners' rights group, Russia Behind Bars. The channel accused her of funnelling donations to the group to a Ukrainian nationalist movement and broadcast an obscenity-littered interview with a former convict who vowed that she would be 'ripped apart'.[21] It came just days after NTV had given airtime to a masked Russian-backed fighter in eastern Ukraine who threatened to murder journalists at Echo of Moscow, a

'HE WAS KILLED BY THE HATRED POURED INTO THE AIR'

liberal radio station. 'And death will look like this!' he shouted, poking his fingers towards his eyes.[22]

If Russian television channels were now openly broadcasting death threats towards the country's own citizens, was it any wonder that an opposition leader could be shot dead just metres from Red Square's famous cobblestones? Even children knew that the payback for opposition to Putin was often sickening violence. Once, I took our daughter, by now almost seven, with me while I reported on a political activist named Roman Roslovtsev who had been holding one-person, peaceful protests in a rubber Putin mask. That afternoon, as Roslovtsev approached Red Square, a smiling passer-by posed for a selfie with him, while other curious onlookers laughed or cheered. M skipped along, filming everything on her new digital camera. Within minutes, two grim-faced police officers stopped Roslovtsev in his tracks. After a brief document check, he was marched off to a nearby police station. It was his seventh arrest in six months.[23] 'Will they chop his head off?' our daughter asked, as we walked home through central Moscow.

By this point I had been living in Russia for almost 20 years. I was 26 when I left London and I was now well into middle age. I travelled relatively frequently back to Britain, but I felt more at home in Moscow, despite the instability and the uncertainty about the future. I had thought during my time at the RIA news agency that progress was possible, that Russia could transform into, if not a genuine democracy, then at the very least into a country where it was safe to oppose the Kremlin without the risk of retribution. But the night of Nemtsov's murder was the first time I began to wonder if it might be time to leave. Did we really want to bring up our daughter in Putin's Russia? In hindsight, that was perhaps the moment when we should have left, rather than hang on, hoping against hope that things would improve.

I was also possessed, I admit, by a morbid curiosity to witness where exactly Putin was leading Russia. Life was growing darker by the day, but the light at the end of the tunnel was still just about visible. What would happen when it was finally snuffed out? I could not have imagined, of course, that the endgame would come so soon or that it would be so catastrophic. Yet we were sheltered, my family and I, at least for a while, from the encroaching shadows. For decades our Old Arbat neighbourhood had been one of the strongholds of Russia's intelligentsia, its dissident class, and while its main street had been tarnished by cheap tourist stalls and tacky restaurants, its quiet, meandering back streets retained a centuries-old calm. I experienced, I suspect, the best years of my life there. At weekends, when our daughter was small, we would sometimes spend all day at the playground, building huge snowmen or walking down to the splendidly named Neskuchny Sad (Not Boring Garden), Moscow's oldest park. After work, I would often cycle for hours through the Old Arbat's almost traffic-free lanes, winding down after a day spent writing about political tensions and human rights abuses. In summer, our neighbours would sometimes stage jazz concerts in their courtyard and we would gather to drink wine, the local kids running among us until they could run no more. Later, during Moscow's coronavirus lockdown, my daughter and I made it a daily routine to walk around the near-deserted streets feeding stray cats, snatching some normality amid the surreal and horrific pandemic.

One year, when I was still on talking terms with my mother-in-law, her cat had kittens and she was unable to find homes for any of them. I travelled to her home in provincial Russia to pick them up, transporting them back to Moscow on the train, five small kittens climbing around my cabin for eight hours. We managed to place most of them, including one with an American woman who later took it back to her home in Pennsylvania. I found homes for the final two kittens by standing on the Old Arbat with a sign that read 'Free to a Good Home'. A police officer and his kids took them off me. He insisted that I take some cash for my troubles.

Anti-Putin sentiments were also high in areas of central Moscow like the Old Arbat: opposition candidates had even managed to defeat the ruling United Russia party at low-level district elections that were, back then, largely free of Kremlin meddling. For a while, one of our neighbours on the Old Arbat

'HE WAS KILLED BY THE HATRED POURED INTO THE AIR'

was Maria Alyokhina, a member of the Pussy Riot activist group. In February 2012, Pussy Riot had performed a 'punk prayer', a musical plea for the Virgin Mary to drive Putin from power, in Moscow's gigantic Christ the Saviour Cathedral. The protest outraged the powerful Russian Orthodox Church and Alyokhina and her accomplices, Nadezhda Tolokonnikova and Yekaterina Samutsevich, were arrested after a city-wide hunt. They were charged with hooliganism motivated by religious hatred. The ensuing trial was a study in judicial absurdity, with dialogue that could have come straight from a medieval courtroom, as Russian prosecution witnesses accused the group of 'waging war on God' and 'twitching like devils' in the cathedral. Alyokhina, handcuffed in a glass and iron cage along with her fellow defendants, observed the proceedings with a mixture of undisguised contempt and amusement. She was still smirking when the judge sentenced her to two years in a remote prison camp.

One sunny afternoon after her release, I met up with Alyokhina in a small square just off the Old Arbat that was dominated by a statue of Alexander Pushkin, Russia's nineteenth-century national poet. The area was her teenage haunt, she told me, and she had spent countless hours here, hanging out with Moscow's punks and hippies in the early 1990s. She may have lost two years of her life for speaking out against Putin, but there was something about the Arbat, once known as the soul of Russia, that kept her tied to Moscow. 'I couldn't live anywhere else,' Alyokhina told me, sitting cross-legged and barefooted on a grassy patch. 'I love Russia. But its story isn't just about those who think they possess the power of the state. It's about us, too. And we dream of a different story.' I admired her bravery and positivity, in spite of everything. Back then, it was still just about possible to dream.

A few weeks after the invasion had begun, I met again with Alyokhina and we walked through the centre of Moscow. By this time, she was living in the apartment block opposite us. One side of the building was dominated by a huge mural of Mikhail Bulgakov, the author of *The Master and Margarita*, the novel about the devil's visit to Moscow that had so intrigued me when I was a teenager.

The mood in the city was as grim as I had ever known it – most opposition figures were already either in exile or in prison and armed police seemed to be on every corner. There was nothing left of the exuberant spirit of defiance that Pussy Riot's protest had once encapsulated: the anti-Putin movement was now simply looking to survive.

Alyokhina had been behind bars again on more protest-related charges as Russia's war drums grew louder, and was expecting to be picked up again any day, as the Kremlin sought to eliminate all dissent. 'My father had always been worried that Putin would attack Ukraine,' Alyokhina said. 'But now he just watches television all day and he has started to say really strange things. Propaganda works. I hate these propaganda agents more than anyone. What they are doing is monstrous – they are killing people's identities and humanity.'

We walked down to the Christ the Saviour Cathedral, the scene of Pussy Riot's famous protest. Several anti-war demonstrators had already been arrested as they held up religious signs, including 'Thou Shall Not Kill.' It was not long after Oksana Baulina, a Russian opposition journalist with whom Alyokhina had been friendly, had been killed in a missile strike on Kyiv while reporting on the war. 'I keep imagining all these buildings in Moscow in ruins after having been hit by missiles,' Alyokhina said, gesturing at the nineteenth-century architecture that dominated the area. 'Like in Kyiv.' We watched in silence as a garbage truck decorated with a huge pro-war Z symbol drove past.

Alyokhina scattered her loathing for Putin and his actions in Ukraine with obscenities and refused to lower her voice, even when we entered a crowded café. 'I haven't been arrested, everything's ok,' she told a friend on the phone. Within weeks, Alyokhina had fled Russia, disguising herself as a food courier to evade police who were watching her building. She has not been back since. To do so would mean certain arrest and a long prison sentence. Or worse.

'HE WAS KILLED BY THE HATRED POURED INTO THE AIR'

But all this was yet to come. Following the 2011–2012 vote protests, central Moscow became extremely liveable, something that would have come as a shock to anyone who had visited the city during the Soviet era or in the early years of Putin's rule. In the wake of the unprecedented show of dissent, officials implemented a massive urban renovation programme that was a barely disguised attempt to pacify the Kremlin's middle-class critics. Cycle paths were built, free wi-fi was everywhere and the city centre was revamped, often to an eye-watering cost. In 2017, the mayor's office spent $122 million on festive lights in Moscow, a sum that was equivalent to the entire annual municipal budget of Tver, a provincial town with a population of almost half a million people.[24] Even though a large chunk of the money ended up in the pockets of corrupt officials, it was clear that no cost was too high to prevent the residents of Moscow from getting uppity again. Karl Marx had once called religion the opium of the people: for Putin's Russia, the modern-day equivalents were sparkling lights, ultra-fast wi-fi and clean streets lined with cosy cafes.

The showcase for the project was Gorky Park, the open space on the banks of the Moscow River that had fallen into decline in the 1990s. Initially known as the Park of Culture and Rest, it was opened in 1928 to promote 'Soviet culture and proletarian art'. Soviet trade unions sent workers to the park for one-day holidays that included group exercise, boating and cycling. In 1932 it was renamed in honour of Maxim Gorky, the Soviet writer. Later, the park was also used by the Soviet authorities to show off Nazi military hardware captured during the Second World War, with jubilant crowds lining up to examine German fighter planes, tanks and other weaponry. During the Cold War, an American U-2 spy plane that had been shot down by the Soviet military over the Ural Mountains was exhibited in Gorky Park to visitors who included foreign diplomats. Gary Powers, its pilot, was exchanged for a Soviet spy in Berlin in 1962. The park also lent its name to the Cold-War era bestselling spy thriller by Martin Cruz Smith.

I first visited Gorky Park in 1997 and my overwhelming memories are of a sad, solitary duck floating in a grimy concrete pond and decrepit Soviet-era amusement rides. It was not a place you felt like visiting very often. Following the vote fraud rallies, the park was rapidly transformed. Its reinvention, which was initially modelled on London's Hyde Park, was bankrolled to the tune of £1.25 billion by Roman Abramovich, the Russian oligarch who owned Chelsea football club. In the summer, skateboarders and cyclists zipped through the crowds, while families and friends gathered for picnics in its magnificently landscaped gardens. In winter, ice-skaters glided around the park's gigantic ice-rink, one of the largest in Europe, to the sound of Russian pop music. Its many cafes and restaurants were usually packed, abuzz with music and conversation, until late in the evening. For more highbrow activities, visitors headed to the Garage Museum of Contemporary Art. For a while, it was possible to imagine you were in western Europe.

Which, of course, was the entire point. When I asked Pavel Trekhleb, Gorky Park's Director, if the famous old park's transformation was motivated by the need to dampen political tensions after the vote fraud protests, he replied: 'There arose a demand for a systematic revamp of the urban environment in Moscow. As the city's central park, it was especially important to show quick and impressive results.' I took that as a yes.

Yet, even as Russians flocked to Gorky Park to spend their weekends in the blissful alternative reality that Abramovich's riches had created for them, the political reality was growing harsher by the day. One of my very last interviews for RIA was with Yevgeny Fyodorov, an MP with Putin's party who also led a pro-Kremlin group called the National Liberation Movement [NOD]. Fyodorov, a former deputy atomic energy minister, and his nationwide network of followers had declared that Russia was being ruled by the United States through American agents of influence embedded within the government. The media, the central bank and even parliament, he said, were controlled from Washington. Opposition figures like Navalny were also, he claimed, working for the CIA. Putin knew all this, Fyodorov insisted, and was attempting to 'liberate' Russia, but he needed help to purge the country of traitors.[25]

'Of course, Putin can't come right out and say all this but just listen to his speeches. It's all there, just cloaked in diplomatic language,' Fyodorov told me during an interview in his parliamentary office, flanked by model Soviet spacecraft and a beer mug with a portrait of Stalin. He also told me that it was time for the Kremlin to draw up a list of 'enemies of the people'. Such language was clearly dangerous given Russia's history, but Fyodorov was unrepentant. At the time, he seemed like little more than a political curio; before long, however, such rhetoric would enter the mainstream, normalizing political violence and inciting hatred.

Fyodorov's NOD later forged a loose alliance with a gang of violent pro-Putin activists called the South East Radical Block, or SERB.[26] The ultranationalist group, which described itself as a 'radical pro-Kremlin movement', had declared on its social media page that it was prepared to use any methods it saw fit in its political struggle. '[We] will not justify ourselves to anyone,' it wrote.[27] The movement was accused of involvement in numerous assaults on people opposed to Putin's long rule. In 2017, Navalny almost lost the use of an eye after a suspected SERB member threw a chemical into his face outside his headquarters in Moscow. His eyesight was only saved after an operation in Spain. Television footage existed of the incident, but Navalny's allies were unable to identify the attacker with 100 per cent certainty because the pro-Kremlin television channel blurred out his face before airing its video of the assault. The group denied any involvement in the attack, which took place the day after SERB activists visited the Russian parliament for a meeting with senior lawmakers who reportedly included Pyotr Tolstoy, the deputy speaker of parliament and the great-great-grandson of Leo Tolstoy, the author of *War and Peace*.[28]

SERB's leader was Igor Beketov, a hulking Putin acolyte from Ukraine's Dnipropetrovsk region who could often be seen harassing opposition activists at protests in Moscow.[29] He and his fellow pro-Kremlin thugs had been accused of hurling urine, excrement and other substances, including a bright green dye known in Russia as *zelyonka*, at Kremlin critics, including opposition journalists.[30] 'Opposition activists are like malign tumours on Russia's body,' Beketov told me when we spoke online. 'It's our job to draw attention to them.'

I was writing an article for *Newsweek* on mounting politically motivated attacks in Russia and I arranged to meet Beketov at a café in central Moscow. I was understandably wary, though. He and his followers were fanatics and their ability to operate with relative freedom indicated that they were under the protection of at least some elements of the security services, if not working for them. Accordingly, when I arrived, I texted Beketov to tell him that I was sitting near the entrance. In fact, I took a seat on the first floor with a view of the front door.

Beketov turned up around ten minutes later but didn't immediately enter the café. He was with a man that I recognized as a fellow SERB activist. His companion opened the bag and Beketov poured an unknown substance into it that I suspected was urine or faecal matter or some other foul and possibly toxic substance. He then walked into the café to look for me. I suddenly recalled that not so long ago, a rabidly pro-Kremlin website had identified me as a 'pathological Russophobe' and called for me to be deported from Russia. It had also included a recent photo.

I went into the toilet and closed the door. I waited for 15 minutes, took out my front door keys, gripped them between my fingers and unlocked the toilet door, ready to fight it out. Beketov was well over six feet tall and heavyset, but I reasoned I might be able to get in a blow or two and escape in the ensuing chaos. Even taking a punch in the head was, I figured, preferable to being drenched in whatever was in that bag. I stepped out of the toilet. Beketov and his accomplice were nowhere to be seen. I left the cafe, jumped on my bicycle and rode home quickly along one of Moscow's wonderful cycle paths.

12

'When They Beat You, Say Thank You for The Lesson'

As with any journalist who writes about Russia, Vladimir Putin looms large in my everyday thoughts. I have written his name thousands of times and spent hundreds of hours reading about him. Allowing Putin to take up space in my head rent-free is undoubtedly one of the downsides of the job. Oddly, though, I do not recall having dreamt about him: perhaps there is only so much space in my brain that Russia's vile dictator can occupy. It is possible, of course, that he is symbolized in my dreams by the occasional nightmares that wake me from my sleep with a jolt.

Many Russians do dream of Putin, though. In 2022, Daria Serenko, an anti-war feminist activist, collected and published anonymous accounts of dreams about the ex-KGB officer.[1] 'I dreamt that Putin was trying to rape me, and to stop me from resisting and destroying him with a fireball, he was holding my husband hostage,' one woman wrote. Another woman dreamt that she was Putin's ex-wife, Lyudmila, and had been imprisoned in their house for a long time. 'He knows everything and all men tremble before him,' she wrote.

'I dreamt that all the monuments erected in his honour around the country were alive, made of flesh and blood, and he himself was hollow and made of metal. That is why it is impossible to kill him,' another Russian wrote. A woman opposed to Putin said that she had 'woken up in a cold sweat' after a nightmare in which her 7-year-old daughter was about to betray her to the police.

The shortest description of a dream was perhaps the most true to life: 'Putin forced all Russians to eat shit.'

One does not have to be a psychoanalyst to see a thread: Putin is all-powerful. It is a message that is amplified by Kremlin officials, who seek to portray him as the living, breathing embodiment of Russia. 'If there is Putin, there is Russia. If there is no Putin, there is no Russia,' declared Vyacheslav Volodin, the speaker of the Russian parliament, in 2014. Patriarch Kirill, the head of the Russian Orthodox Church, a powerful Kremlin ally, has described Putin's rule as a 'miracle of god'. The Kremlin's spin doctors have also sought, with great success, to convince Russians that there is no viable alternative to Putin, an argument that has often been encapsulated in the rhetorical question: 'If not Putin, then who?'

Children are not immune to this relentless deification of the ex-KGB officer. When my daughter was still very young, I took her to one of Moscow's excellent theatres. Halfway through the performance, an actor playing the role of a wizard stretched out his hands and addressed the audience of pre-teens. 'I am the great and all-powerful...' He paused for dramatic effect. A boy in the front row finished his sentence for him. 'Putin!' he said.

Russia is soaked in Putinism. 'When people criticize Putin, I feel as if they are insulting Russia and I get angry,' a pensioner told me during the 2011–2012 vote fraud protests in Moscow. She was not the only one who had conflated Putin with the Motherland. 'I don't particularly like Putin or his United Russia party,' a well-known Russian once told me, on condition of strict anonymity, when I quizzed her about her public endorsement of the Kremlin. 'But I would never dream of criticizing either of them because I am a patriot.'

As we continued speaking, it became clear that this woman, an educated, fluent English speaker who had lived for some time in the West, had never stopped to consider that Putin is merely a temporary representative of the Russian state or that true patriotism does not equal blind loyalty, but rather the desire to improve your country, even if that means pointing out its faults. When I pointed this out to her, she replied: 'That's the cleverest thing I have ever heard.' I assumed that she was joking, but I met her several more times over the years and it soon became apparent that I had overestimated her ability for sarcasm.

She may have been a well-dressed, wealthy Muscovite, but her views were rooted in the instinctive subservience to authority that stretches far back into Russia's long history. During the tsarist era, popular proverbs among the downtrodden Russian peasantry included 'Keep your head bowed and your heart submissive,' 'When they beat you, say thank you for the lesson,' and 'Do the work of seven, but obey just one.' In 1874, during Europe's 'mad summer' of revolt, the Russian intellectuals who tried to foment uprisings in rural areas were handed over to the authorities by the very same peasants they had sought to liberate for having the temerity to speak out against 'God and the tsar'.[2]

Those disillusioned intellectuals would have surely recognized the sentiments expressed by Pyotr Chaadayev, a Russian philosopher, who just 20 years earlier had written: 'Russia is a whole separate world, submissive to the will, caprice, fantasy of a single man, whether his name be Peter or Ivan ... Russia moves only in the direction of her own enslavement and the enslavement of all the neighbouring peoples.'

Vasily Grossman, the Russian author and journalist, who is widely seen as one of the Soviet Union's greatest writers, put it more succinctly: 'The Russian soul,' he wrote in his unfinished novel, *Everything Flows*, '[was] a slave for a thousand years.' This is clearly not true of all Russians, or even all of Russia at all times – otherwise how can we explain the seismic revolts throughout Russian history, not to mention the sporadic protests that have broken out across Russia under Putin? Russian uprisings are unpredictable and often brutal. As Alexander Pushkin, Russia's nineteenth-century national poet wrote: 'God forbid to see a Russian rebellion – senseless and merciless.'

Yet, in between these revolts, most Russians are wearily resigned to placing their fates in the hands of an all-powerful national leader. When I lived in Moscow, barely a month went by without an online video appeal to Putin by ordinary Russians who wanted him to resolve their problems, from housing issues to environmental concerns. The plaintiffs invariably chanted or held up signs reading 'Putin – Pomogi!' ('Putin – Help!').[3] They usually addressed the Russian leader as 'ty' – the informal version of the Russian word for 'you' (the archaic 'thou' in English), which was traditionally also used when appealing to the tsar or God.

This mindset was neatly summed up by an online video that went viral among opposition supporters just before the 2012 presidential elections. The first half of the video featured around a dozen Russians complaining about miserly salaries, corruption, low living standards and other social ills. Then, they were all asked, 'Will you vote for Putin?' They all replied that they would. 'He's someone you can trust,' explained a middle-aged woman, with a smile.

When election day arrived, Putin received 96 per cent of the vote at Butyrka prison in Moscow, a notorious penal facility where Aleksandr Solzhenitsyn, the Soviet dissident, had once been held. But this was no blatant case of poll fraud. 'It was an honest result,' Olga Romanova, an opposition figure and prison reform campaigner who had monitored the vote, told me. 'I talked to all of the inmates as they voted and saw their ballot papers. Instead of just ticking the box next to Putin's name, they had all written their names, cell numbers and the charges against them on the voting slip. They all hoped that it would help them somehow; that someone would come and see they had voted in the "right" way. Russians have a great respect for the boss, for the man at the top.'

Putin's annual televised phone-in with the public reinforced this image of the president as a dominant parental figure quickly able to resolve Russia's problems. Billed as a 'conversation with the people', it frequently featured Putin admonishing officials on air and instructing them to carry out housing repairs or build gas pipelines to remote areas. Once, he gave a dress to a little girl from a poor family and invited her to a New Year party at the Kremlin. '[It's] Putin magic,' Maxim Trudolyubov, a Russian analyst and editor, told me. 'Putin is responsible for all the things that are good and often intangible.'

In 2018, teachers in the Kurgan region, some 1,000 miles from Moscow, appealed to Putin to intervene in a row over unpaid wages and announced they were going on strike until he did. 'This was a desperate act,' Vladimir Kocheulov, the teacher who organized the appeal, told me. 'Teachers in banana republics probably get paid better than we do.' Yet, Kocheulov refused to blame Putin for his woes. 'I'm not going to criticize Putin. What for? I want him to help us. People in Russia have always relied on their kind *batushka* to solve their problems,' he said, using a Russian word that means either 'father' or 'priest'. Kocheulov continued to speak out about salary delays over the next few years until, eventually, he was forced to undergo a psychiatric evaluation. It was never spelled out, but the implication was that only someone who was mentally unsound would continue to fight so stubbornly for their rights. A commission of psychiatric experts ruled that Kocheulov was mentally unfit to work with children and he was dismissed from his job. He had been a teacher for 25 years.

That same year, shortly before Putin secured a new six-year term in rubber-stamp presidential elections that featured a cast of handpicked nominal rivals, I visited a Super Putin exhibition in Moscow that portrayed the Russian dictator as a fearless hero for all ages. There was a portrait of Putin, dressed in a red cape, shooting bullets from a gigantic blaster. Another picture showed him clad in medieval armour, a Russian flag in his hand, while others portrayed him winning an ice-hockey championship and stroking a leopard. The most disturbing image was of Putin holding a portrait of Putin, holding a portrait of Putin, holding a portrait of Putin – and so on, into infinity.[4]

'There is no one else but Putin with the capability to rule Russia right now,' Yulia Dyuzheva, the young journalism student and model who curated the exhibition, told me as she showed me around. A small child when Putin came to power, Dyuzheva had almost no meaningful memories of the chaotic 1990s. Despite this, she insisted she was grateful to Putin for raising Russia from its knees. 'He is a strong leader who has demonstrated great results. We should be grateful to him,' she said. When I asked her about corruption, appalling living standards in the regions and other issues that had been raised by the beleaguered opposition, she said Putin's critics were wrong to only focus on the negatives. 'They just criticize the president rather than acknowledge all the good he has done,' she said, displaying a startling lack of understanding about the role of a political opposition.

As is often the case in Russia, things weren't quite as simple as they seemed. When I made inquiries about the Super Putin exhibition, I discovered that it was essentially an act of political masochism that had been financed and organized by a politician named Alexander Donskoy, the ex-mayor of Arkhangelsk, a city in northern Russia. In 2006, despite being virtually unknown outside his home region, Donskoy had unexpectedly announced that he would run for the presidency. Although he had no chance of victory, his crime was to challenge Putin without the Kremlin's blessing. Retribution was swift: his office was raided and he was hit with fraud charges. He was also the subject of a media smear campaign that claimed he was homosexual. Although Putin's crackdown on Russia's LGBT community was still in its infancy, no openly gay politician has ever held public office in the country. 'He's not gay! He impregnated me!' his wife, Marina, shouted at a press conference in Moscow.[5] Donskoy spent nine months behind bars before being released on parole.

The exhibition, Donskoy told me, when I called him a few days after my visit to it, was an attempt to reconcile himself to the fact that his homeland was not ready for genuine democracy and that his fellow Russians were happy to be ruled for decades by a dictator. 'For me, this exhibition is an act of coming to terms with the fact that Putin will be President for ever,' he said. 'Most people in Russia don't think there is anything wrong with one person being in power for life, like the tsar. They have an infantile belief in the authorities. The "Super Putin" exhibition reflects that. I asked around and found a person who really, genuinely loves Putin and asked her to act as the organizer and censor for the exhibition.'[6]

It was a bizarre act that I struggled to make sense of, but it was hard to argue with Donskoy's grim conclusion about the relationship between Putin and the majority of Russia's citizens. During his first two terms in office, when Putin frequently travelled to the Kremlin from his Novo-Ogaryovo residence near Moscow, it was common for traffic to be held up for almost an hour as police and the presidential guard cleared the route. Once, as Putin's motorcade finally sped past after we had been waiting at a roadblock for around 45 minutes, I complained to a taxi driver about the situation. He looked at me in surprise. 'We have to be patient,' he said. 'There is just one Putin and there are many of us.'

Years later, when Putin's 2018 election campaign offices opened, I spoke to people queuing outside one in Moscow. A sign at the entrance read: 'A strong president. A strong Russia.' But the people in the line were not there to learn about Putin's election programme – he didn't have one – nor were they planning to volunteer to help get the vote out – the result was a foregone conclusion. Instead, they were there to plead for assistance with housing issues and other problems. 'I'm hoping that Putin can help me,' an elderly man who gave his name only as Oleg told me. 'But even if he doesn't, I'll vote for him all the same – I'm a patriot.'

How did Russians become so in thrall to Putin, elevating him from a minor official to a near living god with omnipotent powers in the space of just a few years? Looking for answers, I visited Gleb Pavlovsky, the former Kremlin spin doctor, at his cluttered yet cosy office near Red Square. A softly spoken intellectual from Odesa, the Ukrainian Black Sea port city, Pavlovsky was a dissident during the Soviet era, producing and circulating books that had been banned by the authorities. He was arrested in 1982 but avoided a prison sentence by pleading guilty and renouncing his criticism of the Kremlin, something that was viewed in dissident circles as an 'ethical taboo'. His confession helped him get off relatively lightly: instead of being sent to a prison camp,

Pavlovsky was banished for three years to a small town in the Komi region in northern Russia.

After the Soviet Union's collapse, Pavlovsky transformed himself into one of Russia's most powerful 'political technologists', the men (and they were all men) who orchestrated the machineries of power from behind the scenes. In 1996, he helped engineer Yeltsin's re-election, enlisting the assistance of the country's oligarchs to ensure victory over the resurgent communists, a move that is now seen as undermining Russia's fledgling democracy. He then turned his attention to safeguarding a smooth transition of presidential power to Putin, Yeltsin's hand-picked successor. As Yeltsin's rule juddered to an end, Pavlovsky and his team set up focus groups to determine what Russians thought an ideal leader would look like. The answer was Max Otto von Stierlitz, the codename of a fictional Soviet-era secret agent.

'We enacted a whole story about a spy who had ensconced himself among the authorities and then suddenly emerged and went over to the side of the people,' Pavlovsky told me. 'As if the Kremlin's gates had opened up, and out of them came a people's president, one who – unlike Yeltsin and the Soviet leaders before him – spoke the language of the people. It was like a theatrical production, and Putin quickly learnt his role. He was like an actor who learnt and improved on the part given to him. I was charmed by him. I was his fan.' He sighed and pushed his glasses up. 'He's still playing a role in fact, but now he's playing the role of Putin. You often see the same with ageing actors, they play themselves during their periods of success and it's usually unconvincing.'

Pavlovsky had believed that Russians needed a strong hand after the chaos of the 1990s, one that would ensure a return to at least a modicum of economic and social stability. Yet he had not expected Putin to rule for life. Halfway through Medvedev's presidency, Pavlovsky began pushing for Putin's successor to run for a second term, a move that would have strengthened democracy in Russia. Putin, unsurprisingly, was unimpressed: Pavlovsky was reportedly fired on his personal orders in 2011. By the time I visited him in Moscow in early 2018, Pavlovsky was once again in the role of dissident, spilling the Kremlin's secrets.

'This myth that Putin decides everything, that there is no alternative to Putin, we worked on constantly throughout his first two terms. Just as everyone knew the Soviet Union was Lenin's state, for the majority of Russians today, Russia is Putin's state,' he said. It wasn't quite a confession, but the former Kremlin spin doctor clearly had regrets about his Machiavellian role in bringing Putin to power.

'In the 2000s, during Putin's first term, we consciously stamped down on the political process. We carried out the politics of managed democracy: If you had a major conflict, you had to come to us, to the Kremlin, to Putin, and we would help you resolve it. You couldn't appeal to anyone else. This was meant to be a temporary measure – a temporary therapy – people had to have the chance to recover from the horrors of the previous decade. But then it turned out that this was very convenient, not to mention very profitable, for the authorities. This is one of the things I feel responsible for, unfortunately.'

Putin has never deemed it necessary to debate his nominal rivals, something that Pavlovsky said was also initially partly his doing. 'It wasn't Putin's decision not to participate – it was the decision of his campaign headquarters and his team. There was no point in creating unnecessary risks. Especially when his ratings were so high. It then became a feature of his character; he now hates debates,' he said.

'Another strategy was to prevent Putin being personally associated with any failure. That's why we didn't let him go to the scene of the Kursk disaster,' Pavlovsky added, referring to the death of 118 sailors on board a Russian nuclear-powered submarine that sank in the chilly waters of the Barents Sea in 2000. 'Why would he go there? It's not like he could help. But we still had independent media back then, of course, and he got criticized for that.'

It is a policy that the Russian leader has stuck to down the years. In 2024, when Islamic State gunmen slaughtered almost 150 people at a concert hall in Moscow, Putin did not pay his respects at the scene and only broke his silence about the killings, the worst terrorist attack in Russia for 20 years, the following day. It was left to Dmitry Peskov, the Kremlin spokesman, to try and convince Russians that the president felt their pain.

'Believe me, if you don't see tears on his face, that doesn't mean he isn't hurting,' Peskov said.[7] Yet Putin's purported pain didn't stop him trying to turn the massacre to his own advantage: the bodies had not all been buried before the Kremlin declared that the attack had been organized by Ukraine with Western backing. This was despite the lack of any credible evidence whatsoever pointing towards Kyiv.[8]

After my departure from Moscow, I called Pavlovsky again, this time to ask him about Medvedev's dramatic transformation from the great hope of liberal Russians into one of Moscow's biggest hawks, but he had little interest in discussing his former boss. 'He is not a popular person,' he said, dismissively. That was our last conversation. Pavlovsky died eight months later at the age of 71 after a long illness. His death came almost a year to the day since Putin, the former KGB agent he had helped shape into Russia's undisputed national leader, had unleashed the biggest conflict in Europe since World War Two.

The belief in Putin's omnipotence that Pavlovsky had helped to instil in the national mindset was so deeply entrenched that for many Russians it was psychologically difficult to accept that their leader not only knew about widespread corruption and injustice, but that he was also the root of their problems. The concept of a beneficent ruler whose good intentions are constantly undermined by malign officials has centuries-old roots in Russia. It has traditionally been symbolized by the expression 'Good Tsar, bad Boyars', a reference to the feudal nobility during the tsarist era. I'd known about the saying and the phenomenon before I moved to Russia, but to see such attitudes in real life provided me with a depressing insight into the national character. Perhaps the most extreme example I encountered came when I was reporting on the case of an official with

'WHEN THEY BEAT YOU, SAY THANK YOU FOR THE LESSON'

Putin's ruling party who had been arrested after clashing with the Kremlin and its FSB security service.

Although he had been a member of Putin's ruling party for around a decade, Alexander Shestun, the head of Serpukhov, a small district near Moscow, had an independent and stubborn streak. In 2017, he disobeyed an order to ban protests against a toxic landfill that was said to be controlled by corrupt security officials. He even used his Mercedes to prevent police breaking up a demonstration. He was also locked into a dispute with Andrei Vorobyov, the Kremlin-loyal governor of the Moscow region, who was aiming to abolish direct elections for district chiefs such as Shestun. As his defiance grew, Shestun was summoned to a meeting in Moscow with FSB and Kremlin officials, where he was warned in stark terms what would happen to him unless he got back in line. Ivan Tkachev, a top FSB general, told him that he would be hit with trumped-up criminal charges, his family's home would be seized and, after a show trial to be accompanied by a vicious state media smear campaign, he would be imprisoned for many years. Unbeknown to Tkachev, Shestun was recording the conversation.[9]

'They will steamroll you, and you will have bad fucking problems. You'll go to jail. Don't you want to live anymore?' Tkachev could be heard saying on Shestun's tapes. 'They will bury you.' As Shestun tried to argue his case, a furious Tkachev tried one more time to make him see the seriousness of his situation. 'Listen, this is a command from the president!' he said. 'Move aside.' The conversation was menacing, but also oddly routine. Shestun was not the first insubordinate provincial leader to have been broken this way, the Kremlin's men boasted. These were not empty threats, but Shestun refused to buckle. In a desperate bid to stave off retribution, he published the recordings on YouTube. It made no difference. In 2018, on the eve of the World Cup opening ceremony in Moscow, dozens of armed and masked FSB officers stormed the Shestun family home. Alexander Shestun was charged with illicit property deals and taking bribes, which he denied, and locked up in Lefortovo, a former KGB prison in

Moscow. As promised, his home was confiscated and later seized by the state.[10]

'He believed that once he had made the audio recordings public, the officials who had threatened him would go to prison instead. Like in any normal country,' Shestun's wife, Yulia, told me when we met in a café that was almost in sight of the Kremlin. She refused, however, to blame Putin for her family's tribulations. 'Putin is very involved in foreign policy issues, and he probably doesn't know all the facts about this case,' she told me. She sighed: 'If he did, I think he would help.'[11]

I argued that there was no way that Putin could be ignorant of the case. After all, her husband had been threatened at the presidential office and the recording had been reported on by a number of media outlets. If Putin didn't know about this, then he was surely so ill-informed as to be unworthy of the post of President? Yulia shook her head and repeated her belief that Putin would intervene, once he found out about the terrible injustice that her husband had suffered. The Shestun family had already recorded an appeal to the president and she hoped it was just a matter of time before the case was closed. I wished her good luck and we stayed in touch.

Two years later, shortly before her husband was sentenced to 15 years in a maximum-security penal colony, I spoke to Yulia again. Her views had hardened so much as to be almost unrecognizable. It had taken two years of merciless persecution for her to see the truth. 'Of course, my opinion about Putin has changed. I no longer believe that "kind Putin" will hear about what his security services are doing and save my husband,' she told me. 'I was naive. But that naivety is long gone.'[12]

13

HOLY WATER AND HIV

Leonid Simonovich-Nikshich was dressed in black paramilitary gear festooned with skulls. High above his head, he held a chunky silver crucifix. All around him, thousands of nationalists were chanting slogans calling for the expulsion of migrants from Central Asian countries such as Tajikistan and Uzbekistan. 'Darkies Out of Russia!' they screamed, as a police helicopter hovered above.

The rally, which was called the Russian March, was an annual gathering of nationalists that usually took place in the centre of Moscow. The rallies routinely ended with a few arrests and outraged headlines in the opposition media, as well as a smattering of articles in the West, depending on the size of the crowd.

It was March 2014, shortly after Putin had sent troops into Crimea, and there were bigger stories happening in Ukraine. But I'd made a point of attending that year's rally because I'd known that Simonovich-Nikshich and his Union of Orthodox Banner-Bearers would be there. The Banner-Bearers – whose slogan was 'Orthodoxy or Death!' – were one of the most visible groups that made up Russia's radical religious right, the once fringe movement that had been revitalized by Putin's return to the Kremlin for a third term in 2012 and his adoption of a harsh, ultra-conservative ideology.

The Banner-Bearers were known for attacking LGBT activists on the streets of Moscow and publicly burning books by authors such as J.K. Rowling, who they had accused of promoting witchcraft to Russian children. Since forming the Banner-Bearers in the early 1990s, Simonovich-Nikshich had been honoured twice by the powerful Russian Orthodox Church for his 'tireless' work. He and his movement also had a knack for publicity, wearing black hooded uniforms to the high-profile trial of Pussy Riot and setting fire to a poster of the feminist group outside the courtroom. 'We're going to rip them up and burn them,' Simonovich-Nikshich had said. 'Like in the Middle Ages.'[1]

As anti-Western rhetoric soared, groups like the Banner-Bearers suddenly seemed to be everywhere, whipping up hatred for non-believers and portraying the Kremlin's military actions in Ukraine as a sacred battle against harmful Western ideas. To me, the Banner-Bearers and their fellow Orthodox fanatics seemed like relics of another age, when half-crazed monks and mystics roamed Russia, dispensing God's judgements on peasants and nobles alike. I have always been drawn to the grotesque and the macabre and I often sought out Russia's religious extremists for interviews, fascinated and repulsed in equal measure. Unlike pro-Kremlin politicians and activists, whose motivations for spouting anti-Western rhetoric were often rooted in a cynical desire for money and power, they appeared to be genuine believers. I found it harder to imagine what was going on in their heads and I liked to challenge myself to do so.

As the nationalists roared that afternoon in Moscow, I struck up a conversation with Simonovich-Nikshich, shouting over the noise of the crowd to introduce myself. It was an awkward place for a theological discussion, but I wanted to know how he squared his group's loathing of LGBT people and migrants with the Bible's concept of Christian tolerance. He peered at me over his glasses. 'Tolerance?' he said. 'Where does it say anything in the Bible about tolerance?' I didn't have a Bible to hand, so I was unable to cite scripture back to him and he strode off in disgust.

Instead, I got talking to the movement's second-in-command, Igor Miroshnichenko, an artist and former fashion designer with mournful, deep-set eyes. Igor was responsible for the hooded black uniforms, banners and regalia that had seen the movement's long-haired, bearded members described, at least visually, as a cross between the Grateful Dead and the Ku Klux Klan. I told him I was interested in finding out more about the Banner-Bearers and he invited me to his studio.

A week later, Igor met me outside a metro station on the outskirts of Moscow. 'How come you speak Russian so well?' he asked. I told him I'd been living in the country for many years and was married to a Russian woman. His eyes narrowed, instinctively. 'Where are you from?' he enquired, suddenly aggressive. I told him I was British and he relaxed. 'Ah, that's ok then,' he said. 'We don't have anything against Russian women marrying Britons.' When we got to Igor's studio, a lock-up, he made strong, sweet tea and laid the table with cakes. The walls of his studio were full of paintings, many of them apocalyptic or white supremacist in nature. One of them featured Russia's black and yellow imperial-era flag and the slogan 'Democracy in hell – in the heavens, the empire.'

Some critics had compared the Banner-Bearers to Ivan the Terrible's dreaded secret police, the *oprichniki*, who dressed all in black and had a severed dog's head as their symbol. Others had described the movement and its ideological allies as the 'Orthodox Taliban'. This was an exaggeration, yet they were undoubtedly an ominous indication of the direction Russia was taking. 'We have a bad reputation,' Igor admitted. 'The opposition papers write that we kill and beat people up. That's not true at all. We don't attack anyone.' I began to object, but he held up a hand to cut me off. 'Well, apart from gays, that is, when they try to hold their parades. But they really make us angry and we can't control ourselves.'

'Why not?' I asked. Igor put down his cake and gave my question some thought. 'Gays are being used by certain forces that are attacking Russia. If they are given rights, they will spread the idea that the family is not needed and our birthrate will fall,' he replied. 'It's a plot to lower Russia's birth rate. And then Muslims will come in to fill the empty spaces.' A Western plot? Igor nodded. 'Of course. A plot by Russia's enemies.'

Was there anything about the West that he thought was positive, I wondered. Igor nodded. 'Rock music. 1960s and 1970s stuff, King Crimson, especially. Rock music brought a lot of people to God in the Soviet Union.' It was an odd moment and I pictured Igor as a young man, sitting in a Soviet flat listening to one of the illicit copies of Western rock music that had been smuggled into the communist state, hearing religious messages where perhaps none existed. What album was it, I wondered, that turned him onto God? He couldn't remember, he admitted. When I got home, I set 'Paranoid' by Black Sabbath as the ringtone for his number.

A few weeks later, the dulcet tones of Ozzy Osbourne filled my apartment. It was Igor, calling to invite me to meet Simonovich-Nikshich, the Banner-Bearer's leader, at a café in central Moscow. I think they were as curious about me as I was about them. When I got to the café, Simonovich-Nikshich, Igor and another member of the Banner-Bearers were sitting around a table piled high with coffee cups and blueberry muffins. All of them were dressed in the movement's black paramilitary uniforms, while Simonovich-Nikshich sported a chunky ring on each finger. Even for Moscow, where weirdness was so common it was almost normal, they stood out. Secretaries and office workers cast curious glances in their direction.

'Satanism is a very influential religion,' Simonovich-Nikshich told me, just moments after I had taken my seat. The conversation drifted on surreally. One moment they were calling for Vladimir Lenin's removal from his Red Square tomb ('That Red Dragon needs to go!'), while the next they were urging the establishment of a fundamentalist Christian state from Dublin to Vladivostok. The Banner-Bearers supported Putin, but at heart they were monarchists and longed to see the eventual return of the tsar. 'This is necessary to rescue Russia's lost generation,' Simonovich-Nikshich told me.

But who could claim the vacant crown? He wasn't sure. The modern-day Romanovs, descendants of Tsar Nicholas II, who was executed by the Bolsheviks in 1918, had shown no interest in reclaiming the throne and there were no obvious alternatives. 'How is the tsar going to return, if the Romanovs aren't interested?' Simonovich-Nikshich asked me. This wasn't a rhetorical question. The Banner-Bearers gazed at me intently as if I was going to resolve their problem for them right then and there. 'What about Putin?' I suggested. Would the ex-KGB man make a good tsar? I was being sarcastic, but they had already thought of this.

'Ah, there was some talk about this a few years back,' Simonovich-Nikshich said, sighing. 'And then people started to suggest that it might be better to marry off one of Putin's daughters to Prince William. You know, from your England? To start a new line of the monarchy in Russia, you see?' he sighed again. 'But then he went and got married to that Kate woman? I forget her surname.'

I have zero interest in the British royal family, beyond wishing for the abolition of the monarchy, and I also found myself struggling to recall Kate Middleton's surname. Simonovich-Nikshich looked surprised for a second and then he was off again. This time, he leaned forwards and told me about an alleged Jewish conspiracy to rule the world. I'd been wondering when they would get to the Jews: if I'd had a Banner-Bearers bingo card, it would likely have been the last empty space. 'Stay in touch,' Igor said, as we left the café. 'There are interesting times ahead.' I didn't doubt him for a second.

It was easy to laugh at these muffin-munching members of Russia's religious right, but the muddled and hateful rhetoric they spouted between cups of coffee was slowly entering the mainstream. The Banner-Bearers had been around for over 20 years, but other Orthodox Christian movements, far more radical and far more aggressive, were emerging. Sorok Sorokov, which had been described by its critics as the Russian Orthodox Church's 'combat unit', was formed in 2013 and already claimed to have 10,000 members nationwide. The group's name translated as 'Forty Forties' and was a reference to the 1,600 Orthodox Christian places of worship that had once reportedly existed in Moscow. Some of the group's members were former football hooligans[2] while opposition activists had accused it of attacks on protesters who were opposed to the construction of a new Orthodox church on parkland in the north of the Russian capital. Sorok Sorokov denied the allegations.

'Russia is the last stronghold of humankind on this planet,' Andrei Kormukhin, the leader of Sorok Sorokov,[3] told me when we met at a café in central Moscow that sold traditional Russian food. 'What is happening right now in Europe is a nightmare. Europe has rejected Christian values. Any sin is acceptable now in Europe – zoophilia, incest and paedophilia. As a result, Europe will stagnate and die out.'[4] He was clearly relishing the prospect.

Since my arrival in Moscow in the 1990s, I had encountered plenty of Russians who hated the West and were not shy about telling me. But it had very rarely felt like a personal attack; they were just letting off steam at the nearest Western citizen they could find. Yet Kormukhin clearly felt as if he was morally superior to me and he barely bothered to disguise his disdain. It was uncomfortable and infuriating. He was, like most of Russia's Orthodox fanatics, a very Old Testament kind of Christian. His passion for divine judgement made me wonder if he had even got as far as the New Testament and Christ's exhortations to love one's enemies. If I had got up and punched him in the face as he sat there pontificating on Russia's spiritual superiority, would he have turned the other cheek? Somehow, I doubt it.

This vision of the West as a modern-day Sodom and Gomorrah had been pushed by Russian state media. 'Brothels for zoophiles have existed for a long time in Copenhagen,' read an article that was published by the newly revamped RIA Novosti in 2017. 'Local animal rights defenders, whose voices, however, are almost never heard, [say] that the animals are put in special machines and even have their limbs broken so that they cannot harm those who enjoy such unusual pleasures.'[5] Such propaganda was frighteningly effective, especially for those tens of millions of Russians who had never left the country. 'It's terrible. There aren't enough women [in Europe], so men rape dogs,' a Kremlin supporter claimed in an online video that went viral. 'You walk along the streets there and the dogs are howling everywhere because they are being raped.'[6]

During the Cold War, it was common for American conservatives to describe the Soviet Union, where atheism was an official state policy, as a 'godless' state. During the first two decades of the Soviet era, some 200,000 members of the clergy were murdered, while millions of other Christians were persecuted for their faith, according to a 1995 Russian government committee report. 'The more representatives of the reactionary clergy we shoot, the better,' Lenin once said. Thousands of churches were destroyed under early communist rule, and those that survived were turned into warehouses, garages or museums of atheism. Although a limited Orthodox Christian revival was permitted by Stalin during World War Two, anti-religion propaganda and selected discrimination against believers continued up until the mid-1980s. One Soviet school textbook printed in the 1950s called Christianity a 'perverse reflection of the world'. In 1983, Ronald Reagan, America's first evangelical president, labelled the communist state an 'Evil Empire' over its abandonment of religion.

Decades on, history had come full circle. Although Putin, as president, had never made a secret of what he claimed was his deep Christian faith, his first decade in power was largely free of overtly religious rhetoric. Little or no attempt was made to impose a set of values on Russians or lecture the West on morals. All that changed following his return to the Kremlin in 2012 for a third term. As liberal ideas and LGBT-friendly policies took root in the United States and Europe, Putin and his allies gleefully hurled the 'godless' allegations back at the West. In a keynote speech, Putin accused Western countries of implementing policies that equated 'a faith in God and a belief in Satan', while portraying Russia as a staunch defender of Christian traditional values. Social and religious conservatism, he insisted, was the only way to prevent the world from slipping into 'chaotic darkness'.

Despite the history of religious persecution by Moscow, the Russian Orthodox Church was now one of Putin's biggest supporters. Shortly before Putin reclaimed the presidency from Medvedev, Patriarch Kirill, the head of the church, described the Russian president's rule as a 'miracle of God'. He also lashed out at the West, accusing it of a hostility to religion. 'We have been through an epoch of atheism, and we know what it is to live without God,' he said. 'We want to shout to the whole world, "Stop!"'[7]

Putin backed up his rhetoric with legislation; one new law against 'gay propaganda' in 2013 made it illegal to even suggest to children that there could be anything positive about same-sex relations, while another law approved the same year made it a crime punishable by up to three years in prison to insult the feelings of religious believers. The latter law was used almost exclusively to prosecute those people who had angered the Russian Orthodox Church. The first person to be charged was a man named Viktor Krasnov, who wrote 'there is no God' in an online argument with two Russian Orthodox Christians. 'If I say that the collection of Jewish fairytales entitled the Bible is complete bullshit, then that is that. At least for me,' Krasnov also wrote. He spent a month in a psychiatric ward to determine if he was fit to stand trial after a judge said that 'no one in their right mind would write anything against Orthodox Christianity'.[8]

'Yuri Gagarin said "I travelled into space, and I did not see God there,"' Krasnov told me later, referring to a famous Soviet anti-religion poster. 'And now I'm being charged with insulting the feelings of religious believers?' The charges were eventually dropped after the statute of limitations expired, but the message was clear: questioning the tenets of Russian Orthodox Christianity, one of the bedrocks of Putin's rule, was now dangerous.

Not long afterwards, a 22-year-old blogger named Ruslan Sokolovsky was arrested in Yekaterinburg after he filmed himself playing Pokémon in an Orthodox cathedral. He also posted a video to YouTube that showed him hunting the game's multi-coloured cartoon creatures next to the altar while a priest intoned prayers. Armed police officers raided the flat where he lived with his mother, and he was charged with showing 'disrespect' for Jesus Christ. A police spokesman publicly accused him of blasphemy. He was held in custody for four months and repeatedly beaten by fellow prisoners before being convicted and given a three-and-a-half-year suspended sentence.[9]

The Russian Orthodox Church refused to ask for clemency for anyone charged with insulting religion. In 2012, Patriarch Kirill, who was rumoured to have had ties with the KGB during the Soviet era, even dismissed calls by churchgoers for mercy for the Pussy Riot activists, two of whom were young mothers. Instead, he accused the women of doing the 'devil's work' and criticized those who he said were seeking to 'downplay this sacrilege'. He added: 'My heart breaks from bitterness that amongst these people there are those who call themselves Orthodox.'[10]

Puzzled by Kirill's refusal to forgive his enemies, I went to meet Vakhtang Kipshidze, a spokesman for the Russian Orthodox Church, at Moscow's sixteenth-century Andreevsky monastery. 'Forgiveness is a very tricky thing,' Kipshidze told me, as we sat in a church library. 'Of course, we should follow Christ's examples. However, in all societies, laws are applicable.' Kipshidze was undoubtedly more of a Bible scholar, but I was pretty sure Jesus Christ hadn't described forgiveness as 'tricky'. Then again, I reasoned, his boss wasn't one of Putin's biggest allies.

Kipshidze was a voice of moderation, however, when compared to Father Vsevolod Chaplin, another spokesman for the Russian Orthodox Church. Chaplin, who sported a wispy beard and occasionally visited nightclubs to preach to Moscow's youth, was the leader of the church's radical wing. He was a vocal supporter of Russia's military actions in eastern Ukraine and had ties to Orthodox activists who had taken to destroying 'blasphemous' artworks in Moscow. I had first met him during the Pussy Riot trial, when he had described their anti-Putin protest in Russia's biggest Orthodox cathedral as 'Satanic rage'. He quickly became my go-to whenever I needed a quote from a church official: his remarks were almost always memorable, if grotesque. There was something almost medieval about him and I found it hard to believe that he was just a year older than me.

Chaplin had also supported a Kremlin ban on American families adopting Russian children that was introduced in retaliation for Western sanctions. According to Chaplin, the ban was justified because Russian children brought up in the United States would be unable to receive a 'true Christian upbringing' and would be barred entry to 'the Kingdom of God'. On another occasion, he said that women who wore short skirts and got drunk should 'not be surprised if they are raped'. At times, his rhetoric was so outrageous that I wondered if he was simply trolling Russian liberals. He certainly seemed to enjoy their company. A friend once told me that he had spent an evening drinking vodka with Chaplin at Proekt OGI, an underground music club in Moscow.

In September 2015, Chaplin described Russia's military campaign in Syria in support of President Assad as a 'holy war', a remark that would have horrific consequences. A spokesman for Islamic State cited the comment as evidence that Moscow was engaged in a war against all Muslims and called for jihad against Russia. Two weeks later, a Russian passenger jet full of holidaymakers returning home from a popular Egyptian Red Sea resort exploded in mid-air, killing all 224 people on board. As the aircraft lay smouldering in the Sinai desert, an Islamic State-affiliated group claimed responsibility and celebrated the deaths of the Russian 'crusaders'. It was the deadliest aviation disaster in Russian and Soviet history.

When I visited Chaplin at his office shortly after the destruction of the aircraft, he didn't seem like a man who was tormented by the results of his actions. Sitting at a desk covered in paperwork, chocolates and religious icons, he barely looked up from his documents when I asked him if he regretted his words. 'The plane crash in Egypt was necessary for Russian society,' he told me. 'Society saw death and realized that life in pursuit of entertainment, material well-being, holidays and so on is the incorrect way to live. This is an absurd way to live. If a person does not understand this, then God will remind him of it.' He unwrapped a chocolate and popped it into his mouth. He did not offer me one, I noted.

It was an astonishing statement for one of the Russian Orthodox Church's most high-profile representatives to make in the wake of a period of national mourning. I double-checked that he actually wanted to go on record saying that the loss of over 200 lives, including those of around 20 children, had a positive side. He nodded. 'Wars and catastrophes are necessary to keep people from becoming too convinced that they need to build lives for themselves here, on earth,' he told me. 'That is a false belief. So, while we feel sorry for those people who died, for the rest of society, yes, this was necessary.'[11]

I wrote up my article and included his remarks on the deaths. He was fired by the church from his position as a spokesman around a month after it was published, although it was unclear if there was a link. Shortly before his dismissal, Chaplin had also called for the replacement of the 'tired, corrupt and cynical' Russian political elite with Orthodox believers. In 2016, he praised Stalin, saying: 'What's so bad about destroying some of [Russia's] internal enemies? There are some people you should kill.'[12] Four years later, he died of a heart attack while sitting outside a church in Moscow. He was just 51. I didn't like him or respect him, but it felt strange to think that I would never be able to call him again for a dose of religious fanaticism.

Putin's move to boost ties with the Church was initially seen as a cynical bid to sideline the pro-democracy protesters who had come out in such large numbers after the rigged elections in 2011 by associating them with the 'decadent' West. The protesters had held up western Europe and, to a lesser extent, the United States as role models for Russia's future. Putin's response was to depict Western democracies as the work of the devil. Yet, as the years went by, he appeared to become possessed by his own rhetoric.

As tensions with the West soared after the annexation of Crimea, Putin peppered his threats of nuclear war with religious references.

'An aggressor should know that vengeance is inevitable, that he will be annihilated. Whereas we would become the victims of their aggression, and as martyrs, will go to heaven – they will just end up dead, because they won't even have time to repent,' Putin said in 2018. His remarks came after Orthodox priests wearing cassocks and holding Bibles had sprinkled holy water on Topol-M and Yars intercontinental ballistic missiles as they were being transported to Moscow for the annual Victory Day parade. Amid an uproar, the Russian Orthodox Church defended the actions of the priests, saying that nuclear weapons were Russia's 'guardian angels' and necessary to preserve 'Orthodox civilization'.

But it wasn't only nuclear missiles that priests were blessing – they had also sanctified a vast array of death-dealing devices, including nuclear submarines, tanks and fighter jets. A priest had also blessed a nine-metre-high statue of Mikhail Kalashnikov, the inventor of the AK-47 assault rifle, one of the twentieth century's most effective killing machines, that was unveiled in central Moscow. 'He created this weapon to defend his motherland,' Father Konstantin told me, when I suggested to him that sanctifying a statue of Kalashnikov was an inappropriate use of holy water. Some members of the crowd crossed themselves as the statue was unveiled.[13] It later emerged that a drawing on the base of the statue portrayed a Nazi StG 44 rifle rather than an AK-47. It was removed after the error was discovered.

Even the communists were being gripped by the religious mania that Putin had encouraged. In 2015, on the 145th anniversary of Vladimir Lenin's birth, Gennady Zyuganov, the head of the modern Russian Communist Party, declared that the Soviet Union was an attempt to establish 'God's Kingdom on Earth'.[14] Zyuganov, a former Soviet 'agitation and propaganda' official, made no mention of the communist regime's anti-religion campaign. 'Were you lying back then [in the Soviet era] or is your faith now a lie?' a caller asked him during an interview on the

Echo of Moscow, a liberal radio station. Zyuganov called the station 'a disgrace' and said it should be shut down. Seven years later, as Putin ordered tanks into Ukraine, it was.

At my local grocery store, my favourite brand of dairy products, Russkoe Moloko, had taken to stamping a red cross over the barcodes on its milk cartons and yoghurts. The reason, it explained, was that the ubiquitous barcode was well known to be the 'mark of the beast', as referred to in the Bible's Book of Revelation. ('No one could buy or sell unless he had the mark, which is the name of the beast.') This was a well-established conspiracy theory that is referenced, for example, in the film *Naked*,[15] by Mike Leigh, the British director, as well as elsewhere. 'By placing the cross on the barcode, we want to demonstrate our stance: we are with our Lord, Jesus Christ, and not with the antichrist and his servants,' the company announced. I called the dairy firm and asked the logical question: if they truly believed that the barcode was demonic, why didn't they stop using it altogether? The spokeswoman sighed: 'How would we sell our products, if we did this?' There was certainly no arguing with that.

It was increasingly hard to recognize the Russia that I had flown into all those years ago. In 2000, Putin's first year in power, a pop duo called t.A.T.u. had a massive hit with a song about a romance between two teenage girls. The group's two members were not actually lesbians, but their on-screen kiss in the accompanying music video was a sensation and it was shown regularly on national television. By 2013, public images of same-sex relationships had effectively been barred under the 'gay propaganda' law. After the start of the war in Ukraine, the Kremlin cracked down even further on what it called harmful Western ideologies. In 2023, the Russian Supreme Court outlawed 'the international LGBT social movement' – a deliberately vague designation – as an 'extremist and terrorist' organization, a move that equated it with Islamic State and neo-Nazi movements. The move came shortly before Russia *removed* the Taliban from Moscow's list of banned terrorist organizations. Under the Supreme Court ruling, t.A.T.u.'s video during Putin's first year in power would not only have been barred, but the group and its producers would also have risked being sent to prison.

In a stark illustration of just how dramatically Russia had changed, in 2024, two women who posted an online video of themselves kissing in a café were arrested, forced to apologize on camera and fined. A woman was also arrested and jailed for five days for wearing rainbow-coloured earrings at a café in Nizhny Novgorod, a city east of Moscow. These incidents were just the beginning: in March 2024, masked police brandishing automatic weapons burst into a gay club in the city of Orenburg and forced men to lie half-naked and spread-eagled on the ground. They were accompanied by members of a pro-Kremlin nationalist group. Two of the club's employees were charged with 'extremism' and at the time of writing were being held in a pre-trial detention centre. They faced up to ten years behind bars. 'It's becoming more and more dangerous [to be LGBT in Russia],' a member of a lesbian rock group that played secret gigs in Moscow, told me. 'It's like you are walking along the edge of an abyss and if your rope snaps, you plunge into prison for ten years.'

One of those to support the LGBT ban was Anton Krasovsky, a television presenter who had been fired by his employer in 2013 after he became the first person in Russia to come out on-air as gay. 'Evil is on the rise in Russia,' he warned after his dismissal. 'This can only have one outcome: the deep moral humiliation of society.'[16] Just over a decade later, Krasovsky, by now the director of Russian-language broadcasting for RT, the Kremlin-funded television channel, was one of Putin's biggest admirers. The decision to designate LGBT groups as extremists and terrorists was, he said, necessary 'to make the wheel [of history] turn'.[17] He also called for Ukrainian children who opposed Russian rule to be drowned or burnt alive.[18] Russian investigators said there was nothing criminal about his comments.[19]

As the war in Ukraine raged, it became common for Putin and other officials to declare that God was on Russia's side. Patriarch Kirill described the invasion as a sacred battle against 'the antichrist', and 'forces of evil' that were trying to destroy Russia, while suggesting it was a divine punishment for LGBT pride parades that had been held in Kyiv. He also declared that Russians who were killed fighting in Ukraine would have all their sins forgiven. In Moscow, the defence ministry put up posters that depicted Russian soldiers with the pro-war Z symbol on their uniforms and halos around their heads. One caption read: 'Christ defeated hell and so will Russia.' Another poster asked: 'If God is for us, then who is against us?'

In Ukraine, fellow Orthodox Christian believers watched in horror as Kirill provided Putin with spiritual backing for the war. In Bucha, the town near Kyiv where Russian soldiers had tortured, raped and murdered hundreds of civilians, I spoke to Father Andriy Galavin at the St Andrew Orthodox Church, whose grounds had been used for a mass grave that held the bodies of over 100 people. Its walls were still scarred with bullet holes and shell damage.

'This is very painful for us. [Kirill] is an Orthodox Christian, like us. A brother in faith, at least nominally,' Galavin told me, his voice echoing inside the sunlit church. 'People ask me if he believes in God. I think he believes in the kind of god that he can take out of his pocket when it's convenient for him. Or maybe he has another god, a god that goes by the name of Vladimir Putin.'

In his Easter sermon after Russian troops had been expelled from Bucha, Galavin had urged Ukrainians 'not to become evil when you fight evil'. Yet he admitted that he was not yet ready to forgive the Russian soldiers who had destroyed so many lives. 'It's easy to just say "I forgive". Christ wants us to forgive, but not just to say the words. This should be said with sincerity. And to do that it is going to take a long time. We don't know how many decades it will take.'

Before I left him, I asked Galavin if he and his parishioners struggled with their faith. Did they ever ask themselves how their god could have permitted such atrocities? It was an awkward question to pose to a man who had lived through so much horror, but from his reply it became clear that he had been wrestling with such issues.

'It wasn't god who killed, it wasn't god who raped, it wasn't god who broke down every door and carried out washing machines and televisions and sent them to Russia,' Galavin told me. 'But there is no ready-made answer for this that will satisfy everyone. Whatever words you say, words remain words, they will not take away the pain.'[20]

The Kremlin's intolerance for anything that smacked of 'liberal' Western values also had serious consequences for Russia's national health. In 1986, the year before Russia would register its first official case of HIV, a Soviet health official spoke on state television about the troubling new infection that was making international headlines. 'This is a Western disease,' he said. 'But there is no base here for it to spread, since in Russia there is no drug addiction and no prostitution.'[21]

Over the following decades, it became clear that HIV was also a very Russian disease: by 2020, the number of people living with the virus in Russia was estimated to be at least 1.5 million – around 1 per cent of the total population. In five Russian cities in Siberia and the Ural region, Chelyabinsk, Irkutsk, Samara, Tolyatti and Yekaterinburg, more than 1.5 per cent of the population was HIV positive. Kemerovo, a coal-mining region 2,000 miles east of Moscow, had the unwelcome distinction of being Russia's worst-hit area, with infection rates that were more than 40 times higher than in the European Union. Across Russia, a mere one third of those with the virus were receiving antiretroviral therapy. In 2019, a record 37,000 Russians died of HIV/Aids. The death toll in Britain, which has a little less than half the population of Russia, was 622 or almost 60 times fewer. Russian health officials weren't exactly forthcoming and finding out such figures was time-consuming and often impossible.

Despite the epidemic, the Russian authorities clamped down on almost everything that might have alleviated the crisis. It was almost as if they wanted Russians to die slow and horrible deaths. Attempts to introduce sex education in schools were unsuccessful because of the opposition of the Russian Orthodox Church, which insisted that 'virtue and chastity' provided the best defence against HIV. According to Russia's top official for children's rights, the novels of Leo Tolstoy contained everything that a child needed to know about love and sex.

Moscow also made life as difficult as possible for independent groups that were trying to stem the tide of HIV infections. 'Russia is capable of financing harm reduction programs, but they are not being carried out because the government, including the health ministry, is unwilling to contradict Putin's conservative ideology,' Anya Sarang, the head of the Andrey Rylkov Foundation for Health and Social Justice, a non-governmental organization which sought to reduce the rise in infections, told me. In 2016, the group was designated a foreign agent by the Kremlin, a move that saw it hit with fines, inspections and state media smear campaigns.

One snowy evening in the east of Moscow, I joined two young women from the organization as they handed out condoms and syringes outside a chemist. Incredibly, they were the only source of free clean needles for the city's population of over 12 million people. 'Sometimes we get yelled at by members of so-called patriotic movements, who believe we are undermining Russia's spiritual values or something,' Elena Plotnikova, one of the women distributing the potentially life-saving supplies, told me. She rolled her eyes.[22]

For many Russians, it was more important to project an idea of greatness than exposing problems that would tarnish its international image. Once, after I had told a neighbour in Moscow about my reporting on Russia's Aids/HIV epidemic, he accused me of seeking to sully his motherland's reputation. 'Why would you dig up dirt about our country?' he asked. His attitudes were echoed by officials: in 2022, when the United Nations reported that Russia had the fifth highest number of new HIV infections in the world, Moscow dismissed the international study as 'provocative propaganda'.[23] Meanwhile, Russians continued to die in their tens of thousands, victims of Putin's fixation on shielding his country from 'harmful' Western ideas.

14

Exorcizing Putin

The long-haired shaman, his face daubed with magical symbols, had a warning for humanity. 'Putin is a demon,' he told me, as we spoke in his wooden hut in deepest Siberia. 'He is the antichrist. He will start a big war, if he is not driven off the planet.'

The shaman, whose name was Alexander Gabyshev, clutched a ritual sword as long as his arm. Burning wood crackled in the stove that heated the room. Outside, it was minus 40 degrees Celsius and snow fell steadily, blanketing the icy outskirts of Yakutsk, the coldest city in the world. A black-and-white flag bearing the shaman's image hung next to the front door, stiff with frost.

Yakutsk is the capital of Russia's vast frozen region of Yakutia, a territory that is almost the size of India, but with a population of just under one million people. Ethnic Yakuts, a once semi-nomadic people, are in the majority across the region, known as Sakha in the local language. Despite the efforts of the atheist Soviet authorities, belief in shamanism remains strong, even among local officials.

In April 2019, around half a year before I made the seven-hour flight from Moscow to visit him, Gabyshev had set off on foot from Yakutsk for the Russian capital, a journey of 5,000 miles. His aim was to reach the gates of the Kremlin, where he planned to perform a magical ceremony to 'exorcize' Putin and restore democracy to Russia. He insisted his actions would be entirely peaceful: 'Not a single hair shall fall from his head,' he said.[1]

A former welder who had served in the Soviet army, Gabyshev spent three years as a hermit in the Siberian wilderness following the death of his wife in the early 2000s, sheltering from temperatures as low as minus 55 degrees Celsius in a dug-out and a yurt. When he re-emerged into society, he wore clothes embroidered with the symbols of all the world's religions and taught a self-invented hand-to-hand combat technique that he called Thunderfist in exchange for food. He described himself as 'monk-warrior'.[2]

'The spirits of nature, God, told me to drive out Putin,' Gabyshev told me, shortly after I had arrived at his home in the winter of 2020. 'I checked it all out first, though, to make sure the message was real. I used to vote for Putin, I thought he was a good president, but then I found out the truth. The whole world will be destroyed in a nuclear conflict if he is not stopped. Only the cockroaches will survive.'

When I asked him if his description of Putin as a demon was merely a metaphor, Gabyshev insisted that it should be taken literally. 'The whole world is in danger,' he said, leaning forward as he spoke. 'Putin hides his horns.' One of his followers streamed our conversation live on YouTube, providing a modern-day twist to Russian shamanism. The police were keeping him under constant surveillance, Gabyshev told me. 'I am their biggest enemy,' he said.

Support for Putin in Yakutia was lukewarm: despite the efforts of officials loyal to the Kremlin to rig election results, the remote region often recorded the lowest nationwide vote returns for the president and his ruling party. Closer to Alaska than European Russia's big cities, it often felt like another country altogether. The Kremlin often seemed to view it that way, too, and pumping money into building up the armed forces was clearly more of a priority than investing in crumbling or non-existent civilian infrastructure in remote regions like Yakutia.

During the Siberian summer, when temperatures can soar to above 30 degrees Celsius, vast wildfires frequently break out across the region, shrouding it in toxic smoke and blocking out the sun. One year, I went to report on these apocalyptic blazes, driving for hours along dirt tracks to a remote village where locals were attempting to beat back the flames with little more than shovels and buckets of water. It later emerged that Putin had deployed fire-fighting planes to help quench blazes in Turkey, rather than to Yakutia.

For the first few hundred miles of his quixotic trek to Moscow, Gabyshev walked alone. But as he passed through towns and cities, dragging a yurt and a stove on a cart behind him, he gathered dozens of followers. They ranged from former convicts to students to hippy types and Gabyshev gave them new names, such as Angel, Raven or Owl. He called them 'The Heavenly Squad' and banned them from drinking alcohol. Ordinary Russians, from waitresses at roadside cafés to truck drivers, greeted the shaman and his acolytes like rock stars and donated money and food.[3]

By June 2019, Gabyshev and The Heavenly Squad had covered more than 1,700 miles. Meduza, an opposition website, described Gabyshev as 'a Russified, otherworldly Forrest Gump', while rock and rap musicians wrote songs in his honour.[4] Yet not everyone was so enthralled. At one stage of his trek, Gabyshev was confronted by a group of local pro-Putin shamans who accused him of spreading discord. '[Shamans] do not care about politics. We need harmony. We do not need a bloody war,' one of them said. Gabyshev heard them out and continued on his way.

Early that autumn, the arrest of some of the shaman's followers in Ulan-Ude, a city in eastern Siberia, triggered three days of protests that also saw demands for a rerun of rigged elections for Governor. In Chita, another city in Siberia, Gabyshev spoke at an opposition rally that was one of the biggest there in recent years, despite the Russian Orthodox Church, a key Kremlin ally, threatening to excommunicate anyone who attended. 'From now on, Putin is no longer your law! Live freely!' Gabyshev shouted from a makeshift stage. A banner featured a portrait of the shaman and the words 'Russia is with you.'

Gabyshev's long walk to Moscow coincided with the biggest demonstrations in the Russian capital for a decade, as furious opposition supporters took to the streets to protest yet more election-fixing by the Kremlin. Perhaps inevitably, a government official in Yakutsk alleged that the shaman was working on behalf of the United States to destabilize Russia. As his fame grew, the authorities in Moscow began to get nervous about the prospect of the shaman turning up at the gates of the Kremlin, as well as his epic journey through Russia's most economically depressed regions with an open message of insurrection. 'It was clear that they would clamp down on the shaman sooner or later,' said Alexei Kondaurov, a retired KGB major-general and former lawmaker.[5]

In September 2019, dozens of state security service officers arrested Gabyshev at gunpoint at a makeshift camp in Buryatia, a region in eastern Siberia. The raid on the camp was akin, witnesses said, to an anti-terrorist operation. 'Armed security services blocked the highway, quickly encircled our camp and headed straight to the shaman's tent,' Viktor Yegorov, one of Gabyshev's followers, said. 'They drove him off in an unknown direction.' The heavy-handed response triggered predictable mockery. 'Here he is – the great Putin,' Navalny wrote on social media. 'He was so afraid of the shaman from Yakutia that he had him arrested by 20 people with automatic weapons.'

Having detained Gabyshev, the authorities initially seemed unsure of what to do with him. A trial and a prison sentence would turn the anti-Putin shaman into a martyr, but if he was allowed to remain free, what was there to stop him setting off for the Kremlin again? Gabyshev was flown back to Yakutsk, where he was placed in a psychiatric hospital for examination. He was released two days later, but his movements were closely monitored by the authorities. In May 2020, he was forcibly hospitalized for two months, allegedly because he had refused to be tested for coronavirus. But he refused to back down. In January 2021, a year after I had visited him, Gabyshev announced a new march on Moscow. It was at that point a decision was taken to eliminate the problem of the troublesome shaman once and for all.

Before he could depart for the Kremlin again, dozens of riot police in full body armour and carrying metal shields stormed into his home, knocking Gabyshev to the ground and wrenching his arms behind his back. He was charged with extremism, a catch-all term in Russia for anyone who opposes Putin, and locked up in a grimy pre-trial detention centre, pending a new psychiatric evaluation. Predictably, state-appointed psychiatrists ruled that he was insane, a decision that was challenged by independent experts.

I knew someone was unhinged, but it wasn't Gabyshev. Sure, he was eccentric and unusual, but so were many people, including some of Putin's biggest supporters. He was certainly no more unstable than Zhirinovsky, the ultranationalist politician with a penchant for nuclear war. I had actually felt more comfortable sitting opposite Gabyshev, despite his long, sharp sword, than I had being in the same room with Zhirinovsky.

As one of the few Western journalists who had met the shaman, his lawyer asked me if I would agree to appear in court and testify to his mental health. I was out of the country at the time, however, and could not make the hearing. A few months later, Gabyshev was committed indefinitely to a high-security state psychiatric asylum.[6] I felt bad that I hadn't been able to speak in his defence, even though there was almost zero chance that my words would have influenced the court. As ever in Russia, the decision had been taken elsewhere, before the court hearing had even begun.

Doctors at the psychiatric hospital had reportedly testified that Gabyshev was no danger to himself or anyone else and that he should, at the very least, be transferred to a lower-security facility. Their advice was ignored, most likely on the orders of senior officials.[7] It was depressing beyond words to imagine Gabyshev, a man who loved to commune with the spirits of nature, confined to a Russian state institution for the insane. In a final insult, the shaman's pet dog, Bely, who had been living with a friend in Yakutsk since the police raid on his home, died after someone sprinkled rat poison on its food. The shaman's supporters suspected the animal had been killed to get at him.

Since the start of the war in Ukraine in 2022, the Kremlin has stamped out even the smallest signs of dissent. Yet back then, when Gabyshev and his followers were making their way towards Moscow, there was still some lingering tolerance for opposition. Why then did the authorities move so decisively against the shaman? Alexei Pryanishnikov, a human rights lawyer who defended Gabyshev at great personal risk to his own freedom, believes the answer lies in the widespread belief in Russia in magic and the occult.

'At first, when I first got involved in this case, in September 2019, I assumed that maybe they were afraid of these public events that took place during his trek, when there were [opposition] rallies that were quite well-attended for those regions,' he said.

'But my eyes were opened when I saw how much attention the security services paid to him. After all, it's no problem at all for the Russian government to crush street protests. I'm absolutely convinced now that influential figures in law enforcement and security agencies are afraid of all these not entirely understandable and irrational threats linked to shamanistic rituals. Apparently, there is an understanding that if a shaman is kept away from his land – and he has been locked up in a mental asylum far from his home region[8] – then he loses his power. It seems that the main reason the authorities are not easing the pressure on him is this fear of rites and rituals.'[9]

The suggestion that Russia's security chiefs had felt threatened by the shaman's purported magical powers was entirely plausible. Behind the facade of Putin's Russia lies a world unknown to most Westerners: a place where self-proclaimed urban witches use the dark arts to 'resolve' business and personal problems and political intrigue goes hand in hand with the occult. In 2010, there were estimated to be more occult/faith healers (800,000) in Russia than professional doctors (640,000). Two out of every three Russian women has consulted a psychic or a sorcerer, while in 2013 the national occult industry was estimated to be worth £20 billion a year. It was not at all far-fetched to assume that these beliefs extended to the Russian security services, as well as their bosses in Moscow.[10] 'The most frightening thing is that [the political elite] really saw a threat in the shaman's campaign,' said

Lev Rubinstein, a Russian poet and Kremlin critic. 'They really believe in shamans and wizards. And what if that shaman had stronger connections with important spirits than their shaman? You just never know.'[11]

Russia's mania for the occult and the paranormal has deep roots. In his seminal study of Russian folk culture, *Ivan the Fool*, Soviet-era dissident Andrei Sinyavsky detailed a widespread Tsarist-era belief in superstition, magic and pagan gods. 'In Old Russia, almost everyone resorted to elementary magic help,' wrote Sinyavsky. 'Magic was used on a daily basis.'

When Mikhail Gorbachev's perestroika and glasnost took hold in the late 1980s, these centuries-old occult beliefs flooded into the mainstream, turning society on its head. As Russians clambered for ideas to replace the certainties once supplied by the Soviet system, thousands of occultists offered 'magical services' and state television broadcast bizarre psychic healing sessions. The most famous of these Kremlin-approved psychics was Anatoly Kashpirovsky, a former weightlifter and qualified psychiatrist from Ukraine who achieved national fame.

Dressed all in black, Kashpirovsky 'treated' millions of television viewers every week. 'For those of you with high blood pressure, your blood pressure will lower...whoever has hip injuries, they will heal...' he intoned. In 1990, Kashpirovsky was named Man of the Year by several Soviet newspapers; a few years later, he was elected to parliament, where he served as an MP for two years.

Kashpirovsky's great rival was Allan Chumak, a former journalist who also claimed to possess mysterious healing powers. During his televised show, Chumak would silently and slowly, like some Soviet Zen master, move his hands for half-an-hour or so, 'charging' with healing energy the jars and saucepans full of water that his millions of viewers had placed around their flats.[12]

By the time I got to Russia in the late 1990s, Chumak and Kashpirovsky's stars had faded, but the country's mania for magic and the paranormal was as strong as ever. Over a beer, my new friends would tell me of love spells cast on acquaintances, while businesspeople would confess that they made use of clairvoyants or psychics to aid them in decision-making.

Countless sects sprung up, including one led by a former traffic cop who declared himself the Messiah and relocated with hundreds of followers to a remote spot in Siberia. Grigory Grabovoi, another sect leader, gained nationwide notoriety when he claimed to be able to 'resurrect' the victims of a school siege in Beslan, a small town in southern Russia, in 2004.[13]

Russia's fascination with the paranormal was far removed from the Soviet stereotypes that I had grown up with. Walking home at night through forests of concrete tower blocks, I imagined the occupants of the flats carrying out magical rituals in their bedrooms or casting spells in their living rooms. Flickering shadows behind curtains invariably took on sinister qualities as my imagination, fuelled by my lifelong love of horror films, ran wild. Over the years, I dug deep, visiting occultists and psychic healers across Moscow, from its gritty suburbs to Tverskaya, the glitzy street that leads directly to the Kremlin. Many of the occult practitioners that I spoke to insisted that they had high-level government officials as clients.

'They come in the middle of the night so that no one will see them,' a black-haired 'sorceress' told me at her office in central Moscow, a Soviet-era flat that had been painted black and redecorated with magical symbols. 'I can't name names, of course, but Russian government officials always consult sorcerers before taking major decisions.' A tiny mouse scrabbled in a glass on her desk; behind me, a black rabbit gnawed at the bars of its cage.

'The Russian authorities use psychics in their relations with other states,' another urban witch told me. 'Whenever there are big negotiations going on, Russia always brings a psychic or witch along. To influence things.' Was this something she knew, I asked, or just a hunch? 'It's something I know,' she said, daring me to contradict her.

On top of the usual curses and love spells, the occult industry also offered to magically protect clients against getting the sack by using their powers on unpleasant bosses, ensuring salary increases by bewitching the entire bookkeeping department, and even making sure that loan applications were approved. 'Casting spells on banks is more expensive though,' I was told by the owner of one business when I called to enquire further. Why? 'Because it involves black magic.'

This reliance on the occult was sad and absurd, but it also said much, I think, about the national tendency to abdicate responsibility to a higher authority, be it Vladimir Putin or a middle-aged sorceress on the outskirts of Moscow.

'Under the Soviet system, someone always took care of us, provided free healthcare and education, and, basically, decided everything for us. Where we should live, what we should eat, what we should wear and were we should or should not go,' Doctor Nikolai Naritsyn, an expert on his country's obsession with magical solutions to everyday problems, told me in Moscow. 'When it collapsed, lots of people felt like little children lost on the street. The occultists appeared then and said, "Come and see us! Pay us, and we will solve all your problems!"'

If the aim of occultists is to reshape reality through mantras and magic, then Kremlin propaganda now achieves the same thing through the relentless repetition of falsehoods, fake videos and appeals to memories of lost empire. The result has been widespread support for an irrational, senseless war in Ukraine and the elevation of Putin to something approaching a living god. Russia is teeming with self-proclaimed wizards and witches, but it was the Kremlin's propaganda agents who turned out to be the most powerful sorcerers of them all.

15

A City Soaked in Terror

As I walked the stairways of our apartment block in central Moscow, I sometimes imagined that I could hear the whispered complaints of the building's unhappy dead. Like everywhere in the city centre, our home had a bloody history of political terror. In 1938 alone, during Stalin's purges, three residents were dragged out of their flats by the Soviet secret police and executed on fictitious charges after summary trials at which no witnesses or defence lawyers were allowed.

Their names were: Symon Klimov, a scientist, Pavel Kudinov, a professor, and Alexander Vasilkovsky, a historian and expert on rare coins. Their bodies were all dumped in a mass burial site near Moscow. Vasilkovsky, who was falsely accused of being a member of a terrorist organization, had lived on the floor above ours. He was arrested on 19 March 1938, convicted on 27 April 1938 and executed that very same day. I found a black-and-white photograph of Vasilkovsky in the online archives of Memorial, Russia's oldest human rights group.[1] It showed a balding, white-haired man in his early sixties. His image stared out at me across the long years and I felt some kind of connection.

All three men's names were cleared posthumously, although not until many years after their executions. When I lay awake at night, listening to the nocturnal rumblings of our building, I tried to imagine the fear that Vasilkovsky must have experienced as he was torn from his everyday life by Stalin's sadistic ghouls. The archives did not reveal if he had a family, but I hoped that he did not: under the Soviet system of collective punishment, the spouses of 'enemies of the people' were usually sent to labour camps while their children were packed off to state-run facilities, where they would learn to thank Stalin for their 'happy childhoods'.

Almost every apartment block in central Moscow was haunted by the ghosts of Soviet terror. On our street, 48 people were murdered by the communist regime, with all but four of the arrests and executions taking place in 1937 and 1938, the height of the purges. Yet, while an abundance of commemorative plaques honoured Soviet military men and party officials, the darker side of the street, and indeed the city, was unknown to the majority of its residents, including those who lived in the very apartments that once housed Stalin's innocent victims.

This was not an oversight. Like the Soviet regime, Putin was prepared to deploy ruthless violence and politically motivated criminal charges to eliminate his critics. Reminding Russians of Stalin's crimes would only spark comparisons to his own intolerance of dissent. Instead, Putin sought to amplify Stalin's role in the defeat of Nazi Germany, while downplaying and suppressing the memory of the millions of people whose lives had been destroyed by the Soviet tyrant. Anyone who sought to dig up the past, sometimes literally, risked becoming themselves a victim of Putin's own purges.

In the far north of Russia, Yuri Dmitriev, a historian of the gulag labour camps who had uncovered Stalin-era mass graves, was arrested in 2016 and eventually sentenced to 15 years in prison on charges of sexually abusing his adopted daughter. Human rights groups and independent media said that the allegations were trumped-up as revenge for his refusal to stay quiet about the graves and the grisly warnings they contained about a new era of looming political violence under Putin.' Our state aims to wipe out the individual as if he never existed,' Dmitriev had said before his arrest.[2]

The European Union called the charges against him 'dubious' and urged Moscow to drop them.[3] Tellingly, in a country where fewer than 0.3 per cent of criminal trials result in an acquittal, it took three trials before a judge could be found to convict Dmitriev and hand him a lengthy term behind bars. His prosecution was a clear message from the Kremlin: let the dead lie.

Despite the heroic efforts of human rights groups, the memory of the Soviet purges began to take on a nebulous, almost mythical nature. 'Moscow is a city soaked in terror,' Arseny Roginsky, of Memorial, told me. 'But while everyone knows that lots of people died during the Stalin era, they are largely thought of as almost accidental victims, as if they were wiped out by some medieval-type plague, for which no one can be held responsible. They don't fully comprehend that this was a deliberate crime by the state against its own people.'[4]

In 2014, Sergei Parkhomenko, a veteran opposition journalist and human rights campaigner, decided to try and combat this historical amnesia. Inspired by German artist Gunter Demnig's 'stumbling stones' – tiny commemorative brass plaques installed on the street outside the final addresses of victims of Nazism – Parkhomenko launched a crowdfunded project to commemorate Russians whose lives had been cut short by the Soviet regime. Over the following years, he and other activists at Memorial placed hundreds of steel plaques on buildings where victims of Soviet terror had lived before their executions. In stark black lettering, the plaques stated the victim's date of birth, arrest and execution, as well as when the charges against them were officially recognized as groundless. One afternoon in 2015, I joined Parkhomenko as he drilled one of the plaques onto the wall of a building near our flat. The memorial was in honour of Boris Shternberg, a civil servant who was executed in 1937 after being tortured into confessing to a fabricated plot to poison Moscow's water supply. His granddaughter, Nina Kossman, had flown in from her home in New York, especially for the unveiling. 'We want children to see them and ask their parents about them. And for people to explain,' Parkhomenko told me. 'Russia is heading once more towards totalitarian terror. The aggressive nationalism that we are seeing now leads directly to the idea that the individual's life is worth nothing and that only the state's interests are important. But we say that there is nothing more important than human life.'

Parkhomenko had attempted to gain official permission for the project, but negotiations collapsed when Russia annexed Crimea from Ukraine, sparking a wave of nationalism. 'We have an unspoken agreement – we don't ask for permission and [the authorities] don't stop us. It's anyone's guess how long this will last, though,' he said. When Putin sent tanks into Ukraine in 2022, pro-Kremlin thugs with links to the security services began tearing down the memorial plaques from buildings across Moscow. 'We'll put them all up again when the darkness lifts,' Parkhomenko vowed. When that might be, he could not say.[5]

It had always been dangerous to be an opposition activist in Russia, but after Nemtsov's assassination, the risks escalated sharply. In 2014, Ildar Dadin became the first person to be sentenced under a new law that stipulated prison terms for anyone who was repeatedly detained at demonstrations, including at the peaceful, one-person protests that had led to his arrests. Amid angry scenes at a central Moscow courthouse in December 2015, Dadin, an avowed pacifist, was sentenced to three years in jail, a term that was later reduced by six months on appeal. 'Fascists!' his supporters screamed at the judge and court security, as he was led away in handcuffs. He was initially locked up in Moscow before being sent to a notorious penal colony in Karelia, a remote region in northwest Russia, where prison guards torture inmates to the sound of music by Lyube, Putin's favourite Russian rock group.

In September 2016, two months after Dadin's arrival at Penal Colony No. 7 in Karelia, his wife, Anastasia Zotova, received a letter from him that had been smuggled out of the prison camp by his lawyer. On the second day at the camp, he said, he was beaten 'a total of four times, by 10–12 people at once'. Dadin alleged the torture sessions were overseen by the penal colony boss, one Major Sergei Kossiyev. Worse was to come. '[Penal colony] staff cuffed my hands behind my back and hung me up,' Dadin wrote. 'Being suspended in this way caused a terrible pain in the wrists, twisted out my elbows, and brought about savage back pains. I was hung up like that for half an hour.' After that, he wrote, he was 'beaten regularly, several times a day'.

Zotova, a former journalist, was faced with a terrible dilemma. 'I realized there were three possible scenarios,' she told me, when I met her in a café on a freezing evening in central Moscow. 'One: I wouldn't make the letter public and then they wouldn't find out that Ildar had complained, but they would go on beating him. Two: I wouldn't make the letter public, but the prison camp authorities would somehow find out that Ildar had complained and beat him even worse. Three: I would make the letter public and then they would either stop beating him or beat him until he was half-dead. I decided to risk it.'[6]

Her mind made up, Zotova circulated Dadin's letter among opposition-friendly media and human rights groups. His vivid portrayal of prison camp torture also drew the attention of the European Parliament, which called for his immediate and unconditional release.[7] Russia's prison service and state media accused Dadin of lying, but his torture claims were backed up by fellow inmates who spoke to a visiting human rights lawyer. Prisoners who were kept in cells in different parts of the penal colony and had never met each other related almost identical stories of abuse, including the rock music by Lyube (sample song title: 'Don't Play the Fool, America!')[8] played at a deafening volume by prison staff. Some also spoke of being left almost naked for days on end in freezing punishment cells, while Muslim prisoners said they were tortured for refusing to eat pork or for praying.

Zotova began documenting the numerous allegations of torture at the penal colony. At a press conference in Moscow that she helped to organize, relatives and former inmates testified to widespread beatings at the camp. 'My son arrived on crutches, but he was immediately sent to the punishment cell,' said the mother of a 25-year-old inmate. 'They beat him there with a hammer until he lost consciousness. They hung him up by his legs, beat his feet, stuck his head down the toilet and poured cold water on him,' she said, tears rolling down her face.

Despite campaigning relentlessly for Dadin's release, Zotova was slowly losing hope and taking prescription-strength tranquilizers to cope with the stress. 'Other people think "yes, I know they beat people in prisons, that they hang them up by handcuffs and tear their fingernails out, but, well, I'm going to go and make some borscht. Or go to the cinema." But I just can't do that. I can't forget about it,' she told me. 'I've come to terms with the fact that things are never going to be good. That I might never see my husband again. That they could kill or cripple him in prison.'

I wanted to reassure her, but I also didn't want to give her false hope. Life was cheap in Putin's Russia, especially for anyone locked up in its brutal prison camps. Yet, in February 2017, Russia's Supreme Court ruled to quash Dadin's conviction on a legal technicality. The unexpected move was almost certainly ordered by the Kremlin after Dadin's case became a cause célèbre for international human rights organizations. It was a rare victory over the institutionalized state terror that so often went under the radar. Kossiyev, the head of the penal colony where Dadin had been tortured, was even imprisoned for two and a half years on abuse of office charges. He served just over six months, however, before he was granted a conditional release. He spent some of his time behind bars at a detention facility just 300 metres from his home, Russian opposition media reported.[9]

In an interview with Russian journalists immediately after his release, Dadin had difficulty speaking, stumbling over his words due to a crippling stutter he had developed while behind bars. The stutter was less pronounced when I spoke to him a few days later, but it was clear that his ordeal had left deep emotional scars.

'They beat me for three days, cuffed my hands behind my back and hung me up by the wrists. The prison guards took pleasure from torturing me. These people are sadists who are given the green light by Putin's fascist regime,' Dadin told me, when we met at the headquarters of a human rights group that was later banned by the Kremlin. Occasionally, he rose from his seat to demonstrate the sickening abuse that he had been subject to.

'After they'd broken me, prison guards forced me to shout: "Putin is our president",' he said. 'I was ready to do and agree to anything by this stage. I'd been reading George Orwell's *1984* before I was sent to the camp and I remembered how the hero of the novel had been willing to agree to have his loved one tortured just so they would leave him alone. I realized I was very close to this state of mind. I was considering suicide, because I realized that they had broken me, both physically and mentally, and I couldn't see the sense in living anymore.'

Dadin and Zotova were briefly one of the Russian opposition's most famous couples. Before his release, while she was fighting for his freedom, she had told me how she planned to get him out of Russia if he ever made it out of prison alive. 'I'm going to put him in a car, drive him off somewhere and then hide him for a very long time,' she said. It was not in the stars. Shortly after his release, the couple broke up.

In 2022, after the start of all-out war in Ukraine, Dadin travelled there to join up with Russians who were fighting alongside Kyiv's forces. Although he had insisted on peaceful protest against Putin, Dadin was now determined to take up arms. 'The only effective and remaining way for a Russian to resist Russian crimes is armed resistance,' he said. 'I no longer had any moral strength to achieve anything peacefully.' He dreamt of returning to Russia with a gun in his hands to help bring down Putin's regime.[10]

Putin may be toppled one day, but if he is, Dadin will not be there to see it. Two years later, Dadin was killed in a battle near Kharkiv; just one more life among hundreds of thousands that had been ground up in Russia's senseless war. Zotova did not comment on his death, at least publicly. He was just 42.[11]

Dadin's case was an increasingly rare example of Western pressure being able to alleviate the suffering of opposition activists who were brave enough to stand up to Putin and his thugs. In 2013, ahead of the Winter Olympics in Sochi, Putin had unexpectedly ordered the release from prison of Mikhail Khodorkovsky, the former oil tycoon, and two Pussy Riot activists in a bid to stop the event being overshadowed by protests. But by the time Russia hosted its next major sporting event, the 2018 FIFA World Cup, Putin was largely beyond caring about Moscow's international image. Still, the loved ones of political prisoners continued to speak to Western journalists like me in the hope that international coverage of their fates would force the Kremlin into some kind of compromise, or at the very least ensure that they would not be tortured in custody.

Yet, as the years went by and politically motivated violence became grimly routine, I sometimes worried that by covering the plights of dissidents, we might even be ensuring that they received harsher punishments. It was an uncomfortable, nagging thought. If there was no longer anything that we could feasibly do to help the unfortunate victims of Putin's regime, then what was the sense in all our reporting? I would spend hours, sometimes days, speaking to the relatives of opposition figures who had been tortured by police or prison guards, listening to their horrific stories for an article that would change absolutely nothing. In fact, it seemed more and more as if such reporting had more potential impact as a cautionary tale for readers in the West. This is what happens when a society is strangled; this will be your future, if you allow authoritarianism to take hold. It is also possible, of course, that most people simply shook their heads, thought 'it's so awful in Russia' and then got on with their days, without even reading until the end. After all, political terror was what people *expected* from the Putin regime. Where was the news here?

Years later, in Ukraine, I became briefly desensitized to the dangers of reporting from the war zone. In Russia, I heard so many accounts of torture that my feelings became blunted. In Moscow, I interviewed victims or their family members, recording their accounts of sickening, senseless abuse and then picked up my daughter from her nursery, laughing with her carers as they told me about her day. Once, while sitting in our local children's playground, I finished off an article on my phone about antifascist and anarchist activists who had been tortured into confessing to absurd terrorism allegations, including through the use of electrocution. When I looked down at the screen, horrific violence against defenceless prisoners. When I glanced up, children running and jumping in the sunshine. The thought, unwanted and unbidden, came suddenly: would any of these laughing children grow up to be the Kremlin's torturers? Would any become victims? I closed my eyes and banished the notion.

It wasn't just opposition figures who were being targeted by Putin's enforcers. The authorities didn't release official statistics, but figures collated by human rights activists suggested that hundreds of people were dying every year in police custody, beaten to death by officers who were intoxicated by a deadly cocktail of power and alcohol. Many of the suspect deaths were listed simply as 'a sudden deterioration in health conditions'. In 2019, research carried out by the Levada Center, the country's only independent pollster, indicated that an incredible one in ten Russians had been subject to some form of torture by law enforcement officers.[12] *One in ten*. The Kremlin disputed the figure.

'Torture has become an everyday thing. People are no longer surprised by news that someone was beaten in police custody. It's on the level of online pictures of cats and the weather forecast. It takes something really shocking to arouse interest,' Sergei Babinets, a lawyer with the Committee for the Prevention of Torture, told me at the group's office in Moscow. Like so many other organizations that sought to defend human rights in Russia, the group was forced to close down after the invasion of Ukraine in 2022.

When I travelled to Ukraine's war-ravaged towns and cities, I would frequently hear echoes of the violence that had become so common in Russia. The testimonies of Ukrainians who had spent months under Russian occupation were eerily familiar, the vile handiwork of Putin's troops an unwelcome reminder of the sadistic, monstrous evil that had engulfed Russia and had now extended its reach into Ukraine. The Kremlin's torturers enjoyed it when their victims screamed, I was told time and time again. These men, I suspected, didn't just want to hurt Ukrainians; they were happy to inflict pain on anyone they could. In occupied Ukraine, they were free to live out their sickest fantasies with very little fear that they would ever be held accountable for their crimes.

In a village in the Kherson region, Viktor Kopitok, a low-level Ukrainian official, told me that Russian soldiers had scalded him with a red-hot poker, leaving deep burn marks on his flesh. Every night for three weeks, he was locked in a cold, damp cellar in the yard of his own home. The entrance to the cellar, the soldiers told him, was booby trapped with a tripwire that would detonate explosives if he or anyone else opened it. I descended into the dark cellar; although it was hot outside, the sun's rays penetrated just a few inches under the metal door. There was a rough bed, some tattered books and a candle. I couldn't imagine what it must have been like for Kopitok to have been locked up for weeks down there, alone in the dark, in agonizing pain. 'I considered suicide,' he told me, two days after he had been freed by the Ukrainian army. He wiped away tears. 'Some of the soldiers were just sadists,' he said. 'I might look OK on the outside, but inside, I'm broken.'

In Odesa, I met Natalia, a woman who spent more than a year under occupation in another village in the Kherson region. Russian soldiers had beaten her and forced her to sign a suicide note after discovering that she had been passing on information to the Ukrainian army. They also threatened to torture her four children, the youngest of whom was just 9 years old. She closed the door of the room we were speaking in so that her children would not hear us. 'The soldier who interrogated me said his job was to shake up people's souls,' Natalia said. 'It looked like he enjoyed his work. He was smiling all the time.'

In Kyiv, I met with Anna Makhno, the mother of Leonid Popov, a 23-year-old man with suspected autism who had been seized by Putin's troops in Melitopol, a city in southern Ukraine that was under Russian occupation and beyond the other side of the raging frontlines. The last time he had been seen, Anna told me, Leonid had lost half of his body mass and weighed just six-and-a-half stone. He was 6 foot 5 inches tall. A local who saw Leonid in his cell later told Anna that he had spent most of the time lying on the floor, whispering: 'I want to eat, I want to eat...'. He had been beaten so badly, she said, that he could not go to the toilet for four days.

'He regressed to the developmental level of a 10-year-old. He needs medical and psychiatric help. Instead, they tortured him,' Anna said. Once, during a brief period of freedom that lasted less than an hour, Leonid managed to call his mother. 'I was in hell,' he told her. 'Remember how you used to tell me about hell when I was a child and we went to church? Mum, now I know what hell is.' That was about all he had time for: as he was walking home, he was seized again by Russian troops who forced him to put a bag over his own head and muscled him into a vehicle.

When I met his mother in Kyiv, Leonid's whereabouts were unknown; Anna did not even know if he was alive. After he had vanished, she said, her son's account on the Telegram messaging app had become active and she fired off a message in Ukrainian, hoping against hope. When there was no reply, she wrote in Russian: 'Maybe it's not you? Is my son still alive?' A reply flashed up: 'No.' After she had sent a flurry of furious messages demanding answers, she received another terse message. 'Go fuck yourself,' it read. No further messages were forthcoming.[13]

Anna was trying to stay calm, to tell her son's story, in the hope that someone, somewhere, with the power to help might read it. But once again I felt the same sense of hopelessness that I had when reporting on the miserable fates of Russia's dissidents. The war was so vast, its hunger so ravenous that its victims were soon forgotten by everyone apart from their loved ones. Even as we spoke, I realized and felt ashamed of the knowledge, that my memory of Anna and her son would eventually fade as I encountered more grief and despair across Ukraine.

Around a year later, Leonid was discovered in a Russian jail in eastern Ukraine. He had been charged, absurdly, with espionage and faced up to 20 years in prison. When I heard the news, I thought back to my conversation with his mother. 'I have to stay strong,' she had said. 'Good will triumph in the end. Right?' I had smiled and tried to reassure her that it would. I am not certain that she believed me. But that was hardly surprising, I barely believed it myself.

16

Deliver Us from Evil

On my first trip to Ukraine after the start of the war, following my final departure from Moscow, I visited a humanitarian aid centre in Kyiv for internally displaced people from Mariupol, the port city that was flattened by Russian bombs in the spring of 2022. Some of those seeking assistance at the centre had huddled in basements for three months as missiles pounded the city above them, reducing it to rubble.

'What did we do to deserve this?' Volodymyr, an elderly man, asked me. He repeated the question three more times during our short conversation, gazing blankly at some point over my left shoulder. I had no answer for him besides 'nothing', but he barely seemed to register my reply. He then walked off, unsteadily, to collect a food package from aid workers.

I had visited Mariupol in late 2018, after Russia fired on Ukrainian naval vessels in the nearby Kerch Strait. Just 35 miles from the Russian border, few of Mariupol's residents had believed that the Kremlin was capable of such a devastating, unprovoked attack on their city. The military officials that I spoke to there at the time also seemed sceptical that even Putin could be so unhinged as to launch a full-scale military assault on a city of 450,000 people. We know now, of course, that he was, and more. The final death toll from the onslaught on Mariupol will likely never be known, at least while it remains in Russian hands. Some estimates have put it at 75,000.[1]

It's hard for me to imagine that the streets I once walked in Mariupol have been erased by Russian bombs. For those who once lived there, it is an immeasurable pain that even a lifetime will not diminish. Understandably, many of the people at the humanitarian aid centre were in urgent need of psychological help. One woman who had fled Mariupol had recently flung herself from the 15th floor of a building in Kyiv after succumbing to depression, I was told. Such was the demand that Anna Chasovnikova, a psychologist who had also escaped the carpet bombing of Mariupol, could only spare ten minutes to talk to me.

'Lots of people in Mariupol have relatives in Russia. Some people may even have been pro-Russian,' she told me, as we sat in her office. 'People simply don't understand how a neighbouring country could attack us. We were supposed to be fraternal nations that helped one another, right?' she said, her voice dripping with bitter sarcasm and disgust. 'My godmother in Moscow wrote me a message a few days into the war that said: "Anna, don't worry, we are coming to liberate you." But liberate me from what? From my family, my work, my life? What exactly did they think they were liberating us from?'

I heard of such things over and over again. Millions of Russians had either cut off all ties with friends and family in Ukraine or insisted that they should just sit tight until their army had 'denazified' the country. In Kyiv, Lyubov Zavalnyuk, a presenter with February Morning, a Russian-language media outlet whose broadcasts were aimed at convincing Russians to turn against Putin, told me how she had phoned a cousin in Russia at the start of the war, expecting to hear words of support or concern.

'I told her that I was terrified, but she answered: "It's nothing so awful. Just sit tight for three days and it will all be over." A few days later, I wrote to her and told her that our people were being killed. She replied, "This is all American propaganda, this is all being staged." I wrote her an angry message in reply and we haven't spoken since.'

On one of my trips to Zaporizhzhia, a besieged city in southeast Ukraine, I visited the relatives of a friend from Russia. Svetlana was the only member of her family who had stayed in touch with them, the rest had cut off all contact as soon as the first Russian tanks crossed the border. 'How can my mum think Auntie Olia and her neighbours are Nazis?' Svetlana asked me in a text message. 'We've all spent summers in Zaporizhzhia. Where did they see any fascists?' She later sent another message: 'I feel so ashamed and helpless.'

Olia and her family lived on the tenth floor of a block of flats on the outskirts of the city and they could often hear Russian missiles or drones flying overhead. But, like many families worn down by the war and grimly accustomed to danger, they had long given up running to the air raid shelters when the sirens sounded, as they did almost every night. 'The shelter is in a school across the road. We have to get downstairs and then sprint across an open space to get there,' she told me, as I sat in the family kitchen along with her husband, daughter and grandson. Instead, they were observing the government's rule of two walls, taking shelter in the bathroom or between rooms to protect themselves from any flying glass or debris.

Like millions of Ukrainians, Olia and her family were Russian speakers who had no wish to live under the Kremlin's rule. Her husband, Pavlo, had even taken to watching Russian state television to try and understand what had happened to the people across the border. 'I just don't get it,' he told me. 'Do they really believe all that stuff about us?' He and his wife were confused and upset by the lack of contact from most of their relatives in Russia, as well as in Belarus, the Kremlin's biggest ally in Europe. 'Maybe they are afraid?' Olia asked, charitably. But I could see she didn't believe it.

I felt this sense of betrayal perhaps most keenly in Kharkiv, Ukraine's second biggest city. Just 20 miles from the Russian border, Kharkiv had been targeted relentlessly by the Kremlin's invading forces. The city was so close to Russia that it took less than a minute for missiles to land and they often exploded before the air raid sirens even had time to start up. Indiscriminate rocket attacks were woven into the fabric of daily life. People had been killed in their homes and in the streets, in playgrounds and at bus stops or while queuing for food. On one visit to Kharkiv in

January 2023, I went to the city's so-called rocket graveyard, an area in an industrial estate where prosecutors had gathered over 1,000 Russian missiles that had been fired at the city. None of them, I was told, had hit military targets.

'There are Kalibr cruise missiles, Iskanders, BM-30 Smerch, Grad and Uragan rockets, as well as Kh-101 and Kh-55 cruise missiles here,' Vladyslav Karpov, a spokesman for the city's prosecutor's office, told me, rattling off with grim efficiency the names of the rockets whose shattered, metallic carcasses covered almost every inch of the frosty ground. Kharkiv's 1.3 million residents mainly speak Russian as their first language, but since the start of the invasion some had switched to Ukrainian. 'I regret that I ever spoke Russian,' one local told me, next to the charred ruins of a building that had been destroyed by a rocket. 'The Russians used to come here from Belgorod on day trips and visit the markets and theatres and so on,' she said, referring to the Russian city on the other side of the border. 'And now they are bombing us! I will never speak to any of them again. Are they all brainwashed?'

A crude analogy, it occurred to me, would be if Wales had gained independence from the United Kingdom and, more than 30 years later, English troops based in Bristol had begun bombing Cardiff after the BBC had claimed that the Welsh were a nation of Nazis.

Others in Kharkiv had no intention of switching to Ukrainian, yet their fury was just as great. Again and again, people told me, in flawless Russian, how much they hated Russians. 'They bomb every night as if they have a schedule,' Valentin Turansky, a resident of Saltivka, a sprawling estate on the edge of the city that had been devastated by missile attacks, told me. 'They start at 2 a.m., you try to fall asleep, then at 3 a.m., another blast. Then at 4 a.m. and so on. I get around an hour and a half of sleep a night. I sleep with my windows open because I'm worried about glass shattering if there is an explosion nearby. Once, the sound waves from a blast threw my blanket off my bed.'

We were talking in the bar at Kharkiv's Park Hotel, a popular spot for journalists where I stayed on my first few trips to the city.

Like so many other buildings in Kharkiv, it was later destroyed by a Russian missile. 'You know that song that goes: "Do you want me to kill the neighbours who are disturbing your sleep?"' Valentin asked. I nodded. Yes, I knew it. The song was by Zemfira, a Russian singer-songwriter. A catchy and sentimental rock track called simply 'Do You Want?'[2] it was a big hit in the 2000s across the former Soviet Union. Its lyrics are a litany of outlandish proposals to a lover. 'Do you want the Alps outside the window? The sun instead of a lamp?' and so on, including the proposal to do away with the noisy neighbours. Valentin smiled wearily and took a swig of beer. 'I do,' he said. 'I really want someone to kill the neighbours.' We drank up. I reflected that it was just 170 miles to the north, to Voronezh, where my mother-in-law lived. I could have made the journey in a few hours in peacetime.

It wasn't Putin who was firing these missiles, Ukrainians constantly reminded me. They were being launched by anonymous Russian citizens, men and women whose daily work routines consisted of delivering death to ordinary people on the other side of the border that they had never met. When an exiled Russian opposition journalist tracked down a military commander who was believed to have been responsible for an attack on a block of flats in Dnipro that killed over 45 people to ask him if he felt any shame or guilt, he accused her of being a Ukrainian reporter. 'In Russia, journalists don't ask questions like that,' Colonel Dmitry Golenkov said. 'Journalists don't ask questions at all.'[3] He was later bludgeoned to death in western Russia by an unknown assailant. Ukraine's military intelligence service claimed responsibility for his assassination. The Russian colonel had, it said, been killed by a 'hammer of justice'.[4]

Everywhere I went in Ukraine after the start of Moscow's all-out war, people spoke of their loathing for Russians. 'There is more humanity in the eyes of a homeless dog than there is in the entire Russian nation,' a man told me in Dnipro, as we visited the site of yet another missile attack on a civilian target. In Zaporizhzhia, I was taken into a military hospital ward by a Ukrainian doctor called Dmytro. There were four beds, each occupied by a severely injured soldier. All of them were unconscious, breathing with the aid of machines. At least one had lost a limb. 'And people say we should make peace with the Russians?' Dmytro said. 'My generation, at the very least, will never do this.' He turned away so that we did not see the tears welling in his eyes and walked slowly back to his office.

I understood the hatred and it would have been obscene to try and explain to Ukrainians who had lost loved ones or had otherwise suffered at the hands of the Kremlin's troops that not all Russians supported Putin or approved of his maniacal war. The only thing I could do in such cases was to offer my commiserations while highlighting Russia's war crimes in my articles. Yet, just as it was only natural for me to feel hatred and disgust for the Russians who had killed and tortured so many Ukrainians, as well as those who supported the invasion, it was also natural, in my case at least, to be affected by hearing all Russians referred to as orcs, or slaves, two of the most common slurs. It was unrealistic, of course, to expect cool heads in a country that was fighting off an unprovoked invasion aimed at wiping it from the map, but the rhetoric, often from senior Ukrainian officials, was sometimes hard to understand. In 2023, Oleksii Danilov, at the time the head of Ukraine's national security council, told national television that what he called the lack of humanity among Russians could be explained by one simple fact. 'They are Asians,' he said.[5]

Aside from the troubling racism, it was also hard to see the logic behind Danilov's comments. Was he referring to ethnic Russians? Or Russian passport holders? Either way, it made no sense. There are millions of ethnic Russians in Ukraine, including General Oleksandr Syrskyi, who was at the time the commander of Ukrainian ground forces. If he meant Russian passport holders, then his statement was also confusing; after all, ethnicity is not linked to citizenship.

I was under no illusions about the nature of Russian society and the high level of support for the war, but there was a clear contradiction in recognizing Russia as a brutal, totalitarian state and simultaneously blaming all its people for the sins of the regime. I was wary, though, about raising the issue with civilians and usually only spoke about it with officials, soldiers or journalists whom I felt were open to such discussions. Sometimes, I heard surprising things.

'I no longer consider all Russians to be bad. There are good Russians, just as there are bad Ukrainians,' Major Ivan Skuratovsky, who had been at war since Putin first sent troops into eastern Ukraine in 2014, told me when we spoke near the frontlines in the Donetsk region. 'To say that all Russians are bad is essentially Nazism or fascism. Inciting hatred on the basis of nationality is what they do. If we do the same, then we are no better than them.' He thought for a second. 'I understand that a lot of people will want to draw and quarter me for these words.'

Skuratovsky was correct that such sentiments were relatively rare in Ukraine, as well as controversial. Yet, it was fairly basic stuff, clearly not *all* Russians (Newborn babies? Teenagers who were not even born when Putin came to power? People who went to prison for opposing the Kremlin?) were evil warmongers and not all of them were culpable for the war. 'There are good people and there are bad people, and that's it,' Olia, the relative of a Russian friend, had told me in Zaporizhzhia.

It was also true that there were 'bad Ukrainians', as Skuratovsky put it. Without the collaboration of many Ukrainians, including teachers and officials, it would have been much harder for Russia to impose its rule in the east and south of the country. Many lower-level collaborators were, of course, acting out of fear, but a significant number had gone over to the Kremlin for ideological reasons, succumbing to the insanity that had grown unchecked inside Russia before bursting across the border with such appalling consequences. In 2022, Moscow installed Vladimir Saldo, a former Ukrainian MP, as head of the occupied areas of the Kherson region. He had previously served three terms as the mayor of the regional capital. It also appointed Yevgeny Balitsky, another ex-Ukrainian MP, as the top official in the parts of the Zaporizhzhia region that were under its control.

In Izyum, a town in eastern Ukraine where the Kremlin's forces killed over 400 people, often torturing them to death, a local woman told me that some of the cruellest troops had been from Luhansk, a Ukrainian region that had been under Moscow's control for over a decade. Maksym Chumak, a Ukrainian serviceman and former teacher who had fled Luhansk in 2014, also told me that during the battle for Mariupol, troops from occupied regions of eastern Ukraine had often been 'more brutal in their treatment of civilians and Ukrainian military personnel' than even Russian soldiers. Their cruelty was, he suggested, a result of exposure to the Kremlin's lies about Ukraine and a means of proving their loyalty to Moscow. He also said he knew at least two people from Luhansk, a former classmate and an ex-pupil, who had been killed while fighting for Russia. 'I won't lie – I was glad when I heard that they had died,' he told me.

A belief in Russian collective guilt also suggested the necessity of collective punishment, with all of its awful implications. At the end of World War Two, between half a million and 1.5 million ethnic Germans are said to have died when they were forcibly deported from central and eastern Europe with the knowledge and assistance of the American, British and Soviet governments. The vast majority of the victims were women and children.[6] No one, of course, was suggesting that Russians could meet a similar fate, yet even among Westerners far from the frontlines there was a disturbing level of hatred.

One prominent group on social media, Nafo, had been set up to counter Russian online propaganda, but often seemed to act as an outlet for the bloodlust of its members, many of whom were middle-aged men in western Europe or America. When a 23-year-old Russian tourist was killed by a shark in Egypt, Nafo declared the fish was its 'employee of the month'. When a young Russian woman died in Tbilisi, the capital of Georgia, after falling headfirst into an underpass, Nafo members gleefully mocked her death, even though they knew nothing about her. Despite this, the group was supported by senior government officials in Estonia and Lithuania.[7]

Such blind hatred was self-defeating. As Ukraine's outgunned and outnumbered troops struggled to fight back against the Kremlin's invading army, some officials in Kyiv admitted to me that they believed a revolt in Moscow was the best chance of ending the war. I was unconvinced that Russians would rise up, yet reinforcing Putin's message that they were universally loathed in the West would only ensure that they did not.

Although I was deeply opposed to the idea of collective guilt, I could not bring myself to forgive or maintain contact with the few Russians I knew who were in favour of their country's actions in Ukraine. They were as good as dead to me and I wanted nothing more to do with them. It was pointless to try and convince them that they were being lied to and the attempt, I knew, would only depress me further. I was consumed with a loathing, deep and undiluted, for everyone in Russia who acted as cheerleaders for the invasion. It wasn't a feeling I enjoyed but suppressing it would have been even more damaging, and a lie to myself. So, I embraced the hatred. Some of it, I have sought to leave behind on these pages.

One way, of course, to avoid these conflicting emotions in the war zone would have been to refuse all reporting assignments to Ukraine. Yet that was hardly feasible, unless I quit being a foreign correspondent altogether. And, besides, I felt I had a responsibility to report on the war, on the atrocities committed by the country that I had called home for so very long. I wanted to give the victims of Russia's invasion a voice at the very least. And there were plenty of opportunities for that.

In November 2022, the Ukrainian army forced Putin's troops to withdraw from Kherson, a city in the south of the country. With a pre-war population of 300,000, Kherson was the only regional centre to have been captured by the Kremlin. It had spent eight long months under occupation, its people terrorized by Russian troops for even the slightest pro-Ukrainian sentiments. On the morning after its liberation, I set out towards the city with Kateryna Malofieieva, a Ukrainian journalist and friend.

Kateryna knew very well what it was like to have your home occupied by Russia. In 2014, Donetsk, her home city, had been seized by Kremlin-backed forces who swiftly transformed it into a place of terror where anyone who spoke out risked being thrown into torture chambers. The most notorious was called Izolyatsia and had once been an arts centre before it was taken over by Russia's FSB security service. Its prisoners were physically, sexually and psychologically brutalized by Russian agents, as well as locals who were loyal to Putin. People who lived near to the prison complained that they were unable to sleep because of the constant screaming.[8]

Around three weeks after Russian tanks crossed the border in 2022, Kateryna's mother died after an illness in Donetsk, piling trauma upon trauma. The invasion meant there was no way she could safely return home to place flowers on her mother's grave. With Donetsk on the other side of a raging frontline, the city, just 400 miles east of Kyiv, may as well have been on the dark side of the moon, at least as far as Kateryna was concerned.

The road to Kherson was eerily empty and littered with the unmistakable debris of war. Destroyed villages lined both sides of the motorway and twisted Russian rockets jutted out from the ground. Ukrainian officials had banned journalists from visiting Kherson until it had been cleared of landmines, tripwires and saboteurs, but we reasoned that it couldn't be any more dangerous than the other front-line towns and cities we had visited. Indeed, just a month earlier, we had driven to the outskirts of Lyman, a town in eastern Ukraine, shortly after it had been liberated by Kyiv's forces. The gutted remains of Russian armoured vehicles were strewn across the land like slaughtered metal beasts, while huge anti-tank mines dotted the road in the darkness. Occasionally, a gunshot would sound in the forest that lined the shattered road. The dangers were exacerbated by our driver, who had one eye on the road and the other fixed firmly on nude photos that his girlfriend was sending to his phone. Sometimes, it seemed that all of his attention was fixed on the erotic images. 'A mine!' shouted Kateryna, as an explosive device loomed ahead of us. 'I saw it,' shrugged the driver and swerved to safety. It was a reminder that war was not only horrifying, brutal and senseless, but also, on occasion, utterly surreal.

Through a combination of naked cheek and luck, we managed to talk our way through multiple Ukrainian army and police checkpoints and get into Kherson. Our cover story was so ludicrous – we weren't heading to Kherson, but to a nearby village – that I am still not sure how we managed it. The last of the roadblocks was located on the very edge of the newly liberated city. Inside Kherson, people had already begun tearing down the propaganda posters that had been erected by the Russians. 'Kherson – For ever with Russia!' one read: next to it, a group of gleeful teenagers were posing for selfies, their middle fingers outstretched in joyful defiance. In the centre of the city, on Freedom Square, a crowd of flag-waving locals greeted their victorious soldiers like rock stars. A shout of joy went up as a captured Russian Grad rocket launcher was dragged through the main street by a Ukrainian military truck. A trumpeter played the national anthem and the crowd sang the words, its first line echoing around the square: 'Ukraine's glory and freedom have not yet perished, nor its will…'.

Such scenes, it occurred to me, had not been seen in Europe since 1945 and the liberation of cities across the continent from Nazi forces. I felt privileged to be witnessing them. Putin had thought Ukrainian statehood was so weak, that its people would not resist his troops: instead, his botched invasion had strengthened Ukraine's idea of itself as a united country. Kherson was a Russian-speaking city, yet as was made clear time and time again across wartime Ukraine, language was no indication of political loyalties.

Before they retreated, the Russians had destroyed key infrastructure, leaving the city without running water and electricity, as well as phone and internet service. Desperate to contact relatives, people gathered on the right side of the Dnipro River to try and catch a phone signal from Russian-controlled territory on the opposite bank. As we joined them, Russian soldiers opened fire across the river. The crackle of automatic gunfire filled the air and we beat a hasty retreat. As evening fell, a jubilant chaos descended on Kherson. The Russians had fled and the Ukrainians had not yet deployed enough troops to the city to re-establish order. The sense of unreality was exacerbated by the fact that no one was sure what time it was; the Russians had forced Kherson to live by Moscow time – an hour ahead of Ukraine – and not everyone had reset their watches. In a café near the riverbank, I got into conversation with a man who had escaped from prison when the Russian army undertook its chaotic withdrawal. He had been serving time for robbery, he said, but wanted to get home to western Ukraine. He pumped me for details about the road out of Kherson.

I still had to file my article, which meant heading back to the riverbank and trying to 'hotspot' on the mobile connection of a local who had managed to get a signal with a Russian SIM card. After having done so, I was deep in conversation with an editor in London when the local who had helped us out tapped me on the shoulder. 'Is Birmingham really a dump?' he asked. It turned out that Dmytro was a big fan of *Peaky Blinders*, the British drama that is set in the Midlands. We got talking and he invited us back to his house, which he shared with his father and grandmother. As we sat around a table in their kitchen, Dmytro, a bearded computer programmer, told us stories of life under Russian occupation, of the torture and fear that had become commonplace as Putin's troops prowled the streets, on the lookout for pro-Ukraine activists.

'It was so terrifying to walk along the street and hear the screams of people being tortured. I'll never be able to forget this. The Russians would stop us and check our phones. If they found even a hint that you were pro-Ukrainian, they would lock you up and beat you. When I saw our soldiers entering the city I thought it was a dream,' he said.

As we ate, Dmytro opened a bottle of the family's samogon, the homemade alcoholic drink. 'It's not every day that Kherson gets liberated,' he said, as he poured us all shots. 'Death to our enemies,' he said, and raised his glass. The boom of explosions sounded in the near distance: the Russians had only retreated as far as the other side of the Dnipro River and were already pounding the city with artillery.

We drank more, washing back the samogon with Iranian knock-off Coca Cola that had been brought in by Russian troops. In the bathroom, I noticed that the family had been using scraps of a Kremlin propaganda newspaper as toilet paper. At one stage in the evening, as the Ukrainians spoke of their hatred for Russians, I tried to explain, drunkenly, that not everyone in Russia supported Putin or his war, but it was too early for such things and the pain was too raw. I instantly regretted the comment. 'I hate them all,' growled Dmytro and poured us all another drink. He wasn't offended though: when we left, he handed me a full bottle of samogon to take with me. Somehow, I forgot to pick it up and, as we were walking unsteadily back through a pitch-black park to our accommodation, explosions echoing across the city, he came sprinting down the path after us. 'The samogon!' Dmytro said, breathless from his exertions, holding the plastic bottle aloft like a trophy.

The next day, as locals continued to celebrate, the extent of the horrors inflicted by Putin's troops grew clearer. At a former Ukrainian police detention facility that had been used by the Russians to hold prisoners, a 65-year-old man called Vitali told us how he had been seized by FSB officers who placed a bag over his head. After demanding that he reveal the location of his son, a Ukrainian soldier, they connected a wind-up electric generator to a pair of metal clamps and attached them to his groin. 'Where is your son? Where are the weapons?' they screamed. When Vitali was unable to answer to their satisfaction, they turned on the power. 'The pain was indescribable,' he told us, as he stood in the cell where he had been held. 'It went in waves up my body.'[9]

I'd heard of this torture technique during my time in Moscow: Russian police called it 'a phone call to Putin'. And now, like so much else that was rotten and inhuman in Russia, they had exported it to Ukraine. In some cells, chairs were clamped to the floor, makeshift handcuffs still attached to their frames. A former prisoner sat sobbing in a corner. 'The animals,' he shouted, as he rocked back and forth in the darkness. 'They burnt me,' he said, pulling up his top to reveal red welted flesh on his shoulder. Locals told us the sound of screaming had begun at the detention centre in the early evening and lasted throughout the night. 'They would bring elderly people in, pregnant women, anyone,' said a shop assistant. In one cell, someone had scratched the words of the Lord's Prayer onto a wall. '...forgive us our trespasses, as we forgive those who trespass against us. And lead us not into temptation; but deliver us from evil.' Salvation had come to Kherson eventually, but for many it was too late.

In a garage, Russian troops had scrawled a huge Z and an obscene image of a naked woman as well as the words 'Zele we are coming,' a reference to Zelensky. Elsewhere inside the torture chamber, they had written 'Glory to Russian soldiers' and 'Honour and Glory to our Fallen Brothers' on the walls. It was beyond my understanding what they thought was so honourable or glorious about wiring up a pensioner's genitals to an electric-shock device and cranking up the power. In any case, I'd long stopped trying to make sense of Russia's war.

My insistence that not all Russians were behind Putin may have been inappropriate that night in Kherson, but it was a fact. Protests had broken out across Russia on the same day that the Kremlin began its invasion. From Moscow and St Petersburg to deepest Siberia, thousands of people had taken to the streets chanting

'No War!' Along with opposition figures, celebrities, sportspeople and teachers also spoke out. In Paris, Oleg Anisimov, the head of a Russian delegation to a United Nations climate conference, apologized for the invasion, saying there was no justification for it.[10] But Putin was determined to crush anti-war dissent. Within the first week of the conflict, there were around 5,500 arrests, as riot police moved swiftly to break up rallies and crack heads. The detainees came from a cross-section of society, from students to pensioners, from blue-collar workers to journalists. Protesters were threatened with rape or beaten in custody, while others were handed military draft papers. Yet many were prepared to go to prison rather than stay silent.[11]

Vladimir Kara-Murza, a long-time opposition figure, was sentenced to 25 years on treason charges after travelling specifically from his family home in the United States to try and lead anti-war protests; Alexandra Skochilenko, an artist, was sent to prison for seven years for replacing price stickers in her local supermarket with anti-war messages, while Ilya Yashin, an opposition politician, was jailed for eight and a half years for condemning the Russian army's atrocities in a series of social media videos. 'With one hand, Putin strikes at Ukraine, but with the other he squeezes the throat of Russian society,' Yashin told me later in a handwritten letter from Moscow's notorious Butyrka prison.[12]

An ally of Nemtsov and Navalny, Yashin had been involved in opposition politics since Putin's first term, starting out as a firebrand activist ready to scrap it out on the streets with the Kremlin's acolytes. He had investigated Kremlin corruption, led protest marches and even managed, against all the odds, to get elected as a city councillor in Moscow. I had called him before I left Russia, while he was still free. Upon hearing I was still in the country, he joked, darkly: 'So there's just me, you and Navalny left here.' I was impressed that he could still laugh, despite the inevitable punishment that awaited him for calling out the Kremlin's murderers.

All three of these opposition activists, as well as Oleg Orlov, the human rights activist who had described Russia's 'deal with the devil', were released in a historic East–West prisoner swap in Ankara in August 2024 that also secured freedom for Evan Gershkovich, the American journalist I had known in Moscow. But many more anti-war protesters remained in Russian prisons. Among them was Alexei Gorinov, a Moscow district councillor, who was imprisoned for seven years for saying that it was inappropriate to hold an arts festival while children were dying in Ukraine. Artyom Kamardin, a poet, also got seven years for reciting his anti-war verse in central Moscow. It included lines such as 'Kill me, militiaman! You've already tasted blood! You've seen how your brothers-at-arms dig mass graves for the brotherly nation.' The armed police who raided Kamardin's flat beat him savagely. 'They took photos of him covered in blood on the floor and then showed them to me,' his fiancée, Alexandra, told me. She was held in another room during the raid by officers who kicked her and threatened to shoot her. The youngest person to be imprisoned over their opposition to the war was Arseny Turbin, a 15-year-old who was given a five-year jail sentence after distributing anti-Putin flyers to his neighbours.[13] I didn't know much else about Turbin's case, but I knew enough to understand that he bore no responsibility for Russia's invasion.

Yet many Russian opposition activists were haunted by feelings of guilt. Was there more that they could have done, and should have done, to prevent Putin from unleashing his demons on Ukraine? How had they allowed this to happen? 'I don't know what else I could have done, but when I talk to Ukrainian refugees, I want to cry,' Tatiana Usmanova, an anti-Putin activist whose husband, Andrei Pivovarov, was among those freed in the 2024 prisoner exchange, told me.

On the day that Evan Gershkovich was arrested, I was visiting Mikhail Shishkin, one of Russia's best-known modern writers, at his home in Switzerland. In 2013, Shishkin had refused to represent Putin's 'corrupt, criminal regime' at an international literary event and he had not been back to Russia since the Kremlin annexed Crimea a year later. His novels had been translated into dozens of languages, but the atrocities carried out by the Kremlin's forces in Ukrainian towns and cities such as Bucha had forced him to question the sense of not only his life's work, but also the very meaning of Russia's rich cultural tradition.

'What can we say to Ukrainians whose houses were destroyed, whose family and friends were killed? That there are wonderful Russian writers and that the Russian language is beautiful?' he asked as we sat in his kitchen with its view of his idyllic garden.

'If there is Russian culture, if there is Tolstoy, if there is Rachmaninov and so on, then how was Bucha possible? This means that all the books that I wrote, and that my colleagues wrote over the past 20, 30 years ... we are just losers. What did we write them for, if this catastrophe was possible?'

He was not the only Russian cultural figure having such thoughts. 'We should have fought [Putin] more actively,' a man tells his girlfriend in an episode of *Masyanya*, a satirical Russian cartoon series, that was set at the start of the invasion. 'But you were always "no politics, please, no politics". Here is the result of your "no politics".'

The series, which was created by Oleg Kuvaev, an animator and critic of the war in Ukraine, had been vastly popular in Russia for years, but in the aftermath of the invasion it became darker and more radical. One episode portrays Masyanya, the cartoon's eponymous heroine, goading Putin into killing himself with a ceremonial sword. 'There's only one Nazi here: you,' she tells him. 'You are a monster, Putin, admit it. Thousands of innocent people are dying because of you and your bloated inferiority complex, you moron.'[14]

But many artists struggled to see the point in continuing to create. The despair was best summed up by Nadya Raplya, a Russian dissident artist, who, after fleeing Moscow, scrawled on a canvas the words: '*A Pozdno, Blyat, Risovat.*' (It's Too Fucking Late to Draw.)

Eight months after my meeting with Shishkin, I was in Kharkiv, the war-shattered Ukrainian city, when the news came through that Navalny, the undisputed leader of the Russian opposition, had died in prison. Unlike the assassination of Nemtsov near Red Square in 2015, a killing that signalled the start of Putin's brutal war against the opposition, Navalny's death felt grimly inevitable, a dark coda to the Kremlin's destruction of all dissent inside Russia.

Navalny had already survived one assassination attempt in 2020, when FSB security service agents had poisoned him with Novichok, a Soviet-era nerve agent, in Siberia. After international pressure, Putin allowed him to be airlifted to a clinic in Berlin for treatment. Yet, five months later, having barely recovered from his ordeal, Navalny boarded a flight to Moscow. He was arrested as soon as he landed. It was his last day as a free man.

His death was announced by Russian state television in a news item that lasted just 32 seconds. It was just one of a handful of occasions that Navalny's name had been uttered on national television, yet the report made no mention of who he was or his uncompromising opposition to Putin. Navalny's family and allies accused Putin of giving the order for his murder and leaked documents seemed to indicate that he had been poisoned once more while in prison. Kremlin propaganda initially said that Navalny had died of a blood clot, yet the official cause of death was later given as a 'combination of diseases'.

As we drove through the missile-scarred streets of Kharkiv, I recalled the many opposition rallies I had attended in Moscow, when a single blog post by Navalny had been enough to bring out thousands of protesters. In his speeches and writings, he had spoken of building a 'beautiful Russia of the future'. For a very short time, his dream had almost seemed attainable.

In an act of barely believable cruelty, investigators initially refused to even hand over his body to his family, unless they agreed to a secret burial. His elderly mother, Lyudmila, was forced to trudge from Arctic morgue to Arctic morgue in sub-zero temperatures to try and locate his body. When she insisted on a public funeral in Moscow, she said she was told: 'Time is not on your side, corpses decompose.'[15]

Following an outcry, the Kremlin eventually released Navalny's body and he was buried at Moscow's Borisovskoye Graveyard. His funeral service turned into the biggest opposition rally since the start of Russia's invasion of Ukraine, as thousands of people chanted 'No war!' and 'Russia will be free!' Yet, if such chants had once been infused with a sense of belief, no one was under any illusions anymore: Russia would not be free for a very long time, if ever.

For years, Putin had studiously avoided saying Navalny's name aloud in public, usually referring to him instead as 'this gentleman' or the 'person you mentioned'. The habit was widely ascribed to superstition. A month after the opposition leader's death, the Russian dictator finally plucked up the courage to pronounce the name of his nemesis.

'As for Navalny, yes he passed away, this is always a sad event,' Putin said. He also claimed, without providing evidence, that he had recently agreed to exchange Navalny for an unnamed Russian prisoner in the West. 'I agreed on one condition: we swap him and he doesn't come back,' he said. 'But such is life.'

17

'What Does It Matter If I Am In Pain, If I Am Nothing?'

What must it be like to be Vladimir Putin? Not the Putin of summits with world leaders or televised addresses to the nation, but the Putin in the small moments, when he is alone with himself. Does the Russian dictator ever wake up in a foreign country or at one of his many opulent residences, unable to recall exactly where he is and what he is doing there, his thoughts confused and cloudy? And, when memory returns, does he pause for a moment to consider the misery he has caused and the power he holds in his bloodied hands?

The widespread belief among Russians that everything is decided in the Kremlin's distant corridors means that most people are politically apathetic, accepting Putin's rule as a fact of nature, like the rising of the sun or the changing of the seasons. This is, of course, exactly what the Kremlin wants. It also means, however, that the authorities often have to resort to bribery or threats to boost turnouts at pro-Putin rallies, a vital element of the cult of personality around Russia's leader.

I witnessed these tactics in action for myself in March 2018, when Putin held a rally at Moscow's colossal Luzhniki Stadium, just weeks before he secured a fourth term in tightly controlled presidential elections. The government had methodically eradicated even the slightest chance of a political upset, banning all of Putin's genuine challengers, including Navalny, who had spent months campaigning across Russia to try and force his way onto the ballot. The total lack of any suspense meant that even Putin's most ardent supporters had no reason at all to get excited about an election campaign rally. Putin was going to secure a new presidential term whatever happened, so why waste the afternoon at a windswept stadium?

In the days before the event, workers at companies across Moscow began receiving emails from their bosses. 'Organize yourselves into groups of no less than four and photograph yourselves when you arrive at the stadium. Don't forget to pick up your placards on Friday!' read one message that was forwarded to me by a disgruntled employee. He also told me that he was afraid his wages would be cut if he did not comply.

The authorities also resorted to outright bribery. 'Men and women. 20–55 years old. March 3rd, rally/concert "For a Strong Russia" in support of Vladimir Putin. Payment 500 roubles (£6),' read an announcement posted on a popular 'rent-a-crowd' website. Posing as a Russian citizen, I answered the advertisement and was told to meet the organizer at a location near the stadium. When I got there, a small crowd had gathered around a man who identified himself as Rodion. 'We'll all go to the stadium together, then meet back here and you'll get your money,' he said, before handing out Russian Ecological Party flags and scarves. No one present appeared to have any connection to the party.

'What difference does it make if I pretend to be an Ecological Party member? I mean, I don't support Putin either,' one young man, who declined to give his name, told me. Thousands of people who had been strong-armed into attending were already streaming out of the stadium. 'Let's get out of here,' said one middle-aged man named Pavel, after posing for a group photo with work colleagues. I asked him why he was leaving before Putin's speech. 'I support our President, but I'm not spending all day here,' he replied.

The use of coercion to swell crowd numbers at such rallies is an open secret, although it is unclear if Putin himself is entirely aware of the lengths that his officials go to. But what would attendance look like if the authorities did not pull out all the stops to ensure large turnouts? That's what opposition activists in Tyumen, an oil town with a population of just over half a million people in western Siberia, decided to find out ahead of that year's elections. Posing as Kremlin supporters, they staged a rally that was – on paper – in support of a fourth presidential term for Putin. The event was advertised in local media and online and was held in the afternoon, on a non-workday, in the centre of the city. Yet, because the event had not been arranged by the local authorities, there was no pressure exerted on anyone to turn up and no one was paid to participate. The attendance? Just seven people. 'I figured at least 50 people would turn up', said one of the organizers. [1]

The Kremlin's obsession with proving that Putin enjoys massive popularity also extended to Western countries. Even as relations between Russia and the West sank to their lowest level since the Cold War, Russian state media was curiously enthusiastic about amplifying any foreign approval of Putin, real or invented. Its efforts were often absurd: in 2017, Russian state television announced that a restaurant in New York had created a special burger in honour of Putin's 65th birthday. 'It's not only foreign leaders that are wishing Russia's President a happy birthday, but ordinary citizens too, and in extremely original ways,' gushed a presenter on Channel One, Russia's main TV station. TASS, a state-run Russian news agency, cited what it claimed was a manager of the restaurant saying that Putin was the only world leader whose birthday it deemed worthy of celebrating. Unsurprisingly, the report turned out to be false.[2]

For Moscow, it didn't get much better than when American or European celebrities, even minor ones, endorsed Putin. The biggest names to publicly come out as Putin fans were Gérard Depardieu, the French actor, and Steven Seagal, the star of 1990s Hollywood action films including *Under Siege* and *Hard to Kill*.

'He is one of the greatest world leaders, if not the greatest world leader, alive today. He cares more about Russia than anybody I know, and he's not afraid to stand up and do what needs to get done,' Seagal, who has Russian roots, said in 2013. Moscow was overjoyed: although Seagal's career had tanked in the West, he remained a star in Russia. Over the next few years, the Kremlin granted the actor a Russian passport and named him Moscow's special envoy to the United States for humanitarian issues. Seagal remained on message even after the start of the invasion of Ukraine in 2022, lavishing praise on Putin and attending his inauguration in Moscow for a fifth presidential term. When asked why he supported Putin, he called the question 'stupid'.[3] He also said he would be ready to die for Russia's leader, if necessary.[4]

Another American to praise Putin was Jeff Monson, a mixed martial arts fighter who says he fell in love with Russia during his first trip there in 2011, despite having his leg broken in a televised bout attended by the Kremlin dictator. 'You have the Russian spirit. You never give up,' Putin told him after the fight. Monson soon became a regular feature in Russian state media, slamming US foreign policy and hailing Putin as a 'strong leader'.

In 2018, Monson, who sports tattoos of Karl Marx and Vladimir Lenin and describes his politics as a mixture of anarchism and left-wing principles, was granted a Russian passport. He was also, despite speaking no more than a few words of heavily accented Russian, appointed to the council in Krasnogorsk, a small town near Moscow.[5] The Kremlin was so keen to have Americans endorse Putin that it was willing to appoint them to positions of power, even if they had almost zero command of the language.

I met up with Monson shortly afterwards at a café in Krasnogorsk, where he drew curious glances from locals. After a few pleasantries, I asked him how an 'anarchist-leftist' could support Putin? Did he not realize that Russia was no longer striding towards communism? That Russia had the highest wealth inequality of all major economies? That Putin and his inner circle lived lives of unimaginable luxury? Was this not enough to make his Lenin and Marx tattoos peel away from his skin in revulsion?

Monson sighed. 'I really hate it when people use terms like "useful idiot" to describe me,' he said. 'I'm a smart guy, I know exactly what's going on. Of course, the Kremlin is using me, or trying to use me. But I'm not holding back. I'm speaking my mind, even if there are consequences. Putin is obscenely wealthy for what he's supposed to make as President of Russia. How did he get this wealth? Maybe he's got his hands in some ...' He cut himself short. 'Look, it doesn't take an Einstein to figure out that Russia is an oligarchy. I think Putin's got his wealth because of his connections to oligarchs.'

After the article was published in *The Times*,[6] Monson sent me a smiley face in a text message but asked why I hadn't reported his admiration for Putin's judo skills. I told him there wasn't space and he seemed satisfied by my reply. He said nothing about my inclusion of the comments about Putin or United Russia.

The story would likely have ended there, if my article had not been picked up by Russian opposition media, as well as Western news outlets. A Russian opposition journalist even told me that Monson was now her new hero. His comments were an embarrassment for the Kremlin and I did not have long to wait for state media to respond. A few days later, national television aired a special 'expose' of my article. To give him credit, Monson did not deny that he had made the comments about Putin. He stressed, however, that he supported the Russian leader. 'We are different people!' he told the cameras, somewhat redundantly. 'You can't agree with absolutely everything someone else does. But do I think he wants the best for Russia? I am absolutely sure that he wants only the best for Russia. And so do I!'

A pro-Kremlin media analyst then informed viewers that I had been tasked by my editors at *The Times* with tricking Monson into making statements that would reflect badly on Putin. Watching at home in Moscow, I laughed. My editors hadn't even known who Monson was before I suggested an interview with him. And why would they have? Monson may have been on his way to becoming a household name in Russia, but in the West, he was an obscure figure to anyone outside the world of mixed martial arts. 'We are dealing with a completely new era from the point of view of the media,' the analyst said. '[In the West,] they are transforming information into an instrument for [political] agitation.'[7] It was ridiculous, yet effective. The Kremlin had been hammering home for years the message that Western media was a propaganda tool

'WHAT DOES IT MATTER IF I AM IN PAIN, IF I AM NOTHING?'

and that American and European journalists were engaged in an information war against Russia. Years later, when Putin's army began bombing Ukrainian cities, was it really any wonder that most Russians turned to their own media to find out the 'truth'?

As the report finished, my face flashed up on the screen above a quote from my article about Monson. 'With his shaven-head, tattoos and heavily accented Russian, he stands out on the streets of Krasnogorsk,' it read. I had short hair at the time and a casual viewer would have assumed that I was the person being referred to. I took a photo and used the image as my Facebook profile picture for a while.

As for Monson, he remained in Russia, although he no longer criticized Putin, at least not publicly. In 2022, when Russia launched its all-out invasion of Ukraine, I exchanged messages with him for the first time in years. He told me that Nato had provoked the war and that Russia had no choice but to 'rescue' the people of eastern Ukraine. We have not spoken since.

While the 'pact with the devil' that the Russian people had signed up to with the Kremlin was a very real factor in dampening, if not entirely quashing, dissent, the increased prosperity that Putin had provided in return for acquiescence to his political programme was largely centred on big cities like Moscow and St Petersburg. In remote regions, the Kremlin's success had been to ensure that pensions and salaries were paid on time. No one was getting rich on the miserly sums they were receiving; they were just grateful to be getting paid at all. Living standards in the poorest provinces are often grim, by any measures. By the time Putin ordered tanks into Ukraine, around 1,300 Russian schools had no indoor toilets, including in regions such as Yakutia, in northeast Siberia, where temperatures often fall to minus 40 degrees Celsius and below.[8]

Russia does not have a class system in the sense that Britain has one, but its most privileged citizens are undoubtedly those who were born in Moscow, into families with stable incomes.

In the years before the war in Ukraine, Moscow's middle class had arguably more in common with citizens in European capitals than they did with their fellow Russians in regions thousands of miles and many time zones away. They were also literally closer: Magadan, an impoverished former Gulag labour camp city, is around four times as far from Moscow than Russia's capital is from Berlin, for example.

Although healthcare in Moscow is generally of a European standard, it is woefully unfit for purpose in many other places. Just ahead of the coronavirus pandemic, I visited a hospital in Bogdanovich, a small town in Russia's Ural region, where some service staff were threatening to go on strike over working conditions and pay. I was accompanied on my trip by Anastasia Vasilyeva, the head of the Alliance of Doctors, an independent trade union that was supported by Alexei Navalny. Although trade unions exist in Russia, the vast majority have been coopted by the Kremlin and are as distant from the struggle for workers' rights as Putin is from world peace. Vasilyeva, an ophthalmologist, and her colleagues had been travelling to some of Russia's most underfunded medical facilities to try and draw attention to the pitiful state of healthcare.

Yet even they were shocked by what we saw when we entered the hospital's launderette. Black mould crept along the crumbling walls. Water dripped from the ceiling into plastic buckets that provided a rare splash of colour amid the gloom. Blood- and urine-stained bedding lay in a pile. 'Once, there was no hot water here for an entire year,' Nadezhda Shchipaeva, a middle-aged woman who had worked at the laundry for almost 20 years, told me. A grime-caked sink, the only one in the building, was used for washing dirty sheets and pillows, as well as the staff's cutlery and dishes. The disposable sheets that patients died on were scrubbed and then returned to the wards, even if the patients had died of tuberculosis or other infectious diseases, Shchipaeva said. In the winter, temperatures in the building fell to as low as 9 degrees Celsius. Staff were paid a monthly salary of just 11,000 roubles (around £135 at the time). 'I've ruined my health by working in this place,' said Shchipaeva, who suffered from arthritis and osteoporosis, as well as breathing problems. Hospital officials, she said, treated her and her colleagues 'like trash'. She broke down in tears. Anastasia Shkinder, a nurse at the hospital, told me she was paid 14,000 roubles (around £170 at the time) a month. 'I'm barely surviving,' she said. 'Life is so very hard.'[9]

When I accompanied Vasilyeva to confront Yelena Vdovina, the hospital's chief doctor, we found her sitting in an airy office beneath a large portrait of Putin. She had a smaller one on her desk. When I asked her if she was ashamed of the hellish conditions in the launderette, she refused to comment. Instead, she demanded to see my press accreditation card and took a photo of it. A few days later, an article appeared in the local media alleging that I was part of a nefarious Western plot to discredit the local authorities. I was used to this kind of thing by now and added the article to my growing collection. As we left Vdovina's airy office, I noticed an announcement from the local Kremlin-loyal trade union pinned to a message board. Instead of helping to secure better conditions for the hospital's employees, it was organizing a disco. 'I'm glad to see the local union has things under control,' said Vasilyeva, and rolled her eyes. She and her colleagues were barred from inspecting the hospital wards.

I was astonished that anyone at all chose to work in healthcare in Russia. In 2017, a report by the Centre for Economic and Political Reform in Moscow revealed that average wages for the country's doctors were slightly less than those for supervisors at McDonald's fast-food restaurants.[10] No wonder then that Pavel Astakhov, Russia's former top official for child welfare, once chose to send his wife to give birth in the south of France rather than in Russia. 'I was concerned about my wife and future child. I couldn't take the risk,' he explained.[11] It was a luxury that very few other Russians could afford.

For patients, Russia's hospitals were a microcosm of the state's brutal indifference to their lives. Even though there was no official ban, patients in intensive care units were routinely denied visits from family members, even when they were at death's door.

'These are mainly Soviet-era doctors who think family members and relatives should not be in intensive care units – that they will prevent them from working by asking too many questions,' Lida Moniava, Deputy Director at the Lighthouse, a children's hospice in Moscow, told me. In 2015, a desperate mother forced doctors at gunpoint to let her see her dying 5-year-old daughter. After a public outcry, the health ministry issued a statement confirming that relatives had the legal right to visit loved ones in intensive care. The statement was widely ignored by hospitals, however, Moniava told me.[12]

This pitiless approach to healthcare was reflected in the dire deficit of painkillers for terminally ill people. Strict medical bureaucracy governing the use of powerful pain-alleviating medicines means that hundreds of thousands of cancer patients were simply left to die in agony because doctors were afraid of the legal consequences of prescribing the drugs. For many, suicide was the only way out. In 2014, Vyacheslav Apanasenko, a retired navy admiral, shot himself following a prolonged battle with cancer. 'Do not blame anyone but the Health Ministry and the government. I was prepared to suffer, but watching my loved ones struggle has proven too much,' his suicide note read.[13] The next month, at least eight cancer patients killed themselves in Moscow alone. The situation has improved in recent years, after the government finally made it easier – and safer – for doctors to prescribe painkillers, but it was too late for the untold number of Russians who had taken their own lives to bring an end to their misery.

For some critics, this inability, or unwillingness, to alleviate pain was the logical consequence of decades of authoritarian rule. 'Russians don't want to relieve their suffering and the suffering of those close to them for the simple reason they have been taught to view themselves as replaceable, insignificant screws in the system, whose personal feelings are meaningless,' Alexei Kascheev, a Moscow-based spine surgeon, told me. 'Both doctors and patients are willing to put up with physical and psychological torment. People think, "What does it matter if I am in pain, if I am nothing?"'

18

'Just Switch Your Brains On'

I first met Dani 'Apostle' Akel in an icy military training field strewn with bullet casings in northern Ukraine. Tall, with a gentle smile and a ragged beard, he was clutching an automatic rifle. It was early spring and still cold and ghostly trails came from his mouth as we spoke next to an armoured vehicle. He had just taken part in a live-fire drill, the sound of gunfire echoing across the snowy countryside. There was nothing unusual, of course, about seeing armed men in wartime Ukraine. But Dani was different: he was a Russian citizen who had undertaken a perilous journey to the country with the specific aim of defending it against Putin's invading army.

On the spring morning in 2022 that the Kremlin ordered tanks into Ukraine, Dani was recovering at home from a night out clubbing in Moscow. 'I'd been hanging out all night, I'd met a wonderful girl and she came back to mine. In the morning, I turned on the computer and saw that the war had begun,' he told me. As he watched online videos of Russian missiles raining down on Ukrainian cities, he swiftly realized that his old life was over.

'A missile strike on Kyiv. It was like, I don't know, an alien invasion or something,' he said. 'For the first 10 to 15 minutes I was almost hysterical. There were no tears, but there was this feeling … I jumped up, ran to the cupboard and started to pack my things. There was a lot of hatred inside of me for Putin's regime.'

Within a week, Dani was on a train to the northwest of Russia, where he walked for hours through marshy woodland towards Estonia, fearful all the time that he would be captured by Russian border guards. 'Keep going, don't stop, keep to the plan,' he mumbled to himself as he walked. He eventually clambered over a three-metre fence into the European Union. His departure probably saved him from arrest; after he had left, friends in Moscow said that police were searching for him because of his 'extremist' views, a catch-all term in Russia for anyone associated with the opposition.

Around a year after leaving Russia, following a four-month stint in an Estonian centre for illegal migrants, Akel crossed into Ukraine. He was met there by members of the Freedom of Russia Legion, a military unit made up of Russian citizens who were fighting on the side of the Ukrainian army. 'That was when my new life began,' he said. Once he had enrolled in the Legion's ranks, Dani took on the military call sign of 'Apostle'. Call signs are used by soldiers to quickly identify each other on the battlefield or, if necessary, disguise their identities. Dani's choice of Apostle was a reference to an obscure joke about postmodernism that a friend had made many years ago, he explained. I wondered how many of the Kremlin's bloodthirsty and sadistic troops had taken on call signs inspired by postmodernism. Not many, I guessed.

The son of a Russian mother and a Syrian father, Dani's short life had been shaped by Putin. Born in 1998, just two years before the ex-KGB officer came to power, he had spent part of his early childhood in the city of Aleppo, in Syria, but his family left shortly before the start of the civil war that tore the Middle Eastern country apart. In a foreshadowing of the horrific fates that awaited Ukrainian cities, Aleppo was later razed to the ground by the Kremlin's missiles after Putin ordered in the Russian army to prop up President Assad.

Dani had helped to organize opposition protests in Moscow and several of his friends had been locked up for years on politically motivated charges. 'Just young guys whose lives have been ruined,' he said. 'I've lost them for ever.' His own opposition activities had resulted in him being kicked out of Moscow State University, where he was studying philosophy. Besides a desire to help Ukraine, he was driven, he said, by a belief that the war represented an existential battle between democratic ideals and totalitarianism. I admired his bravery, but it was a damning indictment of Putin's regime that a thoughtful ex-student in his mid-twenties should have felt it necessary to go to war against his own country. 'I would never have picked up a weapon if I hadn't seen a real need for this,' he told me. 'There are values that have become an integral part of me. To put it bluntly, it's easier to die than transgress or go against these values.' Many members of the liberal Russian opposition had said such things to me over the years: Dani was one of the few who backed up his words with action when the time came. It took a special kind of courage to head to the raging frontlines, where life expectancies were sometimes measured in days, or even hours.

Many of the Legion's fighters had family ties in Ukraine and had been living in the country for years on residency permits when the invasion began in 2022. As Russian citizens, they were barred from serving in the Ukrainian army, but the Legion provided them with an opportunity to defend their adopted homeland. The outfit would not reveal its numbers, but it was believed to have a fighting force of several hundred. It had carried out a number of armed incursions into Russian border towns and villages, clashing with the Kremlin's troops and even briefly occupying patches of territory. Before meeting Dani, I had visited one of the Legion's mortar units in Toretsk, a town in eastern Ukraine that was around three miles from the frontline.

The unit was based in one of the thousands of homes in the region that had been abandoned by their owners. I spent the afternoon with the team as they loaded and fired shells, the missiles hurtling across the war-ravaged countryside towards Russia's invading army. The boom of incoming and outgoing artillery was almost constant and I imagined a bird's-eye view of the scene: dozens of mortar teams like this, each one based in someone's once peaceful back garden, firing lumps of explosive metal towards their enemies. It was a grotesque and horrifying image. 'That's war,' shrugged Zhora, the mortar team's leader, when I shared my thoughts.

Zhora had moved to Ukraine with his mother when he was a teenager after his parents split up. His father was still in Russia, and he had had not spoken to him since the start of the full-scale invasion. 'The Kremlin's propaganda is more important to him than his own son,' he said. Like many of the Russians fighting for Ukraine, Zhora's long-term aim was to return home and launch an armed resistance against Putin. 'The only way to bring about a change of power in Russia is with weapons in our hands,' he said.

The Legion's fighters operated under the watchful eye of Ukraine's Gur military intelligence agency, but they appeared to have a large degree of autonomy. It was not going to tip the war in favour of Ukraine, but its raids into Russian border regions forced the Kremlin to redeploy troops from other hotspots along the 600-mile frontline. They are also likely to have aided the Ukrainian military's planning and reconnaissance efforts ahead of its large-scale offensive into western Russia's Kursk region in the summer of 2024. Besides their military value, the Legion's raids played an important psychological role by demonstrating to Russians that Putin, for all his strongman posturing, could not even guarantee border security. The Legion's very existence also acted as a vital counter to Kremlin propaganda by proving to Ukrainians and people in the West that not everyone in Russia supported the war and that some of its citizens were even willing to take up arms to fight back against Putin's occupying forces.

There had been allegations when the Legion was formed that it was a Ukrainian propaganda project whose members did little else apart from post anti-Putin videos on social media. That may have been the case initially, but by the time I met them in the spring of 2024, it was clear that the Legion's troops were fighting and dying in the war. Dani had recently returned from a raid into Russia when I met him and he struggled to hold back tears as he spoke about the death of a comrade-in-arms whose call sign was Sotnik.

'He was blown up by a mine. It was just a second and he was mincemeat,' he told me. He looked away, in the direction of the nearby trees, their branches heavy with ice, as if reliving the scene. 'There was nothing left of him – his legs were like rags. Like a towel when you twist it into a knot. The same with his arms. The young guy who was second in the line lost his legs. He was only 20 or 21.'

Dani was just 26, the same age I was when I first moved to St Petersburg, which meant that we had spent almost the same amount of time living in Russia. It was strange to realize that a child who had been born in Moscow not long after I arrived in the country was now a soldier, fighting against the Kremlin. He seemed older than his years, however, and it was only when he began to talk about how he was still a teenager when the vote fraud protests broke out in Moscow in 2011–2012 that I appreciated how young he was. It was difficult enough for me to accept that I might never be able to go back to Moscow: I couldn't imagine what it was like for someone like Dani. I hoped that he would be able to find a place for himself after the war, in Ukraine or elsewhere. He wasn't making any plans, though. 'Within the Legion, when you start to think about the future, everyone looks at you like "yeah, right",' he said. 'People get torn apart in front of their brothers-in-arms, people we've known for six months. And so we laugh when anyone starts to discuss the future.'

It was grotesque: Dani should have been in Moscow, completing his philosophy studies, hanging out with friends and falling in love. Instead, here he was, holding an automatic weapon and wearing body armour in a field in Ukraine. Before I left him, we exchanged bittersweet memories of our lives in Moscow. Dani sighed. 'I'd give a lot just to be able to spend one more evening at Tsvetnoy Bulvar,' he said, referring to an area of the city known for its summer cafés. But we both knew that he would not be able to return to Moscow in the foreseeable future, if ever. The Legion had been classified as a terrorist organization by the Kremlin and Russians were being imprisoned for up to 20 years for even the slightest association with the group, real or invented.[1]

It would be strange to describe someone I had only met once as a friend, but I was glad to have got to know Dani, even a little bit, and we stayed in touch, exchanging messages about Russian opposition politics and the war. Like most Russians who oppose Putin, he seemed devastated by Navalny's death. 'He was a symbol of the era,' he wrote to me. 'He taught my generation liberal values. Now they will be raised by Putin.' He also asked my opinion on the future of long-term Western support for Ukraine. It wasn't the easiest question to answer, and I promised to get back to him once I'd decided for myself what it might look like. I never had the chance to reply.

The last message I wrote to Dani was on 12 March 2024, exactly a month after our interview. The Legion had crossed over again into western Russia and was engaged in fierce battles with the Kremlin's troops. 'Are you in Russia? Take care!' I wrote. The message appeared to have been delivered, but there was no reply. The following day, Dani appeared in a video that the Legion had posted from the combat zone, holding up its blue flag as he and another fighter stood on a street corner. 'We'll move forward a little later. The street is being heavily shot up,' he said. But he seemed in good humour, winking and flashing the two-fingered peace sign. 'We are alive, but tired,' said his comrade-in-arms. Not long afterwards, when I was back in Britain, I received news that he had been killed in action the day after the video had been filmed and had already been buried in Kyiv. I felt bitter and angry at his death and an overwhelming bleakness. Not only for Dani, but also for Russia, a country that has been so warped by Putin's obsession with Ukraine that there is no longer any place there for many of the young people who should be its pride and joy. Neither of his parents commented on his death, at least not publicly. I wondered how they had found out and if they respected his decisions. I hoped so.

The next time I was in Kyiv, I paid a visit to Dani's grave with Kateryna Malofieieva, the Ukrainian journalist I had made it into Kherson with. Kateryna had introduced me to Dani and they had planned to meet for coffee in Kyiv later that spring. The Legion's spokeswoman had told us that Dani was buried alongside Ukrainian soldiers and gave us rough directions on how to locate him amid the sprawling graveyard. The plot was filled with seemingly endless rows of blue and yellow flags, fluttering in the breeze. The relatives of a fallen soldier embraced, tearfully. We wandered for a while, searching for Dani in the pale afternoon sun.

He was buried under the Legion's blue flag, his grave covered in flowers. The burial plot belonging to the Legion fighter whose grisly death he had recalled to me was just a few steps away. It felt right that they were together. They would soon be joined by Ildar Dadin, the opposition activist who had been tortured in prison in Russia and would later be killed near Kharkiv.

Kateryna had brought along two cups of coffee, one for herself and a symbolic one for Dani that she placed by his headstone. She drank in silence. Before we left, we put a laminated photograph of Tsvetnoy Bulvar, the area of Moscow that Dani had longed to see at least one more time, on his grave. If I am ever able to return to Moscow, I will head to Tsvetnoy Bulvar and toast his bravery there. And the bravery of all the others who died resisting Putin, the resurrected dragon of the murderous Soviet regime. Although I had never lived in Ukraine, Dani was not the only person I knew who was buried in the graveyard. The ex-girlfriend who I had visited in Prague in the years after the break-up of the Soviet Union had later moved to Kyiv and married a Ukrainian man. She had died young of an illness and been laid to rest in the Ukrainian capital. I had already visited her grave the year after her death and it didn't take me long to find it again that afternoon, her name carved into the tombstone in English and Cyrillic. I recalled the time we had spent together in south London, our lives revolving around music and books. It was so very long ago, and so very much had changed. I suddenly felt very old.

Back in my hotel in Kyiv, I listened again to the recording of my interview with Dani at the military training ground. Towards the end of our conversation, I'd asked him if there was anything he would say to his fellow Russians, if he had the chance. He appeared to have anticipated the question: 'How long are you going to keep this up? How long are you going to die for?' he said. 'This is not your war. This is a war of aggression. It would be better to go into the streets and fight for your rights, so that future generations can change things and not sit in factories for the next 20 years building tanks.' He paused. 'Just switch your brains on. That's all I ask.'

19

'Always Cold: Nothing is Allowed'

Spring came late to Moscow in the weeks after Russian bombs had begun falling on Kyiv. One morning in early April, I awoke to heavy snow and a cold snap. I was used to such weather, of course, but the chill that day seemed to bite harder. A thaw, I suspected, would be a long time coming. That afternoon, I trudged through the snow to the nearby Vakhtangov theatre, one of the city's oldest. A pro-war photo display had been installed outside its entrance and I watched for a while as people shuffled past in the sub-zero temperatures, barely giving it a second glance. An ice-crusted billboard advertised the theatre's upcoming adaptation of Nikolai Gogol's novel, *Dead Souls*. Nothing could have been more apt, but the symbolism was so obvious it barely registered, at first.

A few days before I left Moscow, I met up with Stas, one of my oldest friends in Russia and we sat for a while at a café outside a venue where I had once attended record fairs, stocking up on western and Russian vinyl. We then walked through the centre of the city, past a wall where someone had scrawled anti-war graffiti, until we ended up at a small bar that was next to a row of basement shops. In one, I bought a black hoodie decorated with images of barbed wire that read: 'Always Cold: Nothing is Allowed.'

The shop assistant gave the thumbs up to my purchase and when I explained that I was leaving soon, because of the war, she nodded, knowingly. 'You'll have something to remember Russia by, at least,' she said, gesturing towards the garment. Stas and I drank up and said our goodbyes. And then I went home to the Old Arbat, the neighbourhood I had spent more time in than anywhere else on Earth, and packed up my life.

It has now been almost four years since I departed Moscow, my home for a quarter of a century. My thoughts constantly return to that February morning in 2022, when Putin, high on power and long devoid of humanity, gave the order to try and destroy Ukraine. In the process, he has transformed Russia into a neo-totalitarian state and revived Cold War fears of nuclear armageddon.

After so long in Russia, returning to Britain wasn't easy. As I adjusted gradually to the switch, I would sometimes briefly mistake people I saw out of the corner of my eye, or in the distance, for friends and acquaintances in Moscow. The same thing had happened, in reverse, when I had first begun living in Russia, but now my mind was searching for familiar faces from the Old Arbat, rather than the streets of south London. My homesickness for Russia was simultaneously unsurprising and uncomfortable: how could I miss a country that had committed such evils? Yet it is not the propaganda or the political repression that I miss: it is the landscape and rhythms of everyday life in Moscow, a feeling that is accentuated by the knowledge that I am unsure if I will ever be able to live there again. Although I have left Russia, it has not left me: I am still unable to shake hands over the threshold of a door, or while wearing gloves, just two of the Russian superstitions that will likely stay with me for ever.

While I still speak to people in Russia, my memories of Moscow have begun to slowly fade. I wonder if I still see correctly in my mind's eye the paths I once walked in deep snow and searing sunshine to our daughter's music school, or to other places that had become so familiar to me, as my roots in the city grew and took hold. It was a joy to watch our daughter grow up fluent in two languages and knowledgeable about the cultures of two very different countries. During my time in Moscow, I always thought that it was a gift. I hope that it will still prove to be so, eventually. Yet, during the bleakest times since my departure, I have often worried that the link I have established to Russia, these blood ties that could be passed down for generations, might be more of a curse; a dark lodestar in the years to come.

Unless, of course, Russia changes. After the collapse of President Assad's murderous regime in Syria in December 2024, the al-Watan newspaper in Damascus defended its years of pro-government propaganda. 'We simply followed instructions and published the news that they sent us,' an editorial read. 'It is now obvious that it was a lie.'[1] It is so easy to imagine Putin's peddlers of falsehoods claiming the same, if his regime ever falls. But for that to happen, it first has to be pushed and it is hard to see, at least right now, who could do the shoving. As I write these words, there are no credible signs of cracks within the Kremlin elite and the leaders of the fractured opposition are either dead or in forced exile.

Yet Russia is nothing if not unpredictable. I was drinking beer with friends in our back garden in southern England when Yevgeny Prigozhin, the head of the Wagner group of mercenaries, launched an unprecedented armed rebellion in the summer of 2023. Following a vicious row with Russian defence ministry officials, Prigozhin and his heavily-armed fighters seized control of parts of Rostov-on-Don, a city close to the border with Ukraine, and then headed towards Moscow. As events unfolded throughout the next day, Putin vanished from public view, as he has so often done at moments of crisis, and Wagner fighters clashed with the Russian military. I wondered if I would soon be back in Moscow, reporting on civil war. I had barely had time to consider the possibility when Prigozhin abruptly called off his rebellion in return for a pardon. Two months later, he was killed in a plane crash, when his private jet plummeted to earth shortly after take-off from Moscow. It was widely suspected that he had been assassinated on Putin's orders.

It was Joseph Brodsky, the exiled Soviet writer, who said in 1980 that tyranny 'slips into a monstrosity' after 15–20 years of unopposed rule. 'Then you may get the kind of grandeur that manifests itself in waging wars or internal terror, or both,' he wrote. 'Blissfully, nature takes its toll, resorting at times to the hands of the rivals just in time; that is, before your man decides to immortalise himself by doing something horrendous.' Nature, it appears, has been asleep at the wheel when it comes to Putin. Yet, as Brodsky also noted, 'Illness and death are, perhaps, the only things that a tyrant has in common with his subjects.'[2]

For those Russians who oppose Putin, the demise of the Kremlin dictator would be a day of joy. When I asked a woman who had remained in Moscow, why she had not left, she said, half-jokingly: 'I don't want to leave Russia because I want to be here when that *khuilo* finally snuffs it.' When I suggested that she could just fly in for Putin's funeral, she replied: 'There won't be any plane tickets left! They will all be snapped up immediately!'

It is unclear if Putin's sudden death would trigger deep-reaching changes within Russia, or if his allies would simply continue in his bloody footsteps. 'After Putin, there will be Putin,' Vyacheslav Volodin, the chairman of the Russian parliament, declared in 2020. 'Everything that happens after President Putin will happen according to the patterns he laid down.'[3] That may be so, yet it is also worth recalling that following Stalin's death in 1953, the Soviet Union embarked upon a campaign to dismantle and condemn his cult of personality. It was not until Putin's ascent to power that Stalin's reputation was revived, as the Kremlin sought to distract and inspire Russians with myths about the Soviet tyrant. We have already seen Putinist terror: we may one day witness de-Putinization.

If the opportunity for meaningful change does emerge, pro-democracy Russians will need to move fast to ensure that the horrors of Putin's regime are not repeated. In 2024, I met in London with Vladimir Kara-Murza, the Russian opposition politician. He had twice survived near-deadly poisonings by Kremlin agents in 2015 and 2017 before being arrested in Moscow over his outspoken condemnation of the war. He was sentenced to 25 years, the longest sentence ever handed down to a Russian political prisoner. He had thought he would die behind bars; instead he was freed in the August 2024 exchange in Ankara.

Kara-Murza had been a free man for just seven weeks, yet he was already thinking about Russia's future. His biggest fear, he said, upon the fall of Putin's regime, was a repeat of the Yeltsin era, when Stalin's ideological heirs were eventually allowed to return to power, with barely a protest. This time around, he said, Russia would need to ensure that those responsible for the invasion of Ukraine and the crushing of dissent at home were held to justice. Russia, he said, would need a clean break with the past.

'I'm just really, really worried that we're going to mess up the way Yeltsin's people did. This would be a total catastrophe, not just for us, but for everyone else. We need to be preparing for the day after Putin now, because when it comes, it's going to be far too late to start sitting down and scratching our heads and thinking, "okay, what do we do next?" There will need to be justice. There will need to be accountability. There will need to be a genuine reflection, a genuine moral cleansing. And next time we will need to make sure that this evil never, ever comes back again.'

It was not only the future that exiled Russians were thinking about. As the war in Ukraine raged and Putin crushed all independent thought at home, the memory of Galina Starovoitova, the pro-democracy politician who was assassinated in 1998 in St Petersburg, took on a new significance and poignancy. Her bid to bar ex-KGB officers such as Putin from taking power in Russia felt more and more like a missed opportunity, a fork in the road of history that was not taken.

In a strange coincidence, it turned out that Starovoitova's son, Platon Borshchevsky, lived a mere fifteen-minute walk from my new home on the south coast of England. He had been studying in London when Starovoitova was assassinated and had never returned to Russia to live. One spring evening, I visited his family's home and he covered his kitchen table in papers and documents that had been written by or were about his mother. He was already three years older than she had been when she was murdered.

'If my mother's law on lustration had succeeded, and she and other pro-democracy politicians had come to power after Yeltsin, we would have not only a different Russia, but a different world,' he said. 'Without any doubt the war in Ukraine would have been avoided.' When I asked him if the person who ordered his mother's assassination would ever answer in court for the crime, he was sceptical. 'It seems highly unlikely, although one has to hope for justice,' he said. 'Why let them off completely by not believing in the possibility?'

Having observed Russia mainly from a distance since the 1990s, Borshchevsky was clear-eyed about the future of his troubled homeland. 'The desire for freedom and democracy that appeared after the collapse of the Soviet Union was squandered. It will take decades, at least, to restore the drive for the kind of conscious social change that took place in eastern Europe after the fall of the Berlin Wall, or in Germany, after Nazism,' he said. 'We failed as a society.'

In the summer of 2025, with estimated Russian troop deaths at almost 220,000 and the country's economy beginning to buckle, many western leaders, including President Trump, appeared to believe that Putin would choose peace, instead of continuing his war of conquest in Ukraine. There were few such illusions in Kyiv.

'Putin is not a rational person. He does not take into account Russia's losses. He proceeds from a perverted logic and does not think about Russia's future,' Mykhailo Podolyak, a senior advisor to Zelensky, told me just a few days after over 30 people had been killed in Russian drone and missile strikes in the Ukrainian capital.

Despite his claims to the contrary, Putin does not truly love his Motherland. Isolated in the Kremlin and sealed off from his own people in heavily-guarded residences, he no longer even knows Russia. And, after all, in order to love – or hate – something, you have to know it. Indeed, I am certain that even I know modern Russia far better than Putin. How could I not, after so many years in the country and having travelled across its vast breadth to some of its most remote regions?

I would like to go back to Moscow, at least for some time. I invested far too much of myself in the country to never return. As things stand, though, it is unclear if I will ever be able to. In 2022, in response to one of my articles about Putin, the Russian embassy in London wrote on X that I had been banned from entering the country. However, my name did not appear on Moscow's lists of sanctioned British citizens who are subject to Russian travel bans. Curious about my status, I applied for a visa. After a few weeks, when I asked a Russian foreign ministry official if there had been any progress, I was told my documents had been misplaced. Before I had a chance to reapply, Evan Gershkovich, the Wall St Journal reporter, was arrested by the FSB and I forgot any ideas I had about trying to get back to Moscow. At least for now.

I have no regrets about having spent so long in Russia. Unlike Kara-Murza, however, I am not hopeful about its future. Change may come, eventually, but I fear that much of Russian society has been hollowed out of the qualities necessary to build a freer and fairer country. In place of empathy and a sense of civic responsibility, Putin has encouraged cynicism and apathy, as well as an acceptance of violence against anyone suspected of unloyalty towards his regime. Evil and madness hold the upper hand, and the road to normality, or something resembling it, has been rendered almost impassable by bullet-ridden corpses and the charred ruins of Ukrainian towns and cities.

It goes almost without saying, of course, that I hope I am wrong.

ACKNOWLEDGEMENTS

Greetings and thanks to: My wife and daughter for the years in Moscow and beyond. I hope we can one day walk the Old Arbat's lanes again together. Bill and Jo Bennetts (aka mum and dad) for everything. Siobhan Parker and family.

In Russia and elsewhere: Stas, Grisha, Misha and Vera, Yulia and Andrey, Inna, Dima D, Vika, Katya O, Katya B and Katya M, Denis E and family. Extra greetings to Mary Kenway. Everyone who was brave enough to protest the madness.

Tanya N, Daniel Humphries and Matthew Luxmoore for reading parts of the book and offering invaluable advice. Tom Parfitt for suggesting the title.

At *The Times* – Mike Smith for continuing to entrust me with Russia and Ukraine coverage. Roland Watson for taking me on as Moscow correspondent before the war. Samuel Masters, Debbie Mason, David Rose, Madeleine Spence, Gemma Fox, Ben Hoyle, Jack Clover, David Harding, Jim McLean, Suzy Jagger, and everyone on *The Times* and *The Sunday Times* foreign desk I have worked with, past and present. My fellow Ukraine war correspondents. Kasia Sobocinska for the Ukraine videos and the Polish pronunciation tips. Nicola Jeal.

In Ukraine: Kateryna Malofieieva for all the invaluable assistance/advice (sorry about all the Black Sabbath!), Oleksiy Morozov, Oleksiy K, Sasha, and all the people who shared their stories. I wish you victory, freedom and happiness.

At Bloomsbury – Tomasz Hoskins for commissioning the book, and Allie Collins, Octavia Stocker, Rose Wolfe-Emery, Jessica Gray and Fahmida Ahmed for helping to get it ready.

Peter Conradi, Owen Matthews, Peter Pomerantsev, and Anna Reid for the amazing blurbs. Chris Barstow for excellent guidance on the audio version and for spotting so many typos.

ENDNOTES

Chapter 1

1 https://ria.ru/20160907/1476340300.html?fbclid=IwY2xjaw-Mf1mxleHRuA2FlbQIx MQABHprRyTxHgns8N [The original report has been removed, but this is a Russian news article about it].
2 https://www.bbc.co.uk/news/world-europe-47488267
3 https://www.thetimes.com/world/russia-ukraine-war/article/putin-puts-nuclear-deterrent-forces-on-high-alert-hc3dpsc8s
4 https://www.bbc.co.uk/news/live/ck7gwe808yet
5 https://x.com/RussianEmbassy/status/1603724349323845632
6 https://www.youtube.com/watch?v=CYQZ4OoORAg

Chapter 2

1 https://www.youtube.com/watch?v=xmtmWAsoFNU
2 https://www.bbc.co.uk/news/world-europe-59629670
3 https://hbr.org/1994/03/dont-give-up-on-russia
4 https://www.tes.com/magazine/archive/head-sick-leave-after-inspection
5 https://www.livelib.ru/book/1001199339-britaniya-bez-tumanov-vladimir-simonov
6 https://archive.nytimes.com/www.nytimes.com/learning/general/featured_articles/990324Dwednesday.html

Chapter 3

1 *Lenin's Tomb: The Last Days of the Soviet Empire* [Vintage Books, 1994] – David Remnick [page 535]
2 https://www.youtube.com/watch?v=JfaofpDxiKY [The Russian language speech can be seen here, from 1 min 20 sec]
3 There are more details on the failure to prevent servants of the Soviet regime from returning to power in this opinion piece by Vladimir Kara-Murza the anti-Putin activist. https://www.washingtonpost.

com/opinions/2023/09/11/russia-post-putin-democracy-window-nuremberg-lustration/
4. https://www.nytimes.com/2009/05/08/world/europe/08varennikov.html#:~:text=%E2%80%9CI%20have%20no%20regrets%20about,preserving%20and%20strengthening%20his%20country.%E2%80%9D
5. https://holod.media/2023/10/30/galina-starovoitova/
6. I have seen the original letter
7. https://meduza.io/en/news/2023/08/18/head-of-russia-s-central-election-commission-russia-doesn-t-need-democracy-in-the-western-sense
8. http://news.bbc.co.uk/1/hi/world/europe/220722.stm [Both quotes are from this BBC report]
9. https://www.amnesty.org/ar/wp-content/uploads/2021/06/eur460401998en.pdf
10. https://www.svoboda.org/a/27297651.html
11. https://oralhistory.org.ua/interview-ua/566/
12. https://www.themoscowtimes.com/2011/01/26/from-toilet-to-airport-a4524
13. https://www.youtube.com/watch?v=n4h-WpSsXVw
14. https://www.fontanka.ru/2018/06/08/007/
15. https://www.themoscowtimes.com/2019/08/16/20-years-of-vladimir-putin-the-transformation-of-the-economy-a66854
16. https://www.theguardian.com/world/2000/mar/31/russia.iantraynor
17. https://www.france24.com/en/20080509-missile-launchers-tanks-parade-red-square-russia-nuclear
18. https://www.theguardian.com/world/2008/may/10/russia
19. https://www.rferl.org/a/russia-victory-day-celebrations-kids-playing-controversial-roles/27719518.html
20. https://www.ural.kp.ru/daily/27128/4213390/
21. *I'm Going To Run Their Lives: Inside Putin's War on Russia's Opposition:* Marc Bennetts – page 61 [Oneworld 2016]
22. https://novayagazeta.ru/articles/2012/10/08/51800-oleg-orlov-171-my-nikogda-ne-ob-yavim-sebya-inostrannymi-agentami-187
23. https://www.reuters.com/world/europe/putin-is-master-all-he-surveys-russians-head-polls-2024-03-15/

Endnotes

Chapter 4

1. https://www.nytimes.com/2022/03/06/world/europe/ukraine-russia-families.html
2. https://www.thetimes.com/world/russia-ukraine-war/article/russia-demands-nato-remove-all-troops-from-eastern-europe-tdkl-rrvdg
3. https://www.youtube.com/watch?v=ucEs0nBuowE
4. https://treaties.un.org/doc/Publication/UNTS/Volume%203007/Part/volume-3007-I-52241.pdf
5. https://edition.cnn.com/videos/world/2020/06/17/russia-putin-disinfection-tunnel-covid-19-coronavirus-pandemic-chance-intl-ldn-vpx.cnn
6. https://t.me/bazabazon/9666
7. https://www.reuters.com/article/world/russian-war-veterans-quarantined-before-watching-parade-with-putin-says-kremlin-idUSKBN23P1ZO/
8. https://www.nytimes.com/2022/03/10/opinion/putin-russia-ukraine.html
9. https://iz.ru/1507429/2023-05-03/nikolai-patrushev-nazval-samoe-bezopasnoe-mesto-na-zemle
10. https://rg.ru/2023/05/03/nikolaj-patrushev-v-sluchae-izverzheniia-jelloustouna-neizbezhna-gibel-vsego-zhivogo-na-territorii-severnoj-ameriki.html
11. http://duma.gov.ru/en/news/48036/
12. https://www.thetimes.com/article/cc2a38c6-864b-11eb-8b38-e2425c3b9f1b
13. https://theins.ru/en/news/268328
14. https://www.kyivpost.com/post/47742
15. https://www.reuters.com/world/europe/police-detain-more-than-900-people-anti-war-protests-across-russia-monitoring-2022-02-27/
16. https://www.facebook.com/yashin.ilya/posts/pfbid0s1GDQ8k5H-J3SM6HgVRoRbqE3y1opg732jYZbD291vu65ksVRzqZTWE1g-2CjaC9mxl?__cft__[0]=AZU_C-mTmsTf7CJbb_1JG58nNBINhEV5N2V4gkebu8q3kHH9jCP-ccqOSoq8pESI_K0LPW871gp-u7tCyUhLSoUJWyB7BReuKgkmeAOwXNdxnOaIslfkGDsYPQbTDuxqspZW2B5BWBZVcE3CGhhRuv9nPt81IgUMcQT77ZRf_dJPQQ&__tn__=%2CO%2CP-R

17 https://www.youtube.com/watch?v=MtalpBUyl5I
18 https://zona.media/article/2024/08/26/valera
19 https://www.newsweek.com/russian-man-smashes-ipad-response-us-sanctions-viral-video-1684131
20 https://www.currenttime.tv/a/27591360.html
21 https://www.thetimes.com/world/russia-ukraine-war/article/nothing-to-see-here-satire-takes-on-the-kremlin-line-wgd0hqm2r
22 https://www.reuters.com/world/putin-warns-russia-against-pro-western-traitors-scum-2022-03-16/

Chapter 5

1 https://politkovskaya.novayagazeta.ru/pub/2001/2001-31.shtml
2 https://www.declassifieduk.org/when-tony-blair-backed-putins-brutal-war/
3 https://georgewbush-whitehouse.archives.gov/news/releases/2001/06/20010618.html
4 https://www.gazetteandherald.co.uk/leisure/20053034.putin-brought-nuclear-briefcase-paul-mccartney-show/
5 http://news.bbc.co.uk/1/hi/world/europe/3015258.stm
6 https://www.thetimes.com/comment/register/article/blair-fawns-as-russia-gets-ugly-6802wngt7qn
7 https://rm.coe.int/0900001680797f93
8 https://www.kavkaz-uzel.eu/articles/39712
9 https://www.royal.uk/state-banquet-president-russian-federation-24-june-2003
10 https://www.theguardian.com/world/2006/apr/03/russia.stephenmoss
11 https://www.lrb.co.uk/the-paper/v45/n19/vadim-nikitin/saintly-outliers
12 https://www.cbsnews.com/news/bill-browder-vladimir-putin-magnitsky-act-russian-money-laundering/
13 https://www.ft.com/content/46c5b1da-2990-11de-9e56-00144feabdc0
14 http://en.kremlin.ru/events/president/transcripts/24034
15 https://www.nytimes.com/2007/11/21/world/europe/21iht-russia.5.8427399.html
16 https://www.politico.com/blogs/ben-smith/2009/03/peregruzka-016614

17 https://www.rferl.org/a/russia-navalny-profile-anticorruption-crusader-kremlin-foe-putin/32822550.html
18 https://www.rferl.org/a/russia-opposition-leader-navalny-/24948687.html
19 Stanislav Belkovsky, *Chernaya Metka Oppozitsii* (Moscow: Algorithm, 2013).
20 https://www.npr.org/transcripts/1158944377
21 https://www.nytimes.com/2018/02/16/world/europe/prigozhin-russia-indictment-mueller.html
22 https://www.theguardian.com/world/2019/feb/14/darya-burlakova-journalist-quits-over-blacklisting-of-story-about-putin-chef
23 *Football Dynamo: Modern Russia and The People's Game:* Marc Bennetts. Virgin Books, 2009. [page 66]
24 Many of these critical articles were lost when RIA was closed down in 2013. Some were simply transferred, however, to the website of Sputnik, an unashamed propaganda outlet. They now sit rather awkwardly alongside its pro-Putin/pro-war articles, at least until someone gets round to removing them.

Chapter 6

1 https://www.itu.int/en/ITU-D/Statistics/Pages/stat/default.aspx
2 https://abcnews.go.com/blogs/headlines/2012/03/putin-wins-russian-election-cries-during-acceptance-speech
3 https://sputnikglobe.com/20120305/171747756.html [Bizarrely, this article was simply transferred to the Kremlin propaganda website, Sputnik, when RIA Novosti was closed down in 2013.]
4 https://www.washingtontimes.com/news/2014/jan/28/whos-godless-now-russia-says-its-us/
5 https://www.bbc.com/news/world-europe-26839216
6 https://www.bbc.co.uk/news/world-europe-25299116
7 https://www.bbc.com/russian/russia/2013/12/131209_ria_novosti_closing
8 https://www.reuters.com/article/world/putin-dissolves-state-news-agency-tightens-grip-on-media-idUSBRE9B80TF/
9 https://www.indexoncensorship.org/2014/03/crackdown-russian-media/

10 https://www.rbth.com/economics/2013/12/24/ria_novosti_overhaul_sends_shockwaves_31885 & https://www.bbc.com/russian/russia/2013/12/131212_kiselev_journalism_ria_novosti

11 https://www.youtube.com/watch?v=4gZiFjijAsI&embeds_referring_euri=https%3A%2F%2Fl.lj-toys.com%2F%3Fauth_token%3Dsessionless%253A1755601200%253Aembed-content%253A27372819%2526156%2526%2526%2526youtube%25264gZiFjijAsI%253Adc4d6&source_ve_path=OTY3MTQ

12 https://www.economist.com/eastern-approaches/2013/12/10/russias-chief-propagandist

Chapter 7

1 https://www.politico.eu/article/ukraine-pro-russian-former-president-viktor-yanukovych-loses-sanctions-court-battle/

2 https://time.com/archive/6946776/putin-to-the-west-hands-off-ukraine/

3 http://archive.government.ru/eng/docs/1758/print/

4 https://www.theguardian.com/world/2010/apr/21/ukraine-black-sea-fleet-russia

5 http://www.en.kremlin.ru/events/president/news/20603

6 https://www.forbes.com/sites/paulroderickgregory/2014/05/05/putins-human-rights-council-accidentally-posts-real-crimean-election-results-only-15-voted-for-annexation/

7 https://www.politico.eu/article/putin-rap-and-night-wolves-russia-marks-5-years-in-crimea/

8 http://www.en.kremlin.ru/events/president/news/20603

9 https://wciom.ru/analytical-reviews/analiticheskii-obzor/krizis-v-ukraine-chto-delat-rossii

10 https://www.themoscowtimes.com/2023/03/07/navalnys-policy-shift-on-crimea-may-be-too-little-too-late-a80396

11 https://www.newsru.com/russia/30jan2015/yarovaya.html

12 https://www.youtube.com/watch?v=2_Rl_idM0eI

13 https://www.washingtonpost.com/news/worldviews/wp/2014/06/16/khuilo-the-offensive-term-that-has-attached-itself-to-putin/

14 https://www.newsweek.com/2015/03/27/crimea-one-year-314834.html

ENDNOTES

15 https://www.youtube.com/watch?v=tf6nXoc3vMA
16 https://www.newsweek.com/2015/03/27/crimea-one-year-314834.html

Chapter 8

1 https://www.bbc.com/russian/russia/2014/07/140714_tr_tv_fake_child_ukraine.shtml
2 https://www.codastory.com/disinformation/confessions-of-a-former-state-tv-reporter/
3 https://www.rferl.org/a/ukraine-russia-netherlands-australia-malaysia-flight-shoot-down-icao/33412175.html
4 https://www.stopfake.org/en/how-russian-tv-uses-psychology-over-ukraine/
5 https://www.thetimes.com/world/russia-ukraine-war/article/on-putins-zombie-box-tune-into-16-hours-a-day-of-invasion-propaganda-zgds7zzw0
6 https://www.thetimes.com/world/russia-ukraine-war/article/on-putins-zombie-box-tune-into-16-hours-a-day-of-invasion-propaganda-zgds7zzw0
7 https://www.youtube.com/watch?v=2pnlkqaDMoU
8 https://t.me/bloodysx/18929
9 https://www.levada.ru/2024/12/04/konflikt-s-ukrainoj-v-noyabre-2024-goda-vnimanie-podderzhka-otnoshenie-k-peregovoram-trudnosti-i-uspehi-svo-stolknovenie-rossii-i-nato-primenenie-yadernogo-oruzhiya/
10 https://www.levada.ru/2024/07/04/konflikt-s-ukrainoj-osnovnye-indikatory-otvetstvennost-povody-dlya-bespokojstva-ugroza-stolknoveniya-s-nato-i-primeneniya-yadernogo-oruzhiya/
11 https://x.com/francis_scarr/status/1580066665353519104
12 https://www.youtube.com/watch?v=5lIYFvRDxwc&list=PLL-WQyEN3YRo41QwWb7e8J5YjBX80WmGtG
13 https://www.youtube.com/watch?time_continue=158&v=x-hY4-IhUkkI&embeds_referring_euri=https%3A%2F%2Fwww.agents.media%2F&source_ve_path=MzY4NDIsMjg2NjY
14 https://www.youtube.com/watch?v=hyI_7oz5fDc
15 https://www.youtube.com/watch?v=5lIYFvRDxwc&list=PLL-WQyEN3YRo41QwWb7e8J5YjBX80WmGtG

16 https://www.newsweek.com/2015/12/18/spike-russian-treason-trials-spurred-fear-and-loathing-europe-west-402164.html
17 https://www.youtube.com/watch?v=QxIi5KyJBOQ
18 https://www.thetimes.com/comment/register/article/frozen-geese-werent-expecting-the-food-police-9t9rmm0ndw0
19 https://www.theguardian.com/world/2014/mar/03/ukraine-vladimir-putin-angela-merkel-russian

Chapter 9

1 https://www.politico.eu/article/putin-calls-on-ukraine-military-to-overthrow-government-agree-peace-deal/
2 https://www.washingtonpost.com/history/2022/02/25/zelensky-family-jewish-holocaust/
3 https://www.theguardian.com/world/2018/mar/13/ukraine-far-right-national-militia-takes-law-into-own-hands-neo-nazi-links
4 https://www.newstatesman.com/world/europe/ukraine/2023/01/ukraine-stepan-bandera-nationalist
5 *Our Business is Death: The Story of the Wagner Group*, Ilya Barabanov / Denis Korotkov [Straight Forward Foundation] 2025
6 https://www.thetimes.com/uk/obituaries/article/dmitry-utkin-obituary-fqlqnwp6m
7 https://khpg.org/en/1420855493
8 https://x.com/ChristopherJM/status/1344073381830930432?lang=en
9 https://khpg.org/en/1608813918
10 https://censor.net/en/news/3505505/war_crimes_of_rf_neonazis_of_sarg_rusich_plan_to_sacrifice_a_captured_ukrainian
11 https://www.thebarentsobserver.com/borders/neonazi-mercenaries-to-help-fsb-guard-border-with-finland/101159
12 https://x.com/marcbennetts1/status/1578426400091955201
13 https://researchbriefings.files.parliament.uk/documents/SN01982/SN01982.pdf
14 https://english.nv.ua/nation/moscow-court-rules-that-the-slogan-fascism-shall-not-pass-discredits-the-russian-army-50228044.html
15 https://www.itv.com/news/2022-03-07/russian-gymnast-wears-pro-war-z-symbol-ukrainian-medalist
16 https://www.youtube.com/watch?v=ZFsE-1Xs6Ak

ENDNOTES

17 https://theins.ru/en/news/254332
18 https://www.nytimes.com/2023/03/09/world/europe/shaman-putin-russia-ukraine-war.html
19 https://www.youtube.com/watch?v=9myA3HyneHA
20 https://www.thetimes.com/world/russia-ukraine-war/article/russian-singer-shaman-wins-fame-and-favour-with-patriot-pop-9q0t3gn6f
21 https://www.thetimes.com/world/russia-ukraine-war/article/russian-singer-shaman-wins-fame-and-favour-with-patriot-pop-9q0t3gn6f
22 https://www.youtube.com/watch?v=XMMbZh7rrfs
23 https://www.nytimes.com/2021/04/02/world/europe/navalny-butina-prison-taunt.html
24 https://www.nytimes.com/2021/11/19/world/europe/maria-butina-russia-duma.html
25 https://www.theguardian.com/world/2011/mar/27/anna-chapman-agent-provocateur
26 https://www.rferl.org/a/Opposition_Legislators_Say_Russias_Parliament_Is_No_Parliament/2193979.html
27 https://www.pravda.com.ua/rus/news/2022/04/6/7337629/
28 https://meduza.io/news/2022/05/04/proekt-kreml-otkazyvaetsya-ot-termina-denatsifikatsiya-potomu-chto-rossiyane-ego-ne-ponimayut
29 https://www.bbc.co.uk/news/world-middle-east-61296682
30 https://www.themoscowtimes.com/2023/06/16/putin-says-zelensky-a-disgrace-to-jewish-people-a81540
31 https://www.amnesty.org/en/latest/news/2022/02/russia-politician-threatens-to-decapitate-family-members-of-chechen-activist/
32 https://www.themoscowtimes.com/2022/02/02/russian-lawmaker-threatens-to-cut-the-heads-off-chechen-activists-family-a76227
33 https://ombudsman-dnr.ru/obzor-soczialno-gumanitarnoj-situaczii-slozhivshejsya-na-territorii-doneczkoj-narodnoj-respubliki-vsledstvie-voennyh-dejstvij-v-period-s-25-po-30-dekabrya-2021
34 https://www.bbc.co.uk/news/60477712
35 https://ukraine.un.org/sites/default/files/2022-02/Conflict-related%20civilian%20casualties%20as%20of%2031%20December%202021%20%28rev%2027%20January%202022%29%20corr%20EN_0.pdf

36 https://ombudsman-dnr.ru/obzor-soczialno-gumanitarnoj-situaczii-slozhivshejsya-na-territorii-doneczkoj-narodnoj-respubliki-vsledstvie-voennyh-dejstvij-v-period-s-25-po-30-dekabrya-2021
37 https://ombudsman-dnr.ru/obzor-soczialno-gumanitarnoj-situaczii-slozhivshejsya-na-territorii-doneczkoj-narodnoj-respubliki-vsledstvie-voennyh-dejstvij-v-period-s-19-po-25-dekabrya-2020

Chapter 10

1 https://www.youtube.com/watch?v=xvrMUlOR76w
2 https://web.archive.org/web/20240223233059/https://www.compromat.ru/page_25575.htm
3 https://www.thetimes.com/world/russia-ukraine-war/article/putins-stooge-suddenly-wants-the-leading-role-hsghptspp
4 https://www.thetimes.com/uk/politics/article/poverty-in-russia-the-real-threat-to-putins-reign-0tmxt3fmd
5 https://www.nytimes.com/2022/04/06/world/europe/vladimir-zhirinovsky-dead.html

Chapter 11

1 https://www.youtube.com/watch?v=YuMtk75UURc
2 https://www.youtube.com/shorts/JDormQNNmio
3 https://www.newyorker.com/news/news-desk/putins-new-war-on-traitors
4 https://assembly.coe.int/nw/xml/XRef/Xref-XML2HTML-en.asp?fileid=28067&lang=en
5 https://assembly.coe.int/nw/xml/XRef/Xref-XML2HTML-en.asp?fileid=28067&lang=en
6 https://novayagazeta.ru/articles/2016/11/24/70647-geremeev-byl-glavnym-dlya-patsanov
7 https://www.oscepa.org/en/documents/officers-of-the-assembly/margareta-cederfelt-sweden/3971-the-nemtsov-murder-and-rule-of-law-in-russia-report-by-osce-pa-vice-president-margareta-cederfelt-20-february-2020/file
8 https://www.washingtonpost.com/opinions/2019/05/17/us-sanctions-key-organizer-murder-boris-nemtsov/
9 https://home.treasury.gov/news/press-releases/sm691
10 https://www.rferl.org/a/russia-eskerkhanov-nemtsov-murder-pardon/33078234.html

ENDNOTES

11 https://www.thetimes.com/world/article/russia-convicts-murder-ukraine-war-bclvp8b77
12 https://www.thetimes.com/world/russia-ukraine-war/article/putin-pardons-satanist-killer-for-serving-in-ukraine-wlfnkgxds
13 https://www.rbc.ru/politics/10/11/2023/654dfd949a7947e2309a4404?from=from_main_3&ref=en.thebell.io
14 https://www.hrw.org/report/2011/03/10/you-dress-according-their-rules/enforcement-islamic-dress-code-women-chechnya
15 https://www.rferl.org/a/kadyrov-expands-equine-empire/24707109.html
16 https://www.hrw.org/legacy/backgrounder/eca/chechnya0305/chechnya0305.pdf
17 https://www.themoscowtimes.com/2017/02/16/ten-crazy-things-ramzan-kadyrov-has-said-in-his-decade-ruling-chechnya-a57181
18 https://www.rferl.org/a/1074952.html
19 https://www.thetimes.com/comment/register/article/when-chechnyas-hardman-took-on-the-boys-from-brazil-z0ftt35jt33
20 The Facebook post in question has since been set to private.
21 https://www.facebook.com/boris.nemtsov/posts/651319564937647
22 https://www.ntv.ru/novosti/1058436/
23 https://www.newsweek.com/2016/05/13/russia-political-satire-vladimir-putin-ntv-454525.html
24 https://www.facebook.com/profile/100000379272171/search/?q=%D0%BD%D0%BE%D0%B2%D0%BE%D0%B3%D0%BE%D0%B4%D0%BD%D0%B8%D0%B5%20%D0%BC%D0%BE%D1%81%D0%BA%D0%B2%D0%B0%20
25 https://www.rferl.org/a/russia-duma-deputy-sanctions-challenge-more-west-ukraine/26821487.html
26 https://www.currenttime.tv/a/28731830.html
27 https://vk.com/serb_ru?w=club114297047
28 https://www.newsweek.com/2017/11/17/russia-putin-fights-beatdowns-election-navalny-opposition-president-moscow-693388.html
29 https://www.rferl.org/a/urine-feces-zelyonka-russian-radicals-assaulting-kremlin-critics-navalny/28466108.html
30 https://theins.ru/confession/80041

Chapter 12

1. https://femagainstwar.notion.site/5c7b9b90240342d7bf21754cca1c902a
2. Page 13, The Slave Soul of Russia, Daniel Rancour-Laferriere [NYU Press, 1996]
3. https://www.youtube.com/watch?v=kaaD8bXvi_8
4. https://www.newsweek.com/2018/02/16/russians-love-putin-800256.html
5. https://www.nytimes.com/2007/02/25/magazine/25RUSSIA.t.html
6. https://www.newsweek.com/2018/02/16/russians-love-putin-800256.html
7. https://www.dw.com/en/putin-pained-by-moscow-attack-even-if-not-visible-kremlin/a-68704852
8. https://www.bbc.com/news/world-europe-68663043
9. https://amp.meduza.io/en/feature/2018/04/20/a-moscow-district-official-asks-putin-to-save-him-from-moscow-s-governor
10. https://www.rightsinrussia.org/memorial-human-rights-centre-65/
11. https://www.thetimes.com/world/russia-ukraine-war/article/party-official-has-been-silenced-by-kremlin-for-supporting-protests-say-family-gg59b8xn8
12. https://www.thetimes.com/uk/politics/article/this-is-a-command-from-the-president-secret-tape-reveals-putins-role-in-framing-local-leader-lphjqqc2d

Chapter 13

1. https://www.nytimes.com/2012/08/09/world/europe/punk-bands-moscow-trial-offers-platform-for-orthodox-protesters.html
2. https://pravoslavie.ru/99123.html
3. https://www.illiberalism.org/patriarch-kirills-praetorian-guard-sorok-sorokov-as-radical-outreach-for-holy-tradition/
4. https://newhumanist.org.uk/articles/5238/from-here-to-eternity
5. https://euvsdisinfo.eu/from-objective-reporting-to-myths-and-propaganda-the-story-of-ria/
6. https://www.youtube.com/watch?v=Q5zKBKxwYfo&rco=1
7. https://www.washingtontimes.com/news/2014/jan/28/whos-godless-now-russia-says-its-us/
8. https://www.politico.eu/article/putins-holy-war/

ENDNOTES

9 https://globalfreedomofexpression.columbia.edu/cases/case-ruslan-sokolovsky/#:~:text=Sokolovsky's%20videos%20mocked%20Christianity%2C%20Islam,the%20duration%20of%20his%20sentence.
10 https://www.thetimes.com/comment/register/article/russian-patriarch-red-faced-over-miracle-of-disappearing-pound20000-watch-bfxnhkjx6xb
11 https://foreignpolicy.com/2015/11/24/the-kremlins-holy-warrior-chaplin-putin-russia-turkey-syria/
12 https://www.themoscowtimes.com/2016/08/17/there-are-some-people-you-should-kill-the-russian-priests-supporting-stalin-a55006
13 https://www.theguardian.com/world/2017/sep/19/30ft-high-statue-of-mikhail-kalashnikov-unveiled-in-moscow
14 https://www.newsweek.com/russian-communists-are-turning-christ-333410
15 https://www.youtube.com/watch?v=W7nDdS6XrbE
16 https://www.youtube.com/watch?v=g_UqV5MT8oE
17 https://rtvi.com/news/ya-smiryayus-krasovskij-vyskazalsya-o-zaprete-v-rossii-dvizheniya-lgbt/
18 https://www.bbc.com/news/world-europe-63378613
19 https://novayagazeta.eu/articles/2022/12/17/russias-investigative-committee-not-to-consider-case-of-krasovsky-tv-presenter-who-called-to-drown-ukrainian-kids-en-news
20 https://www.thetimes.com/uk/politics/article/it-may-take-decades-to-forgive-russia-for-atrocities-says-buchas-priest-tm2g80ntm
21 https://www.politico.eu/article/everything-you-wanted-to-know-about-aids-in-russia-but-putin-was-afraid-to-ask/
22 https://www.newsweek.com/2016/02/05/russia-aids-hiv-crisis-419397.html
23 https://www.eatg.org/hiv-news/russia-dismisses-data-showing-worlds-5th-highest-hiv-infection-rate/

Chapter 14

1 https://www.thetimes.com/world/russia-ukraine-war/article/kremlin-runs-scared-of-alexander-gabyshev-the-anti-putin-siberian-shaman-sl00pqjld
2 Gabyshev: Identity at the intersection of two cultures: M.B. Bashkirov - Etnograficheskoe Obozrenie, 2021

3 Gabyshev: Identity at the intersection of two cultures: M.B. Bashkirov - Etnograficheskoe Obozrenie, 2021
4 https://meduza.io/en/feature/2019/09/20/here-s-what-we-know-about-the-siberian-shaman-who-set-out-to-battle-putin-s-evil-spirit-and-how-police-finally-got-to-him
5 https://www.politico.eu/article/alexander-gabyshev-anti-putin-shaman-warrior-who-spooked-the-kremlin/
6 https://www.amnesty.org/en/latest/news/2021/09/russia-siberian-shaman-who-marched-against-putin-is-indefinitely-confined-to-a-psychiatric-hospital/
7 https://www.themoscowtimes.com/2025/04/11/far-east-court-rules-to-keep-anti-putin-shaman-in-high-security-psychiatric-facility-a88693
8 Gabyshev was eventually transfered to a psychiatric ward in Yakustk, his home city, in September 2025, four years after he was detained by riot police.
9 https://novayagazeta.ru/articles/2024/06/28/siloviki-vserez-boiatsia-sakralnoi-ugrozy-ritualov-i-mistiki
10 https://newhumanist.org.uk/articles/4862/black-magic-on-red-square
11 https://www.politico.eu/article/alexander-gabyshev-anti-putin-shaman-warrior-who-spooked-the-kremlin/
12 https://www.theguardian.com/world/2010/jun/06/marc-bennetts-anatoly-kashpirovsky-russia-rasputin
13 https://www.themoscowtimes.com/archive/cult-promises-to-resurrect-beslan-children

Chapter 15

1 https://mos.memo.ru/
2 https://www.themoscowtimes.com/2023/06/13/in-the-dmitriev-affair-gulag-historians-persecution-is-a-microcosm-of-putins-russia-a81476
3 https://www.eeas.europa.eu/node/47471_en
4 https://www.newsweek.com/2015/09/18/drive-remember-stalins-victims-being-threatened-putins-push-revise-history-369532.html
5 https://www.dw.com/ru/parkhomenko-o-poslednem-adrese-vsevernem-kogda-mut-osadet/a-66111493

ENDNOTES

6. https://www.politico.eu/article/putins-gulag-ildar-dadin-moscow-russia/
7. https://www.europarl.europa.eu/doceo/document/TA-8-2016-0446_EN.html
8. https://www.youtube.com/watch?v=y_IObE7MIqs
9. https://www.svoboda.org/a/nachaljnik-kolonii-v-kotoroy-pytali-dadina-vyshel-na-svobodu-dosrochno/31428186.html
10. https://meduza.io/en/feature/2024/10/07/imprisoned-tortured-and-killed-at-the-front-the-life-and-death-of-anti-kremlin-activist-ildar-dadin
11. https://www.rferl.org/a/russian-activist-dadin-killed-fighting-ukraine/33148859.html
12. https://www.themoscowtimes.com/2019/06/26/1-in-10-russians-have-been-tortured-by-authorities-poll-a66159
13. https://www.thetimes.com/world/russia-ukraine-war/article/ukraine-soldier-tortured-know-what-hell-is-fmqp5v7k3

Chapter 16

1. https://apnews.com/article/russia-ukraine-war-erasing-mariupol-499dceae43ed77f2ebfe750ea99b9ad9
2. https://www.youtube.com/watch?v=xpJ_fYyAeYk
3. https://storage.googleapis.com/istories/stories/2023/01/16/nachalnik-shtaba-rossiiskoi-aviatsionnoi-eskadrili-chto-ya-pryamo-na-knopku-nazhimal-ili-v-etom-samolete-sidel/index.html
4. https://tvpworld.com/83086476/ukrainian-intelligence-bludgeons-russian-colonel-to-death-with-hammer-of-justice
5. https://www.youtube.com/live/OXwjg3GWsSI
6. *Orderly and Humane: The Expulsion of the Germans after the Second World War:* R.M. Douglas, Yale University Press, 2013
7. https://meduza.io/en/feature/2023/07/10/vilnius-nafo-summit-draws-criticism-from-both-navalny-s-associates-and-russia-s-foreign-ministry
8. The horrors of Izolyatsia are detailed in *The Torture Camp on Paradise Street* by Stanislav Aseyev, a Ukrainian journalist and former inmate. [Harvard Ukrainian Research Institute, 2023]
9. https://www.thetimes.com/world/russia-ukraine-war/article/ukrainians-held-prisoner-in-kherson-describe-torture-by-russian-forces-mfzllz8mh

10 https://www.france24.com/en/live-news/20220227-russian-official-apologises-for-war-in-ukraine-at-un-climate-meet
11 https://www.reuters.com/world/europe/police-detain-more-than-900-people-anti-war-protests-across-russia-monitoring-2022-02-27/
12 https://www.thetimes.com/uk/politics/article/putins-critics-have-a-choice-flee-russia-or-rot-in-jail-93htjnf3k
13 https://en.zona.media/article/2024/06/27/turbin-trl
14 https://www.thetimes.com/world/russia-ukraine-war/article/russias-south-park-turns-tables-on-nazi-putin-9f2cvw0zh
15 https://www.bbc.com/news/world-europe-68374769

Chapter 17

1 https://novayagazeta.ru/articles/2018/01/03/75072-ya-prikidyval-chto-budet-hotya-by-chelovek-50
2 https://www.theguardian.com/world/2017/oct/08/high-steaks-the-vladimir-putin-birthday-burger-that-never-existed
3 https://news.sky.com/story/vladimir-putin-inauguration-steven-seagal-and-other-famous-faces-spotted-at-kremlin-palace-13131109
4 https://united24media.com/latest-news/steven-seagal-claims-hes-ready-to-fight-and-die-if-necessary-for-putin-2938
5 https://www.youtube.com/watch?v=rxcV85Cq-EU
6 https://www.thetimes.com/world/russia-ukraine-war/article/jeff-monson-fighter-who-turned-russian-takes-swipe-at-putin-riches-mfq3cbbgn
7 https://smotrim.ru/article/1485835?utm_source=internal&utm_medium=serp_news&utm_campaign=serp_news
8 https://doxa.team/articles/school-toilets
9 https://www.thetimes.com/world/russia-ukraine-war/article/russias-health-system-is-dying-on-its-feet-kgh9fvh0l
10 https://www.themoscowtimes.com/2017/04/07/russian-doctors-paid-less-than-fast-food-workers-a57667
11 https://www.newsru.com/russia/14mar2013/astakhovnice.html
12 https://www.newsweek.com/2016/12/02/dire-russia-health-care-523380.html
13 https://www.themoscowtimes.com/2015/06/03/driving-russias-cancer-patients-to-suicide-op-ed-a47098

ENDNOTES

Chapter 18

1 https://www.youtube.com/watch?v=8xMjQ8jA0lI [I met Dani Akel during the making of this short film for *The Times*].

Chapter 19

1 https://www.svoboda.org/a/kvintessentsiya-trusosti-i-predateljstva-sotsseti-o-padenii-asada/33231337.html
2 https://vse-svobodny.com/product/brodskiy-o-tiranii/
3 https://duma.gov.ru/news/48844/

INDEX

Abkhazia 18
Abramovich, Roman 138
Akel, Dani 'Apostle' 219–21, 222–6
Akhmad (Chechen) 129–30
Aleksi (Georgian student) 18
Alexandra (Kamardin's fiancée) 206
Alfred, Lord Tennyson 85
Altai region 72
Alyokhina, Maria 134–6
Ametov, Refat 91
Ametov, Rishat 91
Andrey Rylkov Foundation for Health and Social Justice 169
Anisimov, Oleg 205
Apanasenko, Vyacheslav 218
Arctic region 72–3, 84
assassinations 29–31, 57, 229
  in Chechnya 129
  Golenkov 195
  Navalny: assassination attempts 208
  Nemtsov 125, 126–7, 130
  Startovoitova 30, 231–2
Astakhov, Pavel 217
Aven, Petr 33–4

Babinets, Sergei 187
Balitsky, Yevgeny 198
Bandera, Stepan 104
Banner-Bearers 153–7
Baulina, Oksana 136
Bazhanov, Evgeny 80
BBC 69, 81, 118
Beglov, Alexander 48–9
Beketov, Igor 139–40
Belkovsky, Stanislav 63

Bennetts, Marc
  arrival in Russia 16
  early life 16–17, 22–3
  freelance journalism 79
  mother-in-law and propaganda 95
  in Prague 18
  and RIA 79–80, 81
  Starokonyushenny Lane flat 64
  teaching English in Moscow 32, 33, 65
  teaching English in St Petersburg 19–22
  travel-guide assignment 83–4
  in Venezuela 17
Berlusconi, Silvo 65
Biletsky, Andriy 103
Blair, Tony 57, 58
Borshchevsky, Platon 231–2
Brodsky, Joseph 229–30
Browder, Bill 59–60
Bucha killings 112, 167, 206–7
Bukovsky, Vladimir 27
Bulgakov, Mikhail: *The Master and Margarita* 17, 135
Bush, George W. 58, 67
Butina, Maria 110, 111, 112–13, 114–16
Butyrka prison, Moscow 144

Catherine the Great, Tsarina 85
censorship 55
censorship laws 6–7, 8, 111
Centre for Economic and Political Reform, Moscow 217
Chaadayev, Petr 143
Channel One TV station 212

INDEX

Chaplin, Vsevolod 161–3
Chapman, Anna 111
Charles, Prince 58
Chasovnikova, Anna 192
Chechnya 14, 31, 58, 126–30
Cherkesov, Viktor 28
Chernikh, Karolina 36
China 79
Chirikova, Yevgeniya 36–7
Chumak, Allan 176
Chumak, Maksym 198
Clinton, Hillary 61–2
Committee for the Prevention of Torture 187
conspiracy theories 47, 94, 165
contract killings 14, 31
coronavirus pandemic 42, 46–7, 122, 134
corruption 4, 14, 34, 38, 61, 62, 137, 144
  in football 68–9
  in Kremlin 205, 206
  Nemtsov on 124
  in Ukraine 84
Council of Europe 58
crime 13, 51, 105, 160
  contract killings 14, 31
  fake news 6–7, 8, 111
  war crimes 51, 58, 112, 188, 196
Crimea 83–5
  annexation of 86–8
  post-2014 conditions in 90
  referendum 86
  Tatar population 90–2
CSKA Moscow football club 69

Dadayev, Zaur 126
Dadin, Ildar 182–5, 224
Danilov, Oleksii 196
deaths
  assassinations 29–31, 57, 125, 126–7, 130, 195
  contract killings 14, 31
  deaths in prison 60

executions 28, 58, 179–80, 181
  murders 99
  see also war crimes
Delimkhanov, Adam 114, 126
Demnig, Gunter 181
demonstrations 5, 74–6, 93, 132, 136, 151, 172–3, 182
Depardieu, Gérard 212
Deshchytsia, Andrii 89
Dmitriev, Yury 180–1
Dmytro (computer programmer) 202–3
Dmytro (Ukrainian doctor) 195–6
Donetsk People's Republic (DPR) 114–15
Donskoy, Alexander 146–7
Dronov, Yaroslav (Shaman, pop star) 108–9
Durytska, Anna 125
Dynamo Kyiv football club 89
Dyuzheva, Yulia 145–6
Dzerzhinsky, Felix 13
Dzhepparov, Abdureshit 92
Dzhepparov, Islyam 92

Echo of Moscow (liberal radio station) 132–3
economy 14–15, 32–3, 106
  GDP/GDP per capita increase 32
  sanctions 87
election-fixing 74–7, 172–3
Elizabeth II, Queen 58, 59
Eskerkhanov, Temirlan 127–8
executions
  memorial plaques 181
  Soviet era 28, 179–80
  Zumaev 58

fake news 6–7, 8, 111
FBK anti-corruption foundation 62
FC Dynamo Moscow football club 68–9
Federal Security Service (FSB) 5, 30, 150–1

FIFA World Cup (2018) 186
'Final Battle between Good and
   Neutrality, The' blog (Navalny) 62
Flint, Keith 12
football
  corruption in 68–9
  CSKA Moscow football club 69
  Dynamo Kyiv football club 89
  FC Dynamo Moscow football club
    68–9
  Shakhtar Donetsk football club 89
  Spartak Moscow football club 69
  ultras 88–9
Forever Flowing (Grossman) 143
'Forward, Russia!' (Medvedev) 61
Freedom of Russia Legion 220,
   221–2
FSB (Federal Security Service) 5, 30,
   150–1
Fyodorov, Yevgeny 138–9

Gabyshev, Alexander 170–1, 172–5
  arrest 173
  committal to psychiatric asylum 174
  and The Heavenly Squad 172
Gagarin, Yuri 160
Galavin, Andriy 167–8
Garage Museum of Contemporary
   Art, Moscow 138
Gelman, Marat 108–9
Geremeyev, Ruslan 127
Gershkovich, Evan 8, 206, 233
Giner, Yevgeni 69
Girkin, Igor 94
Golenkov, Dmitry 195
Gorbachev, Mikhail 17
Gorinov, Alexei 206
Gorky Park, Moscow 137–8
  Garage Museum of Contemporary
    Art 138
Graboivi, Grigory 176
Grisha (poet) 54
Grossman, Vasily: *Forever*
   Flowing 143

Gryzlov, Boris 111
Gudkov, Dmitry 62
Gudkov, Lev 95–6
Guriev, Sergei 33

healthcare 25–6, 216–18
Hitler, Adolf 126
HIV/Aids 168–9
Human Rights Council, Russia 86
hyperinflation 14

Igor (customer in shopping
   centre) 52
Iran 78
Irina (photographer) 97
Islamic State 149, 162
Islyamov, Dzhevdet 92
Israilov, Umar 129

Kabaeva, Alina 65
Kadyrov, Ramzan 127, 128–9
Kalashnikov, Mikhail 164
Kamardin, Artyom 206
Kapuściński, Ryszard 77–8
Kara-Murza, Vladimir 205–6, 230–1
Karelia 182–4
Karpov, Vladyslav 194
Kascheev, Alexey 218
Kashpirovsky, Anatoly 176
KGB 27–8, 118, 161
Kharkiv, Ukraine 193–5
Kherson, Ukraine 1–2, 199–202
Khodorkovsky, Mikhail 59, 186
Khrushchev, Nikita 85
Kim Jong Il: 64
Kino (Soviet rock band) 9, 52
Kipshidze, Vakhtang 161
Kirill, Patriarch of Russian Orthodox
   Church 142, 160, 161, 166–7
Kiselyov, Dmitry 81–2, 98–9
Klimov, Symon 179
Klitschko, Vitali 84
Kocheulov, Vladimir 144
Kondaurov, Alexei 173

INDEX

Konstantin, Father (Russian Orthodox priest) 164
Kopitok, Viktor 188
Kormukhin, Andrei 158
Kossiyev, Sergey 183, 184
Kossman, Nina 181
Kotlyarov, Vladimir 109–10
Kovalchuk, Yury 47
Krasnov, Viktor 160
Krasovsky, Anton 166
Krechetova, Anna 106
Kryzhanivsky, Volodymyr 31
Kudinov, Pavel 179
Kuliak, Ivan 107
Kuvaev, Oleg 207

Lavrov, Sergey 61–2, 114
LDPR (Liberal Democratic Party of Russia) 104, 118, 119, 120
Lebed, Alexander 118
Lebedev, Vyacheslav 28
Leigh, Mike 165
Lenin, Vladimir 12, 159
Leonid (driver) 76
Levada Center pollster 95–6, 97, 187
LGBT movement 146, 166–7
  outlawed by Supreme Court 165
  persecution of 153, 154, 166–7
Liberal Democratic Party of Russia (LDPR) 104, 118, 119, 120
Lighthouse children's hospice, Moscow 218
Linkov, Ruslan 29
Litvinenko, Alexander 110–11
living standards 215
Lugovoi, Andrey 110–11
lustration 28–30
Luzhniki Stadium, Moscow 210–12
Lyudmila (teaching supervisor) 19

M (MB's daughter) 66–8, 100, 133
McCartney, Paul 58
magic 176–7
Magnitsky, Sergei 59–60

Magnitsky Act 60
Maidan revolution 84–5, 103, 132
Makhno, Anna 188–9
Malaysia Airlines flight MH17 94, 126
Malofieieva, Kateryna 200–1, 224, 225
Mariupol, Ukraine 44, 191–2
Markov, Sergei 81
Marx, Karl 137
Master and Margarita, The (Bulgakov) 17, 135
Masyanya (satirical Russian cartoon series) 207
Meduza (opposition website) 172
Medvedev, Dmitry 60–1, 62, 74, 77, 150
  'Forward, Russia!' 61
  meeting with Kim Jong Il: 64
Memorial (human rights group) 39, 179, 181
Merkel, Angela 101
Milchakov, Alexey 104
Mironyuk, Svetlana 69, 81
Miroshnichenko, Igor 154–6
Mitrofanov, Alexei 86
Monetochka (singer-songwriter) 32
Moniava, Lida 218
Monson, Jeff 213–15
Mukhudinov, Ruslan 126–7
Munich Security Conference (2007) 61
Muratov, Dmitry 61
Murmansk region 83–4
Muzhenko, Viktor 88

Nafo (social media group) 198–9
Naked (film) 165
Naritsyn, Nikolai 178
Naryshkin, Sergei 43
Natalia (Kherson region informant) 188
National Liberation Movement (NOD) 138, 139

National Militia, Ukraine 103
Nato 2, 25, 44, 85, 121, 122
  Russian demands 41
Navalny, Alexei 62–3, 75, 87, 139, 173, 208–9, 210–11
  'The Final Battle between Good and Neutrality' blog 62
Nemtsov, Boris 124–7, 130
Nemtsova, Zhanna 127
New Island restaurant, St Petersburg 67
Night Wolves 132
NOD (National Liberation Movement) 138, 139
North Korea 78–9
Novaya Gazeta 61
NTV (Kremlin-controlled television channel) 132–3
nuclear war threats 88, 96
  Medvedev 61
  Putin 46, 164
  Skabeyeva 97
  Solovyov 98
  Zhirinovsky 117–18, 120, 121

occult industry 175–8
Ogolobyak, Nikolai 128
Old Arbat, Moscow 64, 107–8, 134–5
Olena (Ukrainian, Pavlo's wife) 193, 197
Orlov, Oleg 38, 205–6

Pamfilova, Ella 29
paranormal 175–6
Parkhomenko, Sergey 181–2
parliamentary elections: vote rigging 74–7, 172–3
passenger jet incidents 162
  Malaysia Airlines flight MH17 94, 126
Patrushev, Nikolai 47
Pavel (teacher) 23

Pavlo (Olena's husband) 193
Pavlovsky, Gleb 45–6, 147–9, 150
Penal Colony No. 7, Karelia 182–4
Peskov, Dmitry 128, 150
Pinochet, Augusto 33–4
Pivovarov, Andrey 206
Plotnikova, Elena 169
Podolayk, Mykhailo 232
Politkovskaya, Anna 57, 61
Polyukhovych, Dmytro 99
Ponomarev, Ilya 86, 131
Popov, Leonid 188–90
Popov, Yevgeny 96, 97–8
Pornofilmy (punk group) 109–10
poverty 14–15
Powers, Gary 137
Prigozhin, Yevgeny 67–8, 229
Primakov, Yevgeny 25
Prodigy, The 12–13
propaganda 4, 47, 49–50, 93–7, 102–3, 158–9, 169, 178, 208, 214–15, 221–2
  claims about Nazism 49, 51–2, 102, 104–6, 112–14
  gay propaganda law 160, 165
  mother-in-law and 95
  North Korean 78
  in Syria 229
  in Ukraine 201, 203, 222
Pryanishnikov, Alexey 175
Pushkin, Alexander 143
Pussy Riot protest group 70, 134–5, 136, 154, 186
Putin, Lyudmila 58, 143–4
Putin, Vladimir 14, 30, 31–2
  and assassination of Starovoitova 30
  attitudes to 143–7
  and coronavirus pandemic 46–7
  dreams about 141–2
  economic policies 32–3
  foreign support for 212–14
  nuclear war threats 46, 164
  and religion 159–60, 164

return to power 74–7
rumours about 65–6
and Ukraine 84–5
visits to London 57, 58–9

Raplya, Nadya 207
Reagan, Ronald 159
Red Army parades, Moscow 12, 35
religion
    Putin and 159–60, 164
    see also Russian Orthodox Church
RIA Novosti news agency 69–70, 75, 79–80, 81, 98
    'He Who Sobs with Joy' 77
Roginsky, Arseny 181
Romanova, Olga 132, 144
Roslovtsev, Roman 133
Rossiya 1 channel 94
    60 Minutes current affairs show 96
Rossiya Segodnya (RT, Russia Today) 70, 81
Rowling, J.K. 153–4
Rubinstein, Lev 175–6
Rusich neo-fascist, neo-pagan paramilitary unit 104–5
Russell, William Howard 85
Russia Behind Bars (prisoners' rights group) 132
Russia Profile (RIA online magazine) 69
Russia Today (RT, Rossiya Segodnya) 70, 81
Russian March 153
Russian Orthodox Church 47, 135, 154, 159, 160–1, 163, 167, 172
    blessing of intercontinental ballistic missiles 164
    Kirill, Patriarch 142, 160, 161, 166–7
    Orthodox Christian movements 157–8
    and sex education 168–9
Russian Supreme Court 165

St Petersburg 19–22
    assassinations 29–30
Sakha (Yakutia) 72, 76, 215
    shamanism 170, 171
    wildfires 171–2
Saldo, Vladimir 197–8
same-sex relationships 160, 165, 166
Samutsevich, Yekaterina 70, 135
Sarang, Anya 169
Seagal, Steven 212–13
SERB (South East Radical Block) 139
Serenko, Daria 141
Sergei (Russian friend) 21
Sever batallion 126, 127
Shakhtar Donetsk football club 89
Shaman (Yaroslav Dronov, pop star) 108–9
shamanism 170, 171, 175–6
    pro-Putin shamans 172
    Yakutia 170, 171
Shchipaeva, Nadezhda 216–17
Shestun, Alexander 150–2
Shestuna, Yulia 152
Shishkin, Mikhail 206–7
Shkinder, Anastasia 217
Shternberg, Boris 181
Sidelnikova, Olga 55
Sidyakin, Alexander 70
Simonovich-Nikshich, Leonid 153, 154, 156–7
Sinyavsky, Andrei 176
Skabeyeva, Olga 96–8
Skochilenko, Alexandra 205–6
Skuratovsky, Ivan 197
Slutsky, Leonid 107
Smith, Martin Cruz 137
Sokolovsky, Ruslan 160–1
Solovyov, Vladimir 48, 98
Sorok Sorokov 157–8
Sosnovy Bor 64
South East Radical Block (SERB) 139
Soviet Information Bureau (Sovinformburo) 69

Soviet Union: dissolution of 17–18
Spartak Moscow football club 69
Stalin, Joseph 3
Stanovaya, Tatiana 46
Starovoitova, Galina 27, 28–31, 56, 117, 231
  assassination of 30
Starovoitova, Olga 30, 31
Stas (Moscow friend) 227–8
Super Putin exhibition, Moscow 145–6
Svetlana (Russian) 192–3
Syria 67, 162, 229
Syrskyi, Oleksandr 196

T (MB's wife) 63–4, 66
Taganrog 40–5, 49
TASS news agency 212
t.A.T.u. group 165–6
Telegram messaging app 52
Thaws, Adrian (Tricky) 22
Tikhonova, Katerina 66
Tkachev, Ivan 151
Tolokonnikova, Nadezhda 135
Tolstoy, Leo 169
Tolstoy, Pyotr 139
trade unions 137, 216, 217
Treasures of Sunken Ships, The (Soviet-era cartoon) 107
Trekhleb, Pavel 138
Trudolyubov, Maxim 144
Trump, Donald 67, 118
Tsoi, Viktor 9
Turansky, Valentin 194–5
Turbin, Arseny 206
TV Dozhd (TV Rain, independent online television channel) 63

Ukraine 1–2, 9, 44, 84–5
  Azov military unit 103–4
  Bakhmut 2
  Bucha 112, 167, 206–7
  Donbas region 40, 41, 42, 44–5, 88, 115
  football ultras 88–9
  independence vote 31
  invasion of 44–5, 51, 53, 54
  Kherson 1–2, 199–202
  Kyiv 45, 84, 89, 103, 224–5
  Mariupol 44, 112, 127–8, 191–2, 198
  refugees from 41–2
  2014 annexation of Crimea 93–4
  war with, run up to 40–5
Ukrainian Cultural Center, Moscow 53
Union of Orthodox Banner-Bearers 153–7
United Russia party 110
  'The Party of Crooks and Thieves' 62
Usmanova, Tatiana 206
Utkin, Dmitry 104
Uvarova, Lada 30

Varennikov, Valentin 28
Vasilkovsky, Alexander 179–80
Vasilyeva, Anastasia 216, 217
Vdovina, Yelena 217
Venezuela 17
Vernon, Andy 34–5
Victory Day celebrations 3–4, 34–6, 105–6
  during coronavirus pandemic 47
Vitali (tortured Ukrainian) 203–4
Vitaliev, Vitali 30
Volodin, Vyacheslav 47–8, 142, 230
Volodymyr (elderly Ukrainian) 191
Vorobyov, Andrey 151
Voronezh, Russia 23–4, 25–6
Vorontsova, Maria 66
vote rigging 74–7, 172–3

Wagner Group 67, 104, 229
war crimes 51, 58, 112, 188, 196
We (Zamyatin) 109
Western food imports: destruction of 100

Western media: and legislation 115
Winter Olympics, Sochi (2014) 186

Yakut people 170
Yakutia (Sakha) 72, 76, 170, 215
 shamanism 170, 171
 wildfires 171–2
Yakutsk 170
Yamadayev, Ruslan 129
Yangulbaev, Abubakar 114
Yangulbaev, Saidi 114
Yangulbayeva, Zarema 114
Yanukovych, Viktor 84–5
Yarovaya, Irina 87
Yashin, Ilya 51–2, 125–6, 205–6
Yegorov, Viktor 173
Yekaterina (Ukrainian refugee) 42
Yelan-Koleno: uranium levels 37–8
Yelena (middle-aged woman) 52
Yeltsin, Boris 29, 31, 32, 124, 148
 bans Communist Party 17–18
 economic turmoil of presidency 33
 presidency 13–14

Young Guard (pro-Putin youth movement) 70
Yugoslavia: Nato bombing of 25

Z symbol 106–8, 136, 167, 204
Zakharova, Maria 112
Zaladantsov, Alexander 132
Zamyatin, Yevgeny: *We* 109
Zaporizhzhia, Ukraine 192, 195–6
Zavalnyuk, Lyubov 192
Zelensky, Dmitry 128
Zelensky, Volodymyr 102
 Jewishness of 114
Zhirinovsky, Vladimir 104, 117–23, 174
Zhora (Freedom of Russia Legion member) 221–2
Zhyolud (newspaper) 55
Zolotov, Viktor 43
Zotova, Anastasia 182–4, 185
Zumaev, Sirajdi 58
Zygar, Mikhail 47
Zyuganov, Gennady 164–5